The Family Handyman

BEST
Weekend
PROJECTS

The Family Handyman

BEST Weekend PROJECTS

Reader's Digest

The Reader's Digest Association, Inc.
Pleasantville, New York/Montreal

FOR THE FAMILY HANDYMAN
Editor in Chief: Ken Collier
Executive Editor: Spike Carlsen
Assistant Editor: Mary Flanagan
Design Director: Sara Koehler
Administrative Manager: Alice Garrett
Graphic Designer: Teresa Marrone
Production Manager: Judy Rodriguez

FOR READER'S DIGEST
U.S. Project Editor: Kim Casey
Project Designer: Wayne Morrison
Associate Art Director: George McKeon
Executive Editor, Trade Publishing: Dolores York
Production Manager: Liz Dinda
Vice President, U.S. Operations: Michael Braunschweiger
Associate Publisher: Rosanne McManus
President and Publisher, Trade Publishing: Harold Clarke

ISBN 13: 978-0-7621-0927-2

Previously published as custom publications:
Storage Solutions, Best Weekend Projects,
and *Best Backyard Projects.*

Text, photography, and illustrations are based on articles previously run in *The Family Handyman* (2915 Commers Dr., Suite 700, Eagan, MN 55121), *American Woodworker*, and *Backyard Living* (5400 S. 60th St., Greendale, WI 53129) magazines.

We are committed to both the quality of our products and the service we provide to our customers. We value your comments, so please feel free to contact us.

The Reader's Digest Association, Inc.
Adult Trade Publishing
Reader's Digest Road
Pleasantville, NY 10570-7000

For more Reader's Digest products and information, visit our website:
www.rd.com

Printed in China

1 3 5 7 9 10 8 6 4 2

WARNING
All do-it-yourself activities involve a degree of risk. Skills, materials, tools, and site conditions vary widely. Although the editors have made every effort to ensure accuracy, the reader remains responsible for the selection and use of tools, materials, and methods. Always obey local codes and laws, follow manufacturer's operating instructions, and observe safety precautions.

Contents

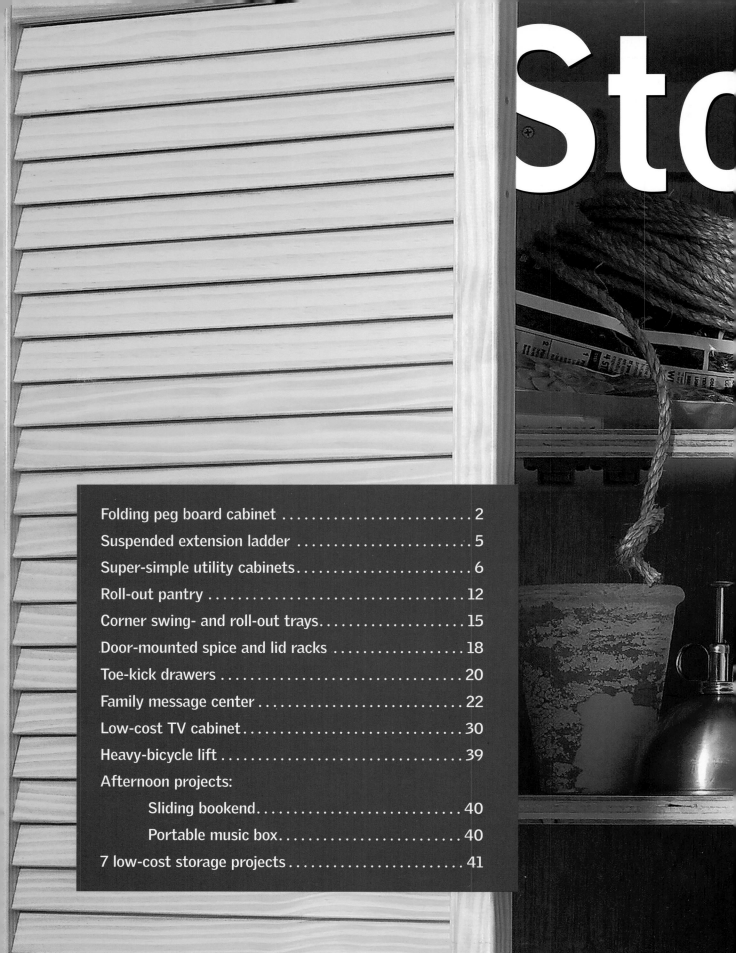

Sto

Folding peg board cabinet

Organize your tools and workshop with this clever cabinet.

Peg board is a great way to organize tools. It displays them in clear view so they're easy to grab and, just as important, easy to put away. This cabinet has the hanging space of almost an entire 4 x 8 ft. sheet of peg board, yet packs it into a compact 24 x 32 in. package. Two overlapping doors open, utilizing the front and back of each for tools. About 4 in. of space separate each panel, leaving a 2-in. depth for tools placed directly across from each other. If you place fat tools across from skinny ones, you can utilize the space even better.

project at a glance

skill level
intermediate

special tools
clamps
drill
circular saw

approximate cost
$110

figure a
cabinet details

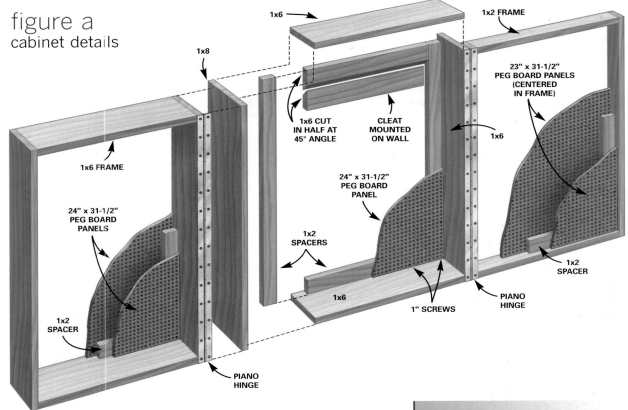

1x6

1x8

1x2 FRAME

23" x 31-1/2"
PEG BOARD PANELS
(CENTERED IN FRAME)

1x6 CUT IN HALF AT 45° ANGLE

CLEAT MOUNTED ON WALL

1x6

1x6 FRAME

24" x 31-1/2"
PEG BOARD PANELS

24" x 31-1/2"
PEG BOARD PANEL

1x2 SPACERS

1x2 SPACER

1x2 SPACER

1x6

1" SCREWS

PIANO HINGE

PIANO HINGE

Materials, cost and tools

This cabinet costs $110 to build. The knot-free poplar boards drive up the price, but the straight, stable wood allows the doors to fit well, minimizes twisting, and keeps the cabinet square. In addition to the materials listed at right, we purchased four eye screws and 2 ft. of small chain to hold the doors open. All the supplies are available at a home center or lumberyard.

You don't need any special tools to build this cabinet, but a pair of 1-ft. clamps are helpful when you're attaching the hinges.

Cut accurately for tight-fitting doors

Cut the 4 x 8-ft. peg board sheet lengthwise into two pieces, one 24 in. wide and the other 23 in.

wide. Then cut the two pieces into 31-1/2-in. lengths. You must cut the peg board panels accurately for the doors to fit evenly. Carefully measure and use a straight-edge to guide your circular saw cuts. Some lumberyards will cut the sheets to size for you. Ask them to be precise.

Then assemble the peg board panels (Photo 1), following the pattern shown in Figure A. You don't have to make fancy joints. Cut and screw on the 1x2 side spacers first, then measure and cut the 1x2 ends to fit between them. You'll have one 23 in. peg board panel left over to hang on the wall for items that won't fit in the cabinet.

Substitute one half of the cleat for the top 1x2 on the back panel (Photo 3 and Figure A). Watch the angle. Orient it so it hooks onto the other half you screw to the wall (Photo 5).

materials list

One 4'x8' sheet of 1/4" peg board

Five 10' lengths of 1x2 poplar

Two 10' lengths of 1x6 poplar

One 3' length of 1x8 poplar

One 6' piano hinge

One lockable hasp

1 lb. of 2" finish nails

1 lb. of 1" screws

Eight 3" screws

cutting list

1/4" peg board panels
  three 24" x 31-1/2"
  two 23" x 31-1/2"

1x2 spacers, 1x6 cleat, and 1x6, 1x8 and 1x2 frames—measure and cut to fit around panels.

tip Punch a starter hole with a nail for the piano hinge screws to keep them centered.

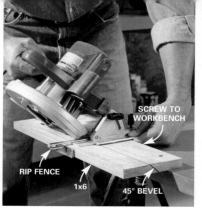
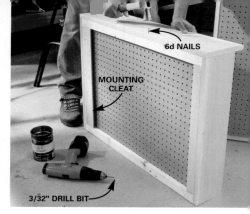

6d NAILS

MOUNTING CLEAT

3/32" DRILL BIT

PEG BOARD

1x2

SCREW TO WORKBENCH

RIP FENCE

1x6

45° BEVEL

1 Cut the peg board to the sizes shown on Figure A with a circular saw guided by a straightedge. Cut the 1x2s to length and fasten the peg board to them with 1-in. screws spaced every 8 in.

2 Cut the 1x6 mounting cleat in half at a 45-degree angle. For safety before cutting, screw it to a firm work surface with one edge overhanging 3 in. Use one half of the mounting cleat in place of the top 1x2 on the back peg board panel.

3 Measure and cut the 1x6 frame boards to fit around each panel. Glue and nail the top and bottom first, then the sides, to the 1x2 spacers with 2-in. (6d) finish nails spaced every 8 in. Fasten the frame board corners with two nails and glue. Predrill all holes with a 3/32-in. drill bit to avoid splitting the wood.

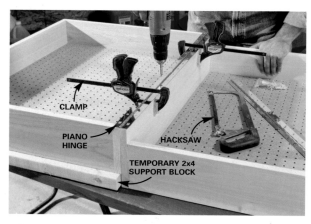

CLAMP

PIANO HINGE

HACKSAW

TEMPORARY 2x4 SUPPORT BLOCK

MOUNTING CLEAT

4 Cut the piano hinge to length with a hacksaw and screw it on with the screws in the hinge package. Support and clamp the hinge sides in position to simplify hinge attachment. Close the doors and attach the hasp.

5 Position the other half of the mounting cleat about 40 in. above the work surface and fasten it to the wall studs with four 3-in. screws. Hang the cabinet and drive two 3-in. screws through the bottom 1x2 into the wall studs for extra strength.

Wrap the panels to form the cabinet and doors

The frames for the three panels are all slightly different. The back panel frame consists of three 1x6s and a 1x8; the middle panel has four 1x2s; and the front has four 1x6s (Figure A). These differences allow them to hinge together.

Measure the lengths and nail on the frames. Make sure to run a bead of carpenter's glue along the panel edges and at the corner joints to make them stronger.

Clamp the piano hinge to a firm surface, and cut it to length with a hacksaw (about 32-5/8 in.). Set the top, bottom, and middle screws to align the hinge, then fill in the remaining holes (Photo 4).

A hasp will hold the doors closed. We used a chest-style one that pulls the doors tight together and has a slot for a lock.

Hang it on the wall

The mounting cleat is an easy way to hang this heavy cabinet. If you're mounting it over a workbench, hang it at least 16 in. above the work surface so you can open the doors without disturbing the project you're working on.

To hold the doors open when working, we installed eye hooks on the bottom of each door and on the wall. A short chain with small S-hooks holds the doors open.

Suspended extension ladder

Up, up and away!

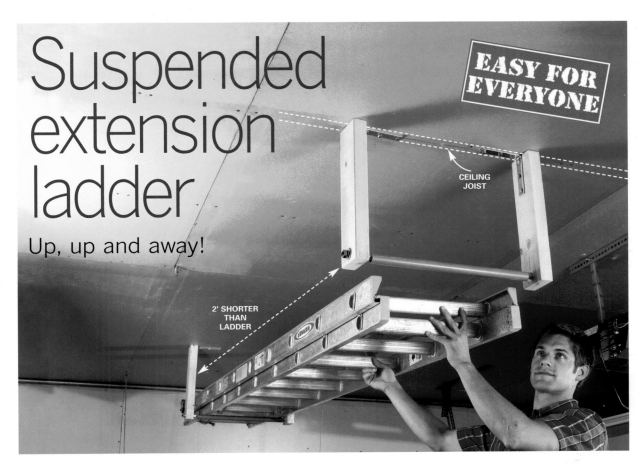

EASY FOR EVERYONE

CEILING JOIST

2' SHORTER THAN LADDER

It's always most convenient to hang an extension ladder on brackets on a wall. But unfortunately that wipes out all other storage potential for that wall. To save that valuable wall space, we designed a pair of 2x4 suspended brackets so a ladder can be stored flat along the ceiling.

Simply slide one end of the ladder into one bracket, then lift and slide the other end into the other bracket. Most people will need to stand on something solid to reach the second bracket. The 2x4 bracket sides are 16 in. long with 5-in. corner braces lag-screwed into the top for attachment to the ceiling joist (Figure A).

The bracket base is a 1/2-in. x 24-in. threaded steel rod ($2.75) that extends through 5/8-in. drilled holes on the bracket sides. It's held in place with flat/lock washers and a nut on each side of both 2x4 uprights. A 3/4-in. x 18-in.-long piece of PVC conduit pipe surrounds the rod for smooth rolling action when you slide the ladder in and out.

project at a glance

skill level
beginner

special tools
drill
drill bits

approximate cost
$10–$15

figure a ladder support detail

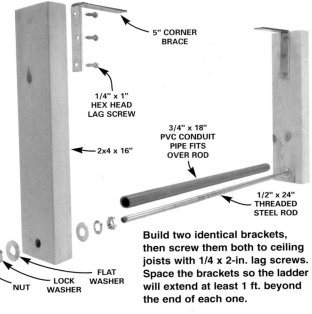

5" CORNER BRACE

1/4" x 1" HEX HEAD LAG SCREW

2x4 x 16"

3/4" x 18" PVC CONDUIT PIPE FITS OVER ROD

1/2" x 24" THREADED STEEL ROD

NUT

LOCK WASHER

FLAT WASHER

Build two identical brackets, then screw them both to ceiling joists with 1/4 x 2-in. lag screws. Space the brackets so the ladder will extend at least 1 ft. beyond the end of each one.

tip*

For extra security, wrap a bungee cord around the ladder and one bracket.

Super-simple utility cabinets

You can knock any of these cabinets together in a couple of hours and have that garage clutter tucked away by dinnertime!

Build 'em and fill 'em. We designed these sturdy cabinets for simple assembly. You just glue and screw plywood together to make the basic box, then add a premade door, actually an inexpensive bifold door panel. Since bifolds are readily available in several styles, including louvered and paneled, you can make a wide range of practical yet handsome cabinets, without the time and hassle of making the doors.

We built a set of five cabinets in different sizes to show you how versatile this design is. You can make them big and deep to store clothing and sports gear; shallow and tall for shovels, rakes, skis or fishing rods; or shallow and short to mount on walls for tools, paint cans and other small items. You can even mount them on wheels and roll your tools right to the job. The only limitation is the size of standard bifold doors.

In this article, we'll demonstrate how to build one of the smaller hanging wall cabinets. You can build the others using the same techniques and the Cutting Lists on p. 8.

You don't need advanced skills or special tools to build this entire set of cabinets. However, you do have to cut a lot of plywood accurately. A table saw helps here, but a circular saw with a guide works fine too. Add a drill or two, a couple of clamps and some careful advance planning, and you're set.

Buying the bifolds and plywood

When planning your cabinets, begin by choosing the bifold door and build the rest of the cabinet to match its dimensions. Standard bifolds are 79 in. high and available in 24-in., 30-in., 32-in. and 36-in. widths. Keep in mind that you get two doors for each of these widths, each approximately 12, 15, 16 or 18 in. wide. Your cabinet can be any of the single-door widths or any of the double-door widths. You can also cut the doors down to make shorter cabinets, as we demonstrate here. Make them any depth you choose.

Bifolds come in several styles and wood species. We chose louvered pine doors ($56 for 30-in. wide) and birch plywood ($40 per sheet) for a handsome, natural look. All the materials for our cabinet, including hardware, cost about $70. The five cabinets cost $320. You can cut that cost considerably by using less expensive plywood, bifolds and hinges.

You can also save by using plywood efficiently. Once you decide on the door sizes, lay out all the cabinet pieces on a scale drawing of a 4 x 8-ft. sheet of plywood (graph paper helps). You can even adjust the cabinet depths a bit to achieve best use. We built the five cabinets shown from four sheets of 3/4-in. plywood and two sheets of 1/4-in. plywood for the backs.

1 Mark the door length and clamp a straightedge to the door to guide your saw. Cut the other cabinet pieces using the straightedge as well.

2 Predrill screw holes through the sides 3/8 in. from the ends. Drive 1-5/8 in. screws with finish washers through the sides into the top and bottom. Stack extra shelves in the corners to keep the box square.

The "partial wrap-around" hinges we used may not be available at home centers or hardware stores. However, woodworking stores carry them. If you don't mind exposed hinges, simply use bifold hinges, which cost less than $1 each at home centers.

Cut out all the parts

Begin by cutting the bifold doors to size (Photo 1). This will determine the exact cabinet height. Be sure to use a guide and a sharp blade for a straight, crisp cut. Center the cut on the dividing rail. Be prepared for the saw to bump up and down slightly as it crosses each stile (Photo 1). Then trim each newly created door so that the top and bottom rails are the same width.

Some bifold door manufacturers use only a single dowel to attach each rail to the stile. If this is the case with your doors, you may find that one of your rails (after being cut in half) is no longer attached to the door. Don't panic. Dab a little glue on each rail and stile and clamp them back together. After 20 minutes or so, you'll be back in business.

Then cut the plywood to size using a guide to keep all the cuts straight and square. If the plywood splinters a bit, score the cutting line first with a utility knife.

tip

Most lumberyards and home centers have a large saw (called a panel saw) for cutting sheets of plywood. For a nominal fee, you can have them rip all of your plywood to proper widths. (You'll cut the pieces to length later.) You have to plan your cabinet depths in advance, but it's quicker than ripping the plywood yourself and makes hauling it home a lot easier.

cutting lists
for cabinet styles shown on p. 9

Storage locker
Door: One 11-3/4" x 79" (half of a 24" bifold)*

Sides: Two 3/4" x 11-1/4" x 79"

Top, bottom, shelf: Three 3/4" x 11-1/4" x 10-1/4"

Cleats: Two 3/4" x 3" x 10-1/4"

Front cleat: 3/4" x 3" x 10-1/4"

Back: One 1/4" x 11-3/4" x 79"

Closet on wheels
Doors: Two 15-3/4" x 79" (32" bifold)*

Sides: Two 3/4" x 22-1/2" x 79"

Top, bottom, shelf: Three 3/4" x 22-1/2" x 30-1/8"

Cleats: Three 3/4" x 3" x 30-1/8"

Back: One 1/4" x 31-5/8" x 79"

Casters: Four 3"

Paneled wall cabinet
Doors: Two 14-3/4" x 32-1/4" (30" bifold)*

Sides: Two 3/4" x 11-1/4" x 32-1/4"

Top, bottom, shelves: Four 3/4" x 11-1/4" x 28-1/8"

Cleats: Two 3/4" x 3" x 28-1/8"

Back: One 1/4" x 29-5/8" x 32-1/4"

Narrow floor cabinet
Door: One 11-3/4" x 79" (half of a 24" bifold)*

Sides: Two 3/4" x 11-1/4" x 79"

Top, bottom, shelves: Nine 3/4" x 11-1/4" x 10-1/4"

Cleats: Two 3/4" x 3" x 10-1/4"

Back: One 1/4" x 11-3/4" x 79"

*Exact door sizes vary. Measure your doors before deciding cabinet dimensions.

Ventilated wall cabinet

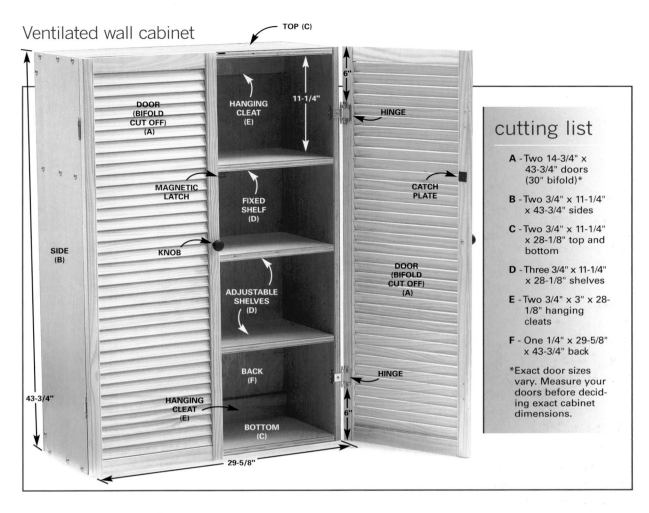

TOP (C)

DOOR
(BIFOLD
CUT OFF)
(A)

HANGING
CLEAT
(E)

11-1/4"

HINGE

6"

MAGNETIC
LATCH

FIXED
SHELF
(D)

CATCH
PLATE

SIDE
(B)

KNOB

DOOR
(BIFOLD
CUT OFF)
(A)

ADJUSTABLE
SHELVES
(D)

43-3/4"

BACK
(F)

HANGING
CLEAT
(E)

HINGE

BOTTOM
(C)

6"

29-5/8"

cutting list

A - Two 14-3/4" x 43-3/4" doors (30" bifold)*

B - Two 3/4" x 11-1/4" x 43-3/4" sides

C - Two 3/4" x 11-1/4" x 28-1/8" top and bottom

D - Three 3/4" x 11-1/4" x 28-1/8" shelves

E - Two 3/4" x 3" x 28-1/8" hanging cleats

F - One 1/4" x 29-5/8" x 43-3/4" back

*Exact door sizes vary. Measure your doors before deciding exact cabinet dimensions.

Other cabinet options (Cutting Lists and dimensions on p. 8)

Storage locker
Compact storage for long items like skis, fishing rods, long-handled tools; either on floor or wall-hung; 12-in. wide door and one fixed shelf.

Closet on wheels
Large storage capacity (about 32 in. wide and 22-1/2 in. deep); fixed shelf; closet rod; 3-in. swivel casters ($6 each).

Paneled wall cabinet
Shorter version of cabinet above; made from the paneled portion of partial louvered doors; one adjustable shelf.

Narrow floor or wall cabinet
Shelf version of storage locker (left); top and bottom shelves fixed; intermediate shelves mounted on adjustable shelf standards ($2 each).

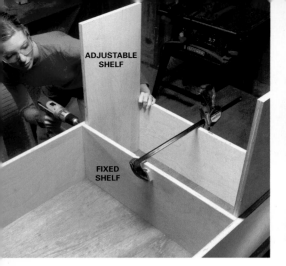

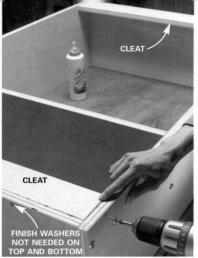

3 **Predrill, clamp and screw the fixed shelf to the sides. Use adjustable shelves as a guide to space it and keep it square.**

4 **Glue and clamp hanging cleats to the top and bottom. Predrill and drive screws through the top, bottom and sides into the cleats.**

5 **Spread a bead of glue on all back edges. Then align the plywood back with the top and nail with 1-in. brads. Align the other sides and nail in the order shown.**

Assemble the box

Assemble the box face down on a flat surface. The garage floor works well for this step.

Mark and predrill screw holes through the sides for the top and bottom pieces (Photo 2). If you've got two drills, this is the time for them both. Use one for drilling holes and the other for driving screws.

We added finish washers (8¢ each; available at full-service hardware stores) for a more decorative look.

Attach the fixed shelf next to stiffen and strengthen the box (Photo 3). Use the extra shelves as guides to help position and square the shelf. Predrill and drive three screws through each side into the fixed shelf.

Attach cleats at the top and bottom of the cabinet to use for screwing the cabinet to a wall (Photo 4). Use three or four screws across the top and bottom. Clamp the cleat into place until you drive the screws. Because the screws won't be visible on the top and bottom, you can skip the finish washers. Use your finger to make sure the cleat sits flush with the side (Photo 4).

The 1/4-in. plywood back stiffens the frame and keeps it square, which is essential for the doors to fit accurately. Spread glue along the cabinet edges, including the fixed shelf and the hanging cleats (Photo 5). Carefully set the back onto the cabinet, keeping the top flush with the cabinet top. Nail in the order and direction shown in Photo 5. Align the edges carefully before nailing each side to keep the cabinet perfectly square. (You cut the plywood back perfectly square, right?)

Shelves, hinges and other hardware

Use a scrap of peg board to help lay out the holes evenly for the adjustable shelf support pins. Mark each hole clearly (red circles, Photo 6) on the front and back of the peg board. Mark each hole position on one side of the cabinet, then slide the peg board across to the other side for marking. Don't flip the peg board over; it can throw the pattern off and the shelves will rock rather than lie flat.

Most shelf support pins require a 1/4-in. hole, but check the pins you buy to be sure. In addition, measure how far the pins are supposed to go into the cabinet sides. Wrap a piece of masking tape around your drill bit at this depth (photo at right). This ensures that you won't drill completely through the side of your cabinet. Check the bit after every few holes to make sure the tape hasn't slipped.

Install your door hinges 6 in. from the top and bottom of the doors (add a third hinge on taller doors). The best type is a "partial wrap-around" hinge (Photo 7). Its hinge leaves are hidden when the door is closed, and the design allows you to avoid driving screws into the weak plywood edge grain.

Begin by installing the hinges on the door (Photo 7). Keep them perfectly square to the door edge and predrill screw holes as precisely as possible. An extra set of hands will be helpful when attaching the doors to the cabinet.

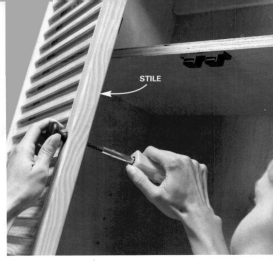

STILE

6 Mark shelf pin locations on both front and back sides of a peg board template. Mark one side of the cabinet, then slide (not flip) the peg board to the opposite side and mark matching holes. Drill the 1/4-in. pin holes.

7 Screw the hinges to the cabinet doors. Align the door edges with the cabinet top and bottom. Then predrill and screw the hinges to the cabinet sides.

8 Attach cabinet knobs to the doors and install a pair of magnetic latches to hold the doors closed. For full-length doors, install latches at both the top and the bottom.

Have your partner align the door exactly with the top or bottom of the cabinet while you mark, predrill and screw the hinges to the cabinet side. Repeat for the other door. Ideally the doors will meet evenly in the center with about a 1/8-in. gap between. You may have to "tweak" the hinge positions slightly with paper shims, or plane the doors a bit to make them perfect.

Choose any type of knob and magnetic latch you like. However, bifold door stiles (the vertical edges) are narrow, so make sure the neighboring door will clear the knob when opened (Photo 8). If you have a rail (the horizontal door frame member), mount the knobs there.

Another problem: Bifold stiles are usually 1 to 1-1/8 in. thick and most knobs are designed for 3/4-in. doors. So you may have to look for longer knob screws at your local hardware store. Or try this trick: With a 3/8-in. bit, drill a 1/4-in. deep hole on the backside of the stile to recess the screwhead.

To mount a magnetic latch, first mount the magnet to the underside of the fixed shelf (Photo 8). Stick the catch plate to the magnet with the "mounting points" facing out (photo below). Close the door and press it tightly against the latch. The points on the catch plate will indent the door slightly and indicate where to mount the plate.

Finishing

That's about it. Now that you've built one cabinet and know the ropes, you can probably build the second cabinet in half the time. We finished our cabinets inside and out with two coats of clear water-based satin polyurethane. It dries quickly (half hour), has little or no odor, and cleans up with soap and water. The first coat raises the wood grain a bit, so you have to sand it lightly with fine sandpaper (150 grit or finer). Whether you use a clear finish, paint or stain, it's generally faster if you remove the doors and hardware first.

Partial wrap-around hinges

The hinges shown are available at woodworking stores such as Rockler Woodworking and Hardware (800) 279-4441; www.rockler.com; No. 31456; $5.99 per pair). Less expensive styles are also available.

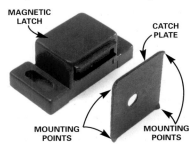

MAGNETIC LATCH

CATCH PLATE

MOUNTING POINTS

MOUNTING POINTS

Roll-out pantry
Twice the storage with half the hassle

Most cabinet manufacturers now include roll-out shelves in their base cabinets. But if you don't have this convenience, this project will one-up those shelves. Here's how to make an entire roll-out pantry.

The hardware consists of two heavy-duty bottom-mounted slides and one center-mounted top slide that together can support 130 lbs. Construct your unit to suit your needs. This bottom tray is 3-1/2 in. tall and the upper ones are 2-1/2 in. tall. You may want to include only two trays if you'll be storing cereal boxes and other tall packages.

Since you'll be converting your door from swinging to rolling mode, you'll need to remove the door and hinges. You'll also have to remove the existing handle, fill the screw holes with putty and reinstall the pull centered on the door. If your hardware mounts from the backside, install it before attaching the door (Photo 6).

SUBTRACT 1/2" FROM CABINET OPENING TO DETERMINE PANTRY UNIT WIDTH

SHELF UNIT HEIGHT (MINUS DEPTH OF TOP BRACKET)

BOTTOM GLIDES

PLYWOOD FILLER

FACE FRAME AND DOOR HINGES REMOVED

TOP OF FRAME OPENING

PLYWOOD FLANGES

1x3 TOP GLIDE SUPPORT

TOP GLIDE

1 Measure the cabinet face frame opening, then subtract the height of the top and bottom glides. Use the guidelines given to arrive at the depth, width and height of your pantry unit. Be sure to install the bottom glides so they run parallel to the cabinet sides. If necessary, use plywood to raise the cabinet bottom even with the bottom lip of the face frame.

2 Install the top glide support and top glide so the support is level and flush to the top of the frame opening. Screw plywood flanges to each end of the 1x3 support beforehand to make it simpler to secure it to the front and back of the cabinet.

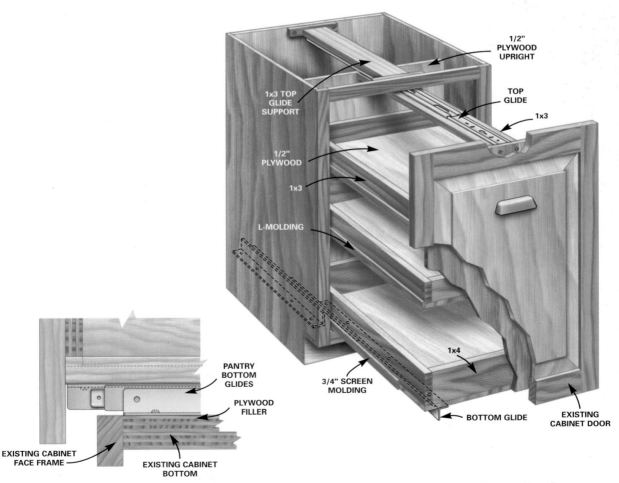

1/2" PLYWOOD UPRIGHT

TOP GLIDE

1x3

1x3 TOP GLIDE SUPPORT

1/2" PLYWOOD

1x3

L-MOLDING

PANTRY BOTTOM GLIDES

PLYWOOD FILLER

EXISTING CABINET FACE FRAME

EXISTING CABINET BOTTOM

3/4" SCREEN MOLDING

1x4

BOTTOM GLIDE

EXISTING CABINET DOOR

● Shelf unit dimensions will vary according to cabinet size.

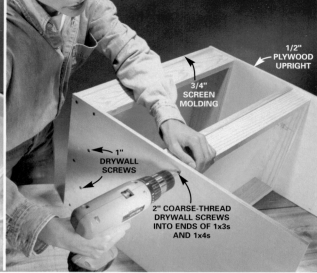

3 Assemble the pantry trays using 1x4s, 1x3s, 6d nails and carpenter's glue. Use the plywood bottoms to square up the trays before nailing them on. L-moldings support and cover the plywood edges of the upper two trays; 3/4-in. screen molding covers the exposed plywood edges of the bottom tray.

4 Secure the trays to the 1/2-in. plywood uprights using glue and drywall screws. Arrange the spacing of the trays to meet your needs.

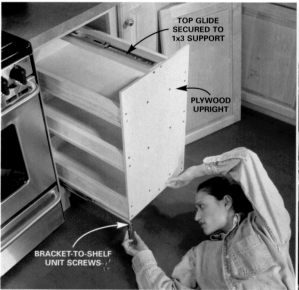

5 Screw the tray assembly to the bottom runners, making sure it's centered in the opening and running parallel to the cabinet sides. The extended portion of the top slide is secured to a 1x3 screwed between the two plywood uprights. You can loosen this 1x3, then adjust the height so the top glide runs flat and smooth.

6 Clamp the cabinet door to the front of the pantry assembly; center it and make the height even with adjacent doors. Predrill eight holes through the plywood upright and drive screws into the back of the cabinet door. After installing two screws, close the door to check its alignment with the adjacent doors. Make adjustments, then install the remaining screws. Use short screws so they don't penetrate the front of the cabinet door.

The key measurements and clearances for the roll-out unit are as follows: The plywood front and back panels should be about 1/8 in. shorter than the distance between the installed top and bottom glides (see illustration on p. 39). The width of the unit should be 1/2 in. narrower than the cabinet opening. The depth of the unit should be 1/2 in. less than the depth of the cabinet (not including the face frame).

Corner swing-
and roll-out trays

Better access for hard-to-reach corners

Blind-corner cabinets—those with a blank face that allow another cabinet to butt into them—may be great for aging wine, but they're darn near impossible to see and reach into. This pair of accessories puts an end to this hidden wasteland. The hinged shelf swings out of the way, and the gliding shelf slides forward so you can access food items stored in the back. You can use the same

project at a glance

skill level
intermediate

tools
miter saw
drill

approximate cost
$40

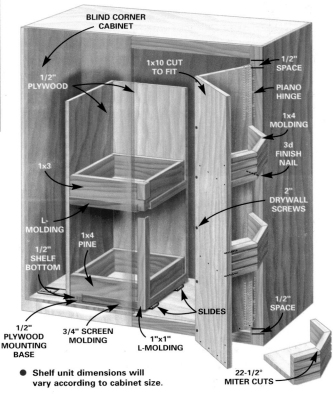

BLIND CORNER CABINET

1/2" PLYWOOD

1x10 CUT TO FIT

1/2" SPACE

PIANO HINGE

1x4 MOLDING

3d FINISH NAIL

2" DRYWALL SCREWS

1x3

L-MOLDING

1x4 PINE

1/2" SHELF BOTTOM

1/2" PLYWOOD MOUNTING BASE

3/4" SCREEN MOLDING

1"x1" L-MOLDING

SLIDES

1/2" SPACE

22-1/2° MITER CUTS

● Shelf unit dimensions will vary according to cabinet size.

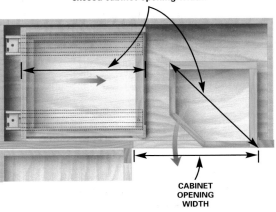

● These two measurements cannot exceed cabinet opening width.

CABINET OPENING WIDTH

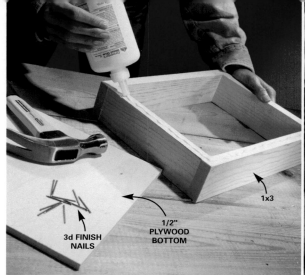

1 Glue and nail the 1x3s together using 4d finish nails, then use 3d finish nails to secure the plywood bottom.

3d FINISH NAILS

1/2" PLYWOOD BOTTOM

1x3

2 Cut out the two plywood sides, then glue and nail the corners. Connect the trays to the two plywood sides using 1-in. drywall screws, then cut and nail L-molding to support the front corner. Cut and install L-moldings to support and cover the exposed plywood edges of the upper tray. Install 3/4-in. screen molding to cover the plywood edges of the bottom tray.

L-MOLDING TO COVER BOTTOM EDGE OF TRAY

1" x 1" L-MOLDING SUPPORT

PLYWOOD SIDES

1/2" PLYWOOD

hardware and techniques for making base cabinets more accessible, too.

The key measurements and clearances:

Glide-out shelf dimensions. You can make the unit only as long as the door opening is wide (or else you can't fit it in). Make the unit about 1/2 in. narrower than the inside width of the cabinet.

Swing-out tray dimensions. The corner-to-corner or diagonal measurement of the unit (see p. 15) can't exceed the width of the door opening (or else that won't fit either). Make the unit about 1 in. shorter than the opening height so it has room to swing freely when installed.

PLYWOOD MOUNTING BASE

METAL SLIDES

COMPLETED TRAY UNIT

3 Cut the mounting base plywood slightly smaller than the other tray bottoms, then secure the two slides parallel to each other about 1 in. from each edge. Slip this mounting base into the opening, extend the slides, then screw them to the cabinet bottom at the rear of the cabinet. Install the slides parallel to the cabinet sides, so the base slides back and forth freely.

Handy Hints®

- Beg, borrow or rent a compressor, finish nailer and brad gun, if you can. You'll work faster, eliminate hammer marks and split the wood less often than you would hand-nailing.

- Use a damp sponge to wipe up glue drips immediately. It'll save hours of sanding down the line.

- Test-fit your shelf units in the cabinet as you work.

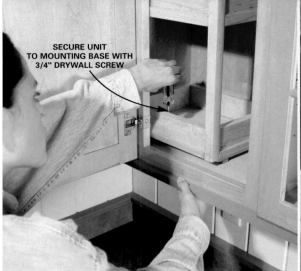

4 Screw the tray unit to the mounting base using 3/4-in. screws. After installing the first screw, slide the unit forward and back, then adjust it until it runs parallel to the cabinet sides and install three more screws.

5 Cut the 1x10 swing-out uprights to length and width (one should be 3/4 in. narrower than the other). Use a countersink bit to predrill holes along one edge, then glue and screw the two edges together. The diagonal measurement (see Photo 7) should be less than the cabinet opening.

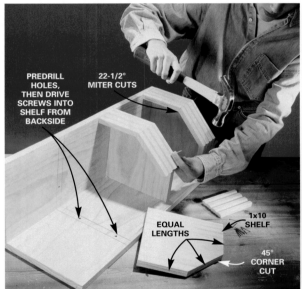

6 Assemble the shelf unit. First mark the shelf positions on the uprights and predrill holes from the front side. Create the three shelves by cutting a 1x10 to length and width, then cutting the corner at 45 degrees. Hold the shelves in place and drive drywall screws through these holes from the backside into the shelves. Cut the 22-1/2-degree angles on the front moldings and secure them with 3d finish nails. You can use any type of wide decorative molding that's at least 1/2 x 3 inches.

7 Screw the piano hinge to the front edge of the swing-out unit, then to the edge of the cabinet face frame. Make certain the swing-out has 1/2 in. of top and bottom clearance. Use an assistant to help you lift and hold the unit at the proper height while you're securing it to the cabinet.

Door-mounted spice and lid racks

There's even storage on the back of a door

These simple racks will help transform those chaotic gangs of spice bottles and pan lids into orderly regiments. Here you'll learn how to build only the spice rack; the lid rack uses the same steps but without the shelves. Each spice rack can hold 20 to 30 bottles, and each lid rack two to six lids, depending on the height and width of your cabinet doors. Before building, measure your spice bottles and lids to determine the spacing of your shelves and dowels.

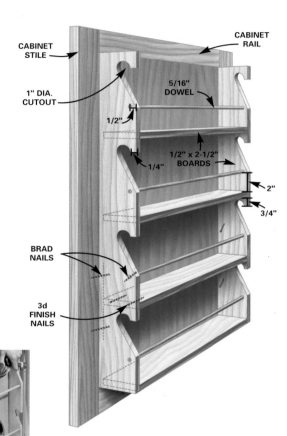

CABINET STILE

CABINET RAIL

1" DIA. CUTOUT

5/16" DOWEL

1/2"

1/4"

1/2" x 2-1/2" BOARDS

2"

3/4"

BRAD NAILS

3d FINISH NAILS

The key measurements and clearances:

Existing shelf depth. If the existing cabinet shelves are full depth, narrow them by about 2 in. to accommodate each door-mounted rack. Shelves that are permanently affixed in grooves in the cabinet sides will need to be cut in place with a jigsaw. Adjustable shelves can be removed, cut along the backside with a circular saw or table saw, then replaced. You may need to move brackets or add holes to remount narrowed shelves.

Spice rack depth and positioning. Make certain the new rack won't hit the cabinet frame when the door

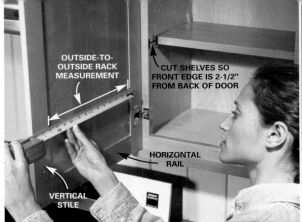

1 Measure the distance between the two vertical stiles and the two horizontal rails to determine the outside dimensions of your spice rack. Cut existing shelves back 2 in. so they don't interfere with the rack when the door is closed.

2 Transfer dimensions from the illustration on p. 48 onto 1/2 x 2-1/2 in. side boards. Cut out the sides of the spice rack. Drill 1-in. holes to create the circular shape, then finish the cutout with a jigsaw. Drill 5/16-in. holes for the dowels. Sand parts smooth.

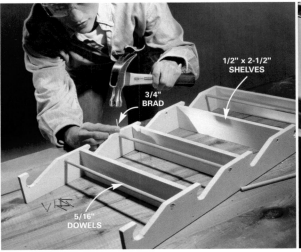

3 Glue and nail the shelves in place one at a time, using 3d finish nails. Then use 3/4-in. brads to pin the dowels in place. Sink all nailheads using a nail set. Apply polyurethane or other finish to match the cabinets.

4 Clamp the finished rack to the door, then drill angled pilot holes through the rack and into the door every 8 in. Secure with brad nails (remove the door for this step if you find you need a more solid surface for hammering). Use carpenter's glue for a more permanent installation.

swings. In this case, fitting the rack between the two 2-in.-wide vertical stiles (Photo 1) provided adequate room. If your doors are solid wood or laminate, hold in place a scrap of wood the same depth as the spice rack (2-1/2 in. was the depth used here) and swing the door. Move it away from the door edge until it no longer makes contact with the cabinet frame, then mark the door. This will determine the overall width of your spice rack.

Use soft, easy-to-nail pine and basswood for both the spice and the lid racks. If you're using a harder wood, like maple or oak, position the pieces, then predrill holes through the side pieces and into the shelf ends. This will prevent splitting and make nailing easier. Install your shelves one at a time so you don't have to balance and juggle multiple pieces as you work. Always nail on a flat, solid surface.

Handy Hints®

Use high-gloss polyurethane for natural wood and high-gloss enamel for painted wood. These finishes are more scrubbable.

Toe-kick drawers

Make every nook and cranny count

The toe-kick under the cabinets shown here was just a strip of 1/4-in. plywood backed by 5/8-in. particleboard (Photo 1). You might run into something different, like particleboard without any backing at all. In any case, opening up the space under the cabinet is usually fairly easy.

To determine the dimensions of the cradle, measure the depth and width of the space and subtract 1/16 in. from both to provide some adjustment room. If your floor covering is thicker than 1/4 in. (ceramic tile, for example), you may have to glue plywood scraps to the underside of the cradle to raise it and prevent the drawer from scraping against the floor when extended. Size the drawer to allow for slides and the cradle's sides.

Don't worry too much about an exact match of the finish with your existing cabinets. In that dark toe space, nobody will be able to tell. For hardware, consider handles instead of knobs so you can pull the drawers open with your toe.

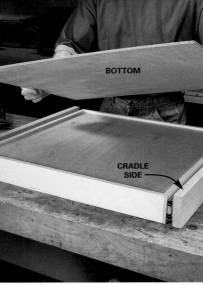

BACKING

DRYWALL SAW

BOTTOM

CRADLE SIDE

CRADLE

1 Pry off the toe-kick and remove the backing by drilling a large hole near the center, cutting the backing in half and tearing it out. Then grab a flashlight and check for blocks, protruding screws or anything else that might interfere with the drawer.

2 Build a cradle, simply two sides and a bottom, to hold the drawer. Attach the cradle's sides to the slides and drawer, then add the plywood bottom.

3 Slip the cradle under the cabinet. Then drive a pair of screws through each side and into the cabinet box as far back as you can reach.

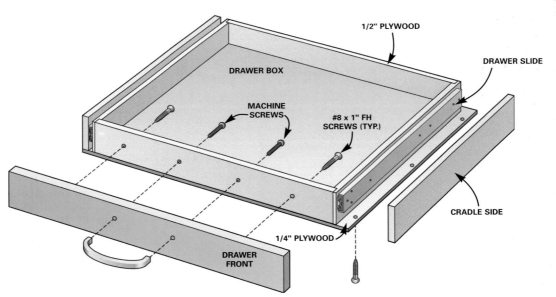

1/2" PLYWOOD

DRAWER SLIDE

DRAWER BOX

MACHINE SCREWS

#8 x 1" FH SCREWS (TYP.)

CRADLE SIDE

1/4" PLYWOOD

DRAWER FRONT

personally speaking

I always looked at the toe space under the cabinets in my too-small kitchen and thought it would be a great place to add drawers. After some head scratching, I found a way to do it without having to install drawer slides in that dark, cramped space. I mounted the drawer and slides in a self-contained cradle that slips easily under the cabinet.

Because the cabinet overhangs the toe-kick by 3 or 4 in., full-extension slides are a necessity for this project. Better yet, use "overtravel" slides that extend an extra inch.

–Gary Wentz, editor
The Family Handyman

Family message center

This cabinet keeps everyone's schedule within easy reach... without cluttering up the kitchen

Busy family? If you have trouble keeping track of the kids' or your spouse's schedule, and you want to make sure your messages are read, build this simple organizing cabinet. It has an erasable calendar for busy schedules and immediate messages; plenty of cork for photos, invitations, coupons and permission slips; a pull-down door with a notepad for short messages and shopping lists; and storage for a good supply of pens, postage stamps, tissue and other items that usually clutter nearby table tops. It also has hooks for keys and shallow bins for magazines, mail, dog leashes, address books and homework (completed, no doubt).

This cabinet was designed to slip back into the wall between empty stud spaces, so you won't bump it as you go by and knock stuff off the board. And the closed doors keep most of the clutter out of sight.

You'll need a table saw, a miter saw and a pneumatic brad nailer for this project, in addition to standard hand tools, but you could also build the project with just a circular saw (with a cutting guide for straight cuts) and a drill.

Detective work comes first

Before cutting into the wall, try to get an idea of what's concealed inside it. Find stud locations with a stud finder or by tapping on the wall and listening for variations in tone. Be aware that blank walls can conceal a wide variety of framing—especially in older houses. Note: Locating studs in old plaster walls may require a more sensitive, higher-priced stud finder. If you absolutely can't find the studs, try removing a section of baseboard and opening the wall where you can hide the hole. Or tap a finish nail through the wall until you hit a stud, then measure over about 16 in. and tap the nail through again to find the next stud.

Once you've located studs, check both sides of the wall and the rooms above and below for heat registers, plumbing and electrical fixtures. If you find potential obstructions on adjacent floors, use an outside wall for a reference point to estimate if it'll obstruct your cabinet. Even if the location looks clear, you never know what's inside, so cut small holes in both cavities and double-check for obstructions. Cutting the hole with a utility knife is difficult, but it's safer than using a saw because you can keep the cuts shallow and away from any electrical wires (Photo 1). If you find obstructions, don't despair. Half of this message center is only 3/4 in. deep (not including trim). It may fit over the obstructions without any problem. Another option is to make the box shallower. You may also be able to extend wires around the boxes by rewiring, but consult an electrician or electrical inspector first.

making it fit your space

The message center fits inside a standard interior wall, which is usually constructed of 2x4s spaced 16 in. on center, with 14-1/2 in. of space between studs. Exterior walls won't work, because they have insulation in them. And some interior walls won't work either, if they have heating ducts, pipes and wiring running through them. You can easily adapt this project to any size and as many open cavities as you want. The basic concept is simple—just cut a hole in the drywall, insert a wooden box and add trim to it.

Cut the openings

Draw plumb lines at stud locations, then mark the rough opening height (34 in. from the floor to the bottom and 83 in. to the top). Adjust this height above the floor, if necessary, so the message center lines up with nearby door or window trim.

Check the studs for plumb (Photo 3) and adjust the box dimensions as needed to fit cleanly between them. In this situation, the center stud was plumb, but the left and right sides were out of plumb by 1/8 in. in opposite directions, so the two boxes were made 14-1/4 in. wide instead of 14-1/2 in. wide and left 1-5/8 in. between them. It's generally best to leave the center stud in place.

Build the boxes

This message center spans two stud cavities, with a deep side for shelves and miscellaneous storage and a shallow

materials list

One 4' x 4' x 1/2" birch plywood (A, B, C)

One 2' x 4' x 3/4" birch plywood (K, L)

Two 1/2" x 3/4" x 8' pine (A1, B1, J)

One 3/4" x 3/4" x 4' pine (D)

One 1x4 x 6' pine (E)

One 1x3 x 4' pine; two 1x3 x 8' pine (F, G)

One 1x2 x 6' (H)

1" brads

1-1/2" brads

2-1/2" finish nails

Wood glue

cutting list

KEY	PCS.	SIZE & DESCRIPTION
A	2	3-1/2" x 47-7/8" x 1/2" birch plywood (sides for deep box)
B	2	3-1/2" x 13-1/4" x 1/2" birch plywood (top and bottom for deep box)
A1	2	1/2" x 3/4" x 47-7/8" pine (sides for shallow box)
B1	2	1/2" x 3/4" x 13-1/4" pine (top and bottom for shallow box)
C	2	14-1/4" x 45-7/8" x 1/2" birch plywood (backs for both boxes)
D	4	3/4" x 3/4" x 10" pine (nailers for top and bottom trim F)
E	4	3/4" x 3-1/2" x 13-1/4" pine (shelves)
F	2	3/4" x 2-1/2" x 34-1/8" pine (top and bottom trim)
G	3	3/4" x 2-1/2" x 44-3/8" pine (center and side trim)
H	2	3/4" x 1-1/2" x 35-1/8" pine (top and bottom sill)
J	2	1/2" x 3/4" x 34-1/8" pine (bottom crossbars)
K	1	3/4" x 13-1/8" x 20-1/8" birch plywood (upper door)
L	1	3/4" x 13-1/8" x 12-1/4" birch plywood (lower door)

figure a
message center details

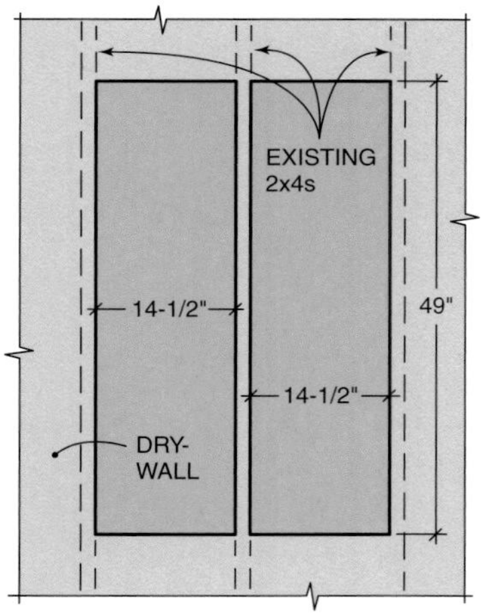

WALL OPENINGS

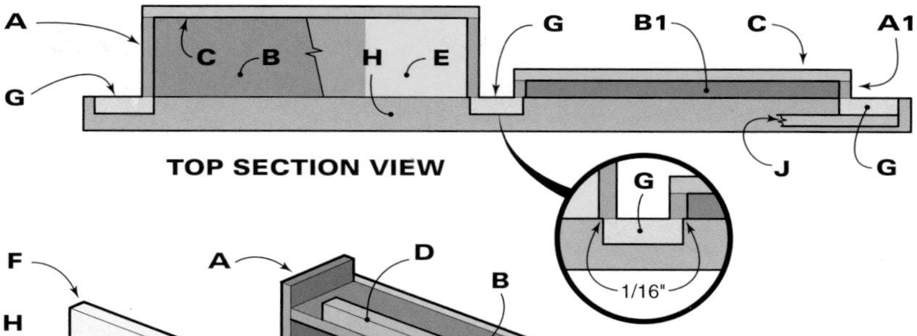

EXISTING 2x4s

14-1/2"

14-1/2"

49"

DRY-WALL

TOP SECTION VIEW

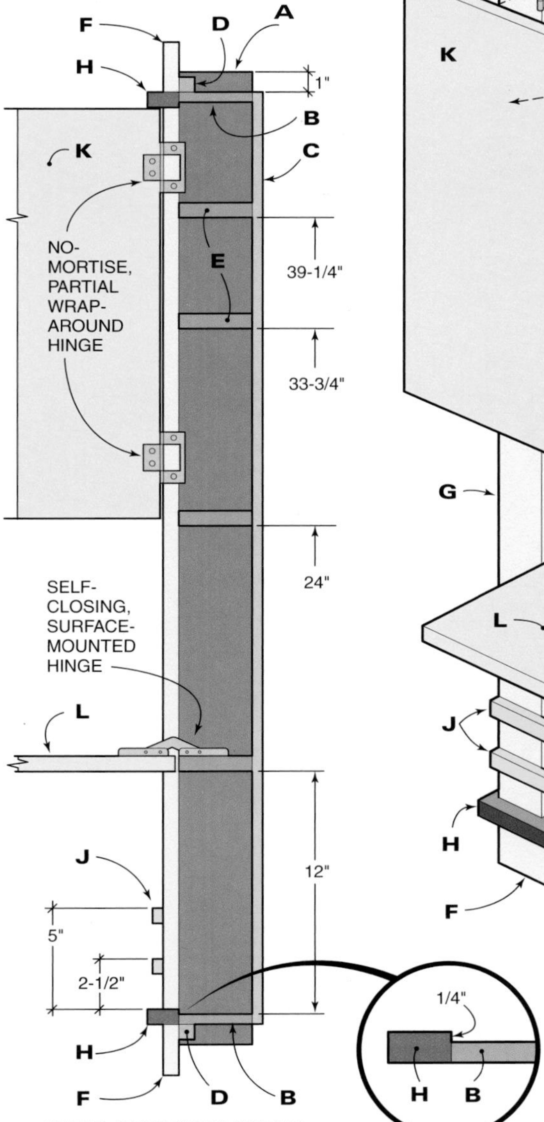

A

G

C

B

H

E

G

B1

C

A1

J

G

G

1/16"

SIDE SECTION VIEW

F

H

D

A

1"

K

B

C

NO-MORTISE, PARTIAL WRAP-AROUND HINGE

E

39-1/4"

33-3/4"

SELF-CLOSING, SURFACE-MOUNTED HINGE

L

24"

J

12"

5"

2-1/2"

1/4"

H

F

D

B

H   B

F

H

A

D

B

E

K

E

E

E

G

G

L

KNOBS

J

C

B

C

G

G

C

D

A1

B1

D

B

B1

D

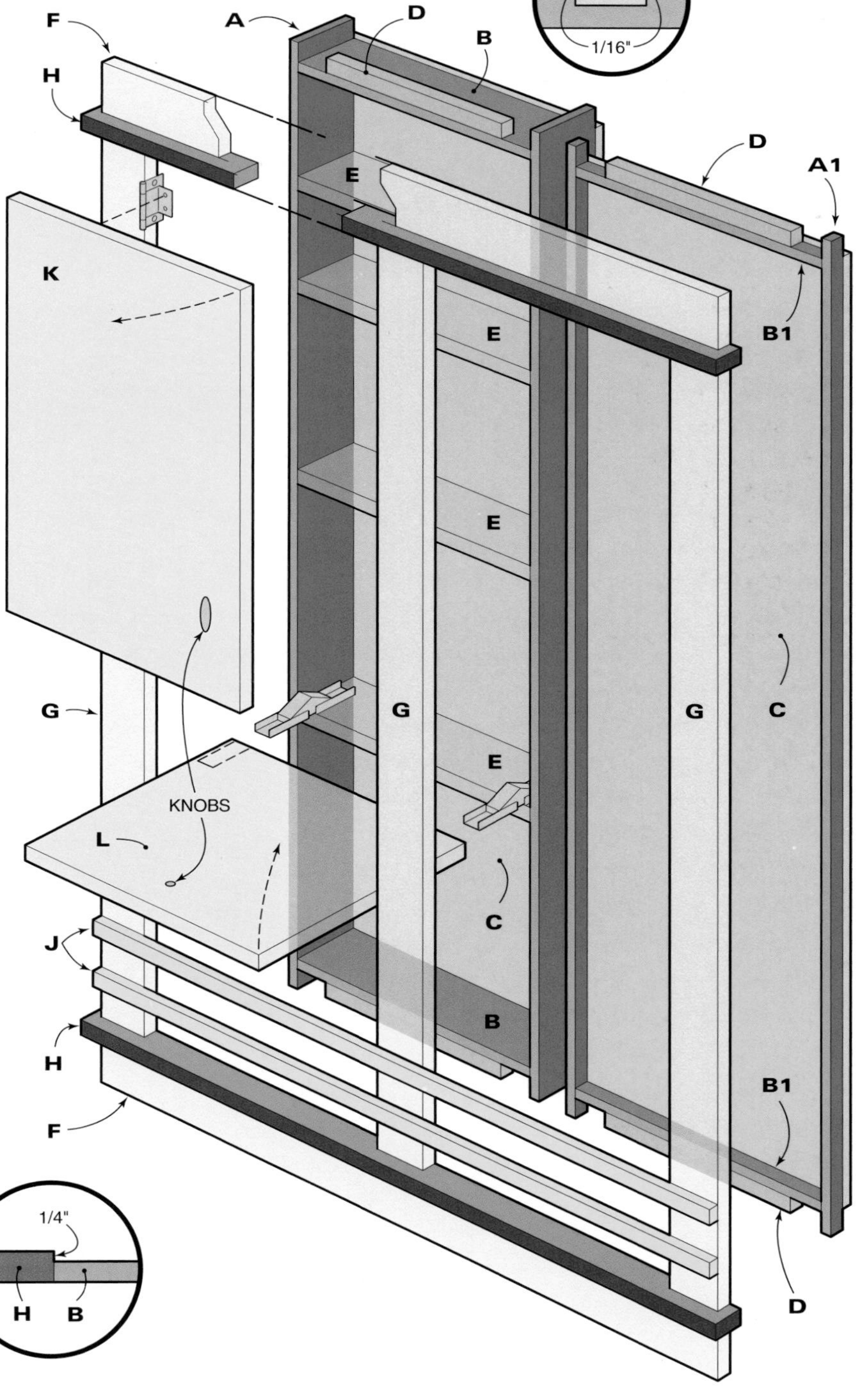

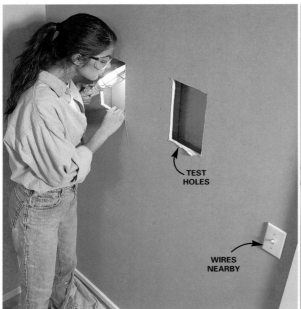

1 Find nearby studs with a stud finder, then cut a small opening with a utility knife in each stud cavity and check for obstructions. Save the cutouts in case you have to repair the wall.

2 Cut the opening to the desired height and size of your message center, following the studs with the drywall saw. Smooth ragged edges with a rasp or knife.

side for a cork message board and calendar. To maximize space, make the sides of the deep box from 1/2-in. birch plywood and the sides of the shallow message board from 1/2-in. x 3/4-in. pine. Nailing trim to a 1/2-in. edge is finicky work, so use a brad nailer or predrill the nail holes.

Cut the backs and side pieces from a 4 x 4-ft. sheet of 1/2-in. birch plywood using a table saw or a circular saw with an edge guide. If you use a circular saw, cut from the backside to avoid chipping the birch veneer. If possible, gang-cut pieces that are the same length (Photo 4). Use 1/2-in. plywood for the back for rigidity and give solid support for the cork board and any other items you want to mount.

Cut the long sides of the boxes 47-7/8 in. (A, A1, Figure A, p. 25), and nail the top and bottom pieces (B, B1) 1 in. in from the end to create nailer legs for the top and bottom trim pieces (F); see Photo 5. Glue and nail the back (C) down onto the box, aligning the edges and squaring the box as you nail (Photo 5). Tack down the back with 1-in. brad nails; longer nails might angle and break through the plywood sides. Use a damp cloth to wipe off any glue that oozes to the inside.

Install shelves

Nail the shelves (E) into place before joining the two boxes (Photo 6). Gang-cut the shelves from 1x4 pine, then slide them into position and hold them tight against square blocks of wood clamped to the sides. Mark the center of the shelf on the outside of the box frame to ensure accurate nailing (Photo 6). Use four 1-1/2-in. brads on each side and then flip the box over, connect the nailing lines from each side across the back and shoot a few brads in through the plywood back for extra strength and rigidity.

Join the boxes with the trim

Line the two boxes up with each other, then glue and nail the center trim (G) to join the sides, leaving a 1/16-in. reveal on each side. Center the center trim lengthwise to leave it about 1/4 in. short of each end. When you attach the top and bottom sills (H), this will give you a 1/4-in. lip to help keep papers and odds and ends from sliding out the bottom (Photo 8). Remove the spacer blocks after nailing the center trim.

PLUMB

NOT PLUMB

SPRING CLAMP

3 Check the studs for plumb and adjust the width and spacing of the boxes as needed in your plan to allow them to slip in easily (Photo 10).

4 Cut out all the pieces, following the dimensions in the Cutting List or your own plan. Clamp and gang-cut matching parts when possible.

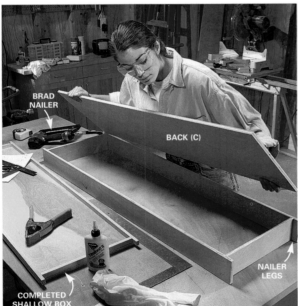

BRAD NAILER

BACK (C)

NAILER LEGS

COMPLETED SHALLOW BOX

CLAMPED BLOCK

SHELF (E)

CENTER LINES FOR NAILING

CAUTION

Keep hands

well away from

the power nailer.

5 Glue and nail the sides, top and bottom first, then glue and nail on the 1/2-in. plywood back (C) to square each box. Wipe off excess glue with a damp rag.

6 Cut and nail the shelves into the deep box. Clamp square blocks to the sides to hold the shelf at a right angle while you nail it.

Glue and nail the sills (H) at the top and bottom edges of the boxes (Photo 8). Center them on the center trim. They'll overlap the side trim by about 1/2 inch.

Then glue and nail the side trim (G) flush with the edges of the boxes. Nail the sills to the side trim as well with 1-1/2-in. brads. Cut the nailers (D) and nail them to the tops and bottoms of the boxes to support the top and bottom trim (Photo 8). Finally, glue and nail on the crossbars (J); see Photo 9 and Figure A.

Take a break and let the glue set up. Then sand out all the rough edges. Paint it now, rather than waiting until it's up.

Set the message center into the wall

The message center should slide right into the opening that you cut in the wall and cover all the rough edges as well (Photo 10). Level it and adjust the height before nailing it to the studs through the trim with 2-1/2-in. finish nails.

You can install doors after mounting the cabinet in the wall, but it's easier to do it before. Install a door (K) on the upper part of the deep box, and a small, drop-down writing surface (L) below it. Special hinges hold the drop-down door at 90 degrees without supports (photo, at right). These doors are both inset, so they have to be aligned with each other and evenly spaced in relation to the trim. This can take some time and patience. At first, install the hinges with only one screw in the adjustable slot, then lock them into place with additional screws after all adjustments are complete.

Fill and sand all nail holes, then paint the message center if you haven't already done so. Finally, install knobs on the doors and put the message center to use.

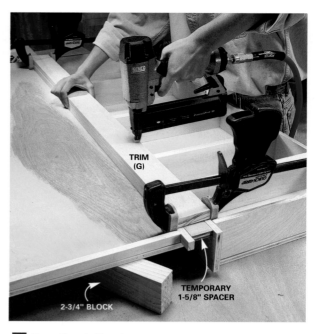

TRIM (G)

TEMPORARY 1-5/8" SPACER

2-3/4" BLOCK

7 Prop the shallow box even with the deeper one, space them with a 1-5/8-in. block and clamp them. Nail on the center trim (G).

UPPER DOOR HINGE

Use a no-mortise, partial wrap-around hinge for the upper doors and a self-closing surface-mounted hinge with a 90-degree stop for the drop-down desk. See Resources, p. 186, for suppliers.

LOWER DOOR HINGE

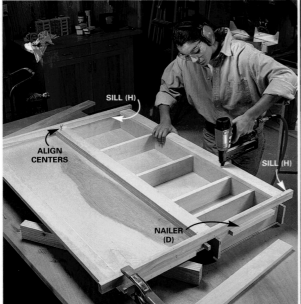

SILL (H)

ALIGN CENTERS

SILL (H)

NAILER (D)

8 Center the top and bottom sills (H) and glue and nail them to the center trim. Glue and nail the side trim (G) to the sides and to the sills. Glue and nail 3/4-in. x 3/4-in. blocks to the top and bottom for nailers (D).

CROSSBARS (J)

BOTTOM TRIM (F)

9 Nail on the top and bottom trim (F). Position and clamp the two 1/2-in. x 3/4-in. crossbars (J). Nail with 1-in. brads.

10 Set the completed message center in the opening and level it. Then nail through the trim into the studs to secure it.

11 Screw hinges to the doors and align them in the openings. Inset doors can be fussy to adjust—use just one screw per hinge until you complete the alignment (see Handy Hints®, p. 28).

Low-cost TV cabinet

Simple joinery makes it fast—plywood makes it inexpensive

The striking style of this cabinet was inspired by visits to upscale furniture stores where similar pieces can be found selling for $1,500 or more. This unit was designed so you can build and finish it in about three weekends for a cost of less than $300! That will leave you more money for what you put inside the cabinet.

Design features

- The TV space is 39 in. wide by 30-1/2 in. tall by 23-3/4 in. deep, and will accommodate most 36-in. TVs, but measure your TV before building this cabinet.
- The two large component openings will accommodate stacks of high-tech TV gear. Each one measures 19-1/8 in. wide by 11-1/4 in. tall by 23-3/4 in. deep.
- Cutouts in the back of the TV shelf make it easy to run wires between the TV and the components.
- Two deep drawers provide lots of room for videotapes, DVDs or video-game junk.
- To create the bold color contrast, you can stain the stiles and top with a dye before assembly.

Tools and materials

This project requires a jigsaw, table saw and router. You'll also need a dado set for your table saw, a pattern bit for your router and clamps with a reach of at least 25 inches.

It takes only three sheets of 3/4-in.-thick plywood, one sheet of 1/4-in.-thick plywood and about 6 bd. ft. of lumber. Shop for plywood sheets that are similar in color and grain on at least one side, and be sure to face these sides out when you build your cabinet. The sheet of 1/4-in. plywood for the back is less critical, since it will

project at a glance

skill level
intermediate

special tools
jigsaw
table saw
router
clamps

approximate cost
$300

be almost totally hidden once you install your TV and components.

You can buy the birch plywood for this cabinet at most home centers, but you may have to sort through half the pile to find three sheets that are similar. It's easier to find matching plywood at a lumberyard. It will probably cost you more, but it may also save you some time and hassle.

You may need to buy the birch lumber from a lumberyard if your home center doesn't carry it.

Prepare the plywood parts

Cut out plywood parts A through G according to the Cutting List, p. 32, and Figure D, p. 35. Rough-cut your sheets of plywood into manageable sizes with a jigsaw or circular saw, and then do the final cutting on your table saw. Use a router and straightedge on parts that are too big for your table saw.

Edge band the plywood edges that will be visible when the project is complete (see Notes column in Cutting List). Pre-glued edge banding is simple to apply with an old iron and easily trimmed with a utility knife (Photos 1 and 2). Rubbing the banding with a wood block helps it adhere to the plywood edge.

Screw the cabinet half of the drawer slides to the drawer divider and sides (F). It's easier to attach the slides now with the parts flat and before the cabinet is all assembled (Photo 3). Use ball-bearing slides with a weight rating of 100 pounds. Glue and clamp the rails (L) to the front edge of the bottom and sub top (C). Cut out the wiring slots in the TV shelf (D) with a jigsaw.

Sand all of the plywood parts before moving on to assembly; 180-grit paper on an orbital sander is all it usually takes.

Assemble the inner drawer and component boxes

Screw together the upper and lower sections of the inner boxes separately (Photo 4). Then add the cleats (H) and join the two sections together (Photo 5). Use a 5/32-in. drill bit for pilot holes and a countersink bit for the screw heads. Be careful that you don't go too deep when drilling pilot holes.

Rabbet the sides and rout the feet

Rout the rabbet on the back edges of the sides (B) to accept the 1/4-in. plywood back. Stop the rabbet 4 in. from the sides' bottom.

Trace the foot profile on the bottom of the sides using the foot template (Figure B, p. 35). Rough-cut the foot detail with a jigsaw. Leave about 1/8 in. of extra material. Then trim this rough edge with a router and the template (Photo 6). You'll need a pattern bit for this routing.

File the inside corners at the top of the feet square, then edge band the exposed plywood edges around the foot opening. The edge banding will help protect the veneer on these edges from chipping due to bumps from shoes or a vacuum cleaner.

Add the sides

Fasten the sides to the inner box assembly (Photo 7). They attach at the bottom with the cleats (J) and screws through the component and drawer section sides (E, F, Figure A, p. 33). The front edges of the sides (B) must be aligned flush with the front edge of these inner boxes. The back edges of the component and

cutting list

Overall dimensions: 46-3/4" W x 27-3/4" D x 61" T

PART	ITEM	QTY	T	W	L	NOTES
			FINAL DIMENSIONS			
A	Top	1	3/4"	27-3/4"	46-3/4"	Edge band all four edges.
B	Sides	2	3/4"	24"	60-1/4"	
C	Bottom and sub top	2	3/4"	23"	40-1/2"	
D	TV/component shelves	2	3/4"	23-3/4"	40-1/2"	Edge band front edges.
E	Component sides/ divider	3	3/4"	23-3/4"	11-1/4"	Edge band front edge of center divider only.
F	Drawer sides/divider	3	3/4"	23-3/4"	10"	Edge band front edge of center divider only.
G	Back	1	1/4"	41-1/2"	55-1/2"	Drill holes for power cords after assembled.
H	Cleats for inner box	6	3/4"	3/4"	20"	Miter front ends to make less visible when installed.
J	Bottom/sub top cleats	4	3/4"	3/4"	23"	
K	Long top cleat	1	3/4"	3/4"	38-1/2"	
L	Rails	2	3/4"	1-1/2"	40-1/2"	
M	Stiles	4	3/4"	2-1/2"*	60-1/4"	Tapered width is 2-3/8" at top and 1-5/8" at bottom.
N	Drawer fronts/backs	4	3/4"	8-1/2"*	16-5/8"*	Measure drawer opening to determine exact length.
P	Drawer sides	4	3/4"	8-1/2"	22"	
R	Drawer bottoms	2	1/4"	17-1/8"*	21"	Check width before gluing drawers together.
S	Drawer faces	2	3/4"	18-7/8"*	9-3/4"*	
T	Wood knobs	2	1-1/4" dia.			

*Approximate

personally speaking

Drilling a pilot hole is no time for guessing, especially when there's a risk of drilling too deep and going through the other side. To avoid this, mark the correct depth on the bit with a masking tape flag. When the flag gets close to the wood, slow down until it touches, and then stop drilling.

I got lucky on this drill-through. The bit pushed out the veneer, but it didn't break off. I was able to work some glue behind the veneer with a tiny nail and stick the veneer back in place. After the first coat of clear finish, I added a speck of matching wood filler for a near-perfect repair.

–Gary Wentz, editor
The Family Handyman

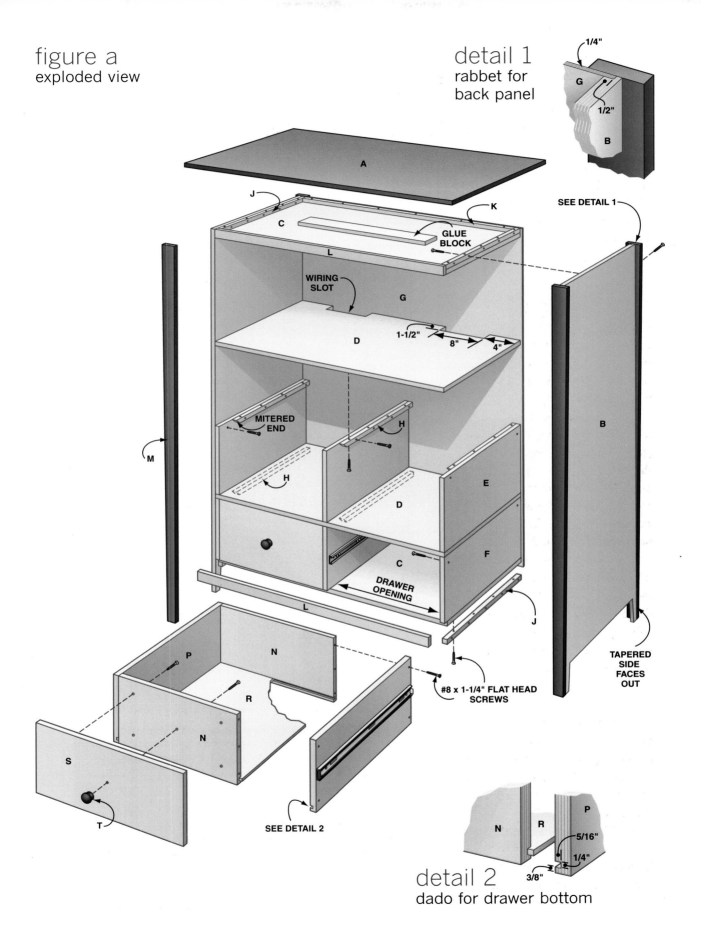

figure a
exploded view

detail 1
rabbet for
back panel

1/4"

G

1/2"

B

A

J

C

K

SEE DETAIL 1

GLUE
BLOCK

L

WIRING
SLOT

G

1-1/2"   8"   4"

D

MITERED
END

H

H

D

B

E

F

C

DRAWER
OPENING

L

M

#8 x 1-1/4" FLAT HEAD
SCREWS

J

TAPERED
SIDE
FACES
OUT

P

N

R

N

S

T

SEE DETAIL 2

detail 2
dado for drawer bottom

N   R   P

5/16"

1/4"

3/8"

1 Iron on edge banding to cover the exposed edges of the uprights, shelves, top and drawers. A cheap or old iron works for this.

2 To trim the banding, set it on a flat surface and use a *sharp* utility knife. MDF or hardboard makes the best trimming surface because it has no grain. Wood grain can steer your knife off course.

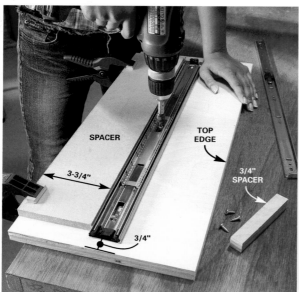

3 Screw the drawer slides onto the sides and center divider of the drawer section. It's easier to do it now while the parts are lying flat. A spacer makes centering the slides foolproof. Set the slides 3/4 in. back to allow for the inset drawer faces.

4 Assemble the drawer and component storage separately. Drill a pilot hole for each screw and make sure the front edges of the parts are flush.

drawer sections should now align with the rabbet at the back of the sides.

Attach cleats (J, K) to the sub top. Then screw the sub top (C) to the sides. Stand the unit up and mark the location for the screws that will attach the back (G, Photo 8).

Then lay the unit down and attach the back with screws every 6 in. (Photo 9).

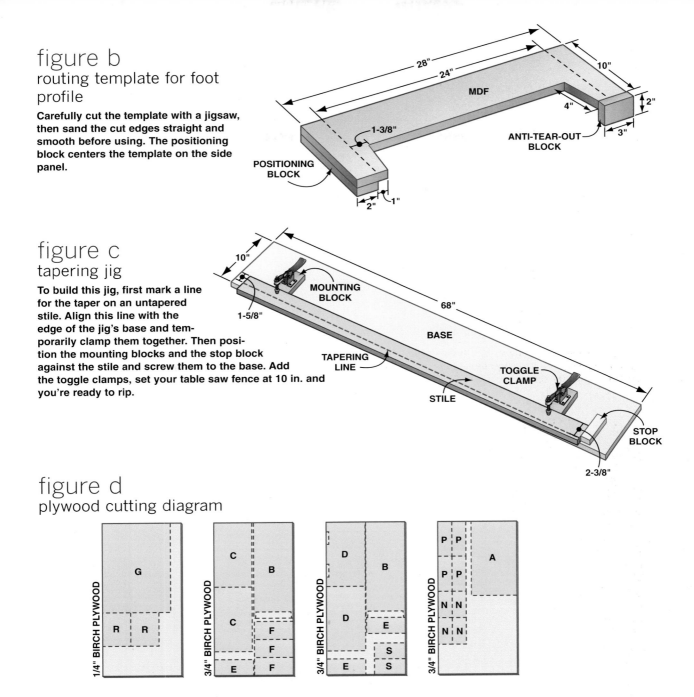

figure b
routing template for foot profile

Carefully cut the template with a jigsaw, then sand the cut edges straight and smooth before using. The positioning block centers the template on the side panel.

28"
24"
10"
MDF
1-3/8"
4"
2"
ANTI-TEAR-OUT BLOCK
3"
POSITIONING BLOCK
2" 1"

figure c
tapering jig

To build this jig, first mark a line for the taper on an untapered stile. Align this line with the edge of the jig's base and temporarily clamp them together. Then position the mounting blocks and the stop block against the stile and screw them to the base. Add the toggle clamps, set your table saw fence at 10 in. and you're ready to rip.

10"
MOUNTING BLOCK
1-5/8"
68"
BASE
TAPERING LINE
TOGGLE CLAMP
STILE
STOP BLOCK
2-3/8"

figure d
plywood cutting diagram

1/4" BIRCH PLYWOOD
G
R R

3/4" BIRCH PLYWOOD
C
B
C
F
F
E F

3/4" BIRCH PLYWOOD
D
B
D
E
E S S

3/4" BIRCH PLYWOOD
P P
A
P P
N N
N N

Attach the stiles and the top

Build the stile-tapering jig (Figure C, above). You'll spend an hour making the jig, but it's worth it, because it makes quick and easy work of tapering the stiles (Photo 10). Before you remove each stile from the jig, label the tapered edge. This taper must face out when attached to the cabinet, and it's easy to mix up the tapered edge with the straight edge. Completely sand the stiles at this time.

Next stain the stiles, the top (A) and the drawer knobs

(T). A dark brown alcohol-based dye stain was used for this cabinet. Dye stain is easy to work with, and it won't interfere with gluing.

Use 12 oz. of alcohol and add 1 oz. of dye. This makes a very dark dye solution, but that's what it took to get the wood as dark as that shown. Let the dye dry thoroughly before moving to the next step.

(If you plan to use an oil stain, skip the previous step. An oil stain will interfere with the gluing that takes place

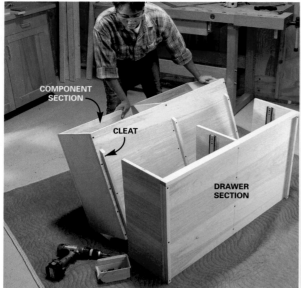

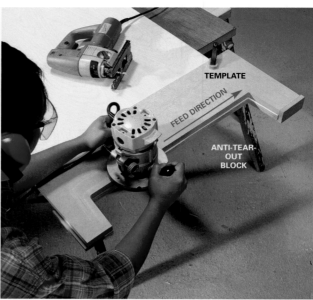

5 Join the component section, which is simply a screwed-together plywood box, to the drawer section. The cleats keep the parts aligned.

6 Rough-cut the feet with a jigsaw and then trim the rough edge using a template and a pattern bit in your router. A small block glued to the right end of the template will prevent the plywood from tearing out at the end of the cut.

7 Screw the sides to the component and drawer sections from the inside. Fasten the cleat along the bottom edge. It should align flush with the foot opening.

8 Temporarily install the back panel with a couple of screws, but put it in backward. Then trace around the shelves and sides to show you where the screws should go when you turn the back around.

in Photos 11 and 12. Instead, wait until the front stiles and top are glued on. Then tape around them to keep stain off the rest of the cabinet.)

Glue the front stiles in place (Photo 11). Attach the rear stiles with screws. This allows you to remove them and the plywood back for easier finishing later on.

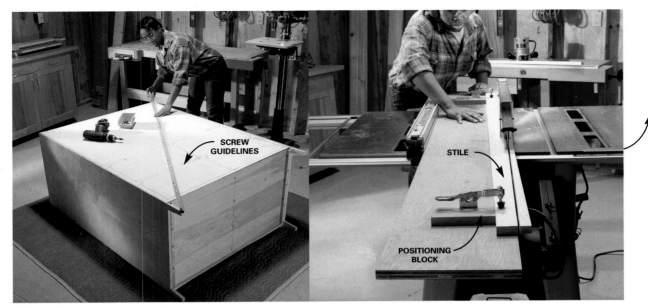

9 Screw on the back. Begin by fastening one edge with a few screws. Then nudge the unit one way or the other until you get equal diagonal measurements, which means it's square. Then fasten the other edge, top, bottom and shelves with screws.

SCREW GUIDELINES

10 Taper the stiles that will be applied to the sides of the cabinet with a shop-made tapering jig. After sanding, stain the stiles.

STILE

POSITIONING BLOCK

Glue the top in place (Photo 12). Don't use too much glue around the perimeter of the case; you want to avoid a squeeze-out mess. Masking tape is still a good idea to catch any drips. The top should overhang the front by 2-1/4 in., each side by 2-7/8 in. and the rear stiles by 3/4 inch. Use spacers to help center the top on the case. Once the top is aligned, weight it down and then immediately remove the spacers, or any squeezed-out glue might bond them to the top. Leave the weight on the top until the glue is dry.

Build and install the drawers

Cut out drawer parts N through R. Make the length of the drawer fronts and backs (N) so that when the drawers are assembled, they are 1 to 1-1/16 in. narrower than the width of the cabinet drawer opening (Figure A). This is the space required for most ball-bearing-type slides.

Cut dadoes in drawer parts N and P and then edge band the top edges of these parts. Sand these drawer box parts at this time.

Install the drawer bottoms (R) in the dadoes and assemble the drawer sides with glue and screws. Strips of masking tape along the joints will protect the sanded parts from glue squeeze-out. Wipe any glue squeeze-out off the tape, but leave the tape on until the glue in the joint has set up. Center the drawer half of the drawer slides on the outsides of the drawers and attach them with screws. Put the drawer boxes into the cabinet. Cut the drawer faces (S) 1/4 in. smaller than the drawer opening, and edge band all four edges. This will produce a clearance space around the sides of the drawer faces that is slightly less than 1/8 inch. Attach the drawer faces to the drawer boxes with screws (Photo 13).

Add the finishing touches

Seal the whole cabinet with spray-on shellac. The spray-on shellac will seal the dye stain, which will bleed and smear onto the unstained parts if you try to brush or wipe a finish over it. Use shellac in a well-ventilated area and wear a respirator with organic vapor cartridges. Lightly sand the shellac after it is completely dry and then topcoat the cabinet with a brush-on satin polyurethane varnish. Shellac makes a good seal coat, but polyurethane is a lot more durable.

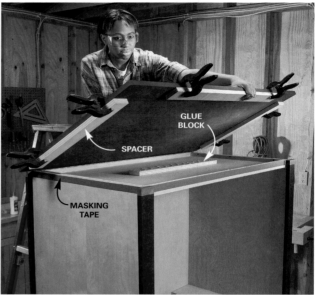

11 Glue and clamp the front stiles in place with the tapered edge facing out. Position the stiles flush with the inside of the drawer and components cabinet. Overhang the stile by 3/4 in. on the inside of the TV space.

12 Glue on the top. Spacers position it exactly, and masking tape catches any glue squeeze-out. A plywood glue block provides extra bonding area. Stack weights on the top and then remove the spacers before the glue dries.

13 Position inset drawer faces using spacers and drive a temporary screw though the center of the front, where the knob will be attached later. Then pull out the drawer and add screws from the inside.

14 Spray on a light coat of clear shellac. This seal coat keeps the dark dye stain from bleeding onto unstained wood areas and makes a good sealer for the polyurethane topcoat.

EASY FOR EVERYONE

Heavy-bicycle lift

More space with less hassle.

WALL CLEAT

Hanging bikes by one or both wheels on bicycle storage hooks is the quickest and cheapest way to get them off the floor and out of the way. But the hooks won't always work if your bike is too heavy to lift easily. Then the best solution is a convenient pulley system that allows you to quickly and easily raise the bike out of the way.

We couldn't design a system much cheaper or better than a purchased system like the Hoist Monster from ProStor (about $40 through Ace, TrueValue, or www.racorinc.com). It can lift up to 100 lbs. with its quality mechanical system of pulleys and hooks, and its dual safety design (locking mechanism and rope tie-down cleat) keeps the bike secure.

Attach the pulley brackets to a ceiling joist with wood screws. Position the hooks the same distance apart as the distance from the handlebar to the seat rear. Choose a location that's convenient yet doesn't interfere with vehicles or people, since the bike will hang down about 4 ft. from the ceiling. If the joists aren't spaced just right, lag-screw 2x4s to them and then screw the brackets to the 2x4s.

project at a glance

skill level
beginner

special tools
drill

approximate cost
$40

1 **Attach the lift assembly** hardware to the center of the ceiling joists with the screws provided. Mount the safety rope cleat to a garage wall stud, out of a child's reach. Wrap the cord around the cleat to secure the bike (photo at top of page).

CEILING JOIST

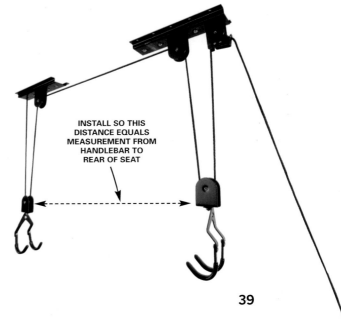

INSTALL SO THIS DISTANCE EQUALS MEASUREMENT FROM HANDLEBAR TO REAR OF SEAT

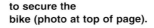

Sliding bookend

To corral shelf-dwelling books or CDs that like to wander, cut 3/4-in.-thick hardwood pieces into 6-in. x 6-in. squares. Use a band saw or saber saw to cut a slot along one edge (with the grain) that's a smidgen wider than the shelf thickness. Stop the notch 3/4 in. from the other edge. Apply a finish to the bookend and slide it on the shelf.

Portable music box

Keep your portable CD player and CDs ready for use, but out of harm's way, with this sturdy case. This was designed to fit a specific CD player, and since yours may be different, measure it carefully and modify the dimensions accordingly. Cut 1/4-in.-thick walnut or other attractive plywood into sides, a bottom and a lid. Round the ends of the lid and bottom. Make three partitions out of 3/4-in.- to 1-in.-thick hardwood. Clamp the middle partition vertically in a drill press and carefully drill two 9/16-in. holes 4 in. deep in the upper end for spare batteries. With No. 6 brass screws (countersunk), secure the partitions to the bottom, then attach the sides. After sanding and finishing, put self-adhesive hook-and-loop fastener strips under the lid ends and the outside partition ends to hold the lid closed.

Cutting List
Sides: 14-1/2 in. x 6-1/2 in.
Top and Bottom: 14-3/4 in. x 2-1/2 in.
Partitions: 6 in. x 2-1/2 in.

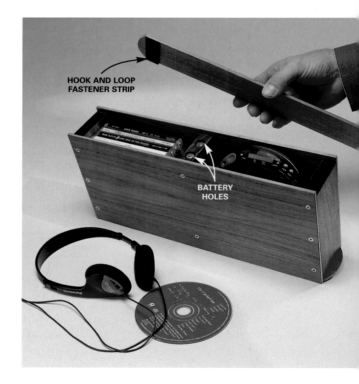

HOOK AND LOOP FASTENER STRIP

BATTERY HOLES

7 low-cost storage projects

Ideas for every room in the house.

Shoe-bag storage

Expand the limited storage space in your garage by hanging clear plastic shoe bags on the wall. They take up very little room and are great for holding garden sprays, spray paints, lubricants and other bottles and cans. And, since the items are in plain sight instead of buried at the back of a shelf, you always know what you've got and where it is.

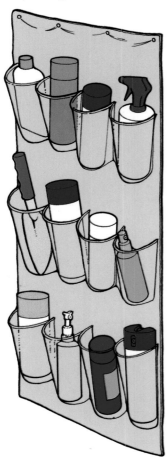

project at a glance

skill level
beginner

special tools
circular saw, jigsaw, drill

approximate cost
$10–$25 each

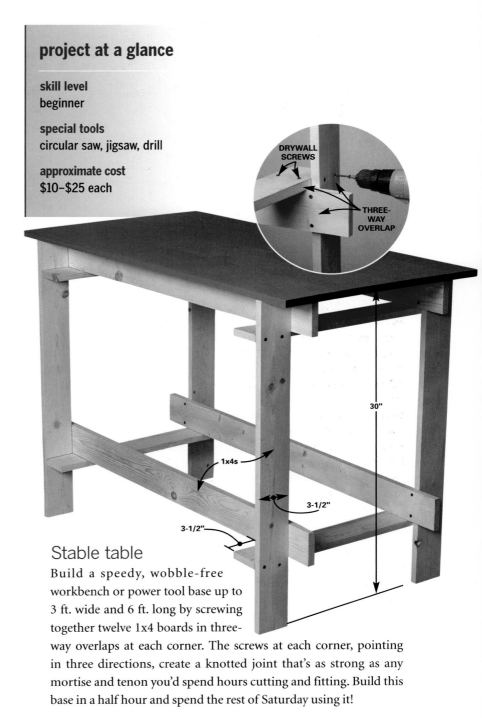

DRYWALL SCREWS

THREE-WAY OVERLAP

30"

1x4s

3-1/2"

3-1/2"

Stable table

Build a speedy, wobble-free workbench or power tool base up to 3 ft. wide and 6 ft. long by screwing together twelve 1x4 boards in three-way overlaps at each corner. The screws at each corner, pointing in three directions, create a knotted joint that's as strong as any mortise and tenon you'd spend hours cutting and fitting. Build this base in a half hour and spend the rest of Saturday using it!

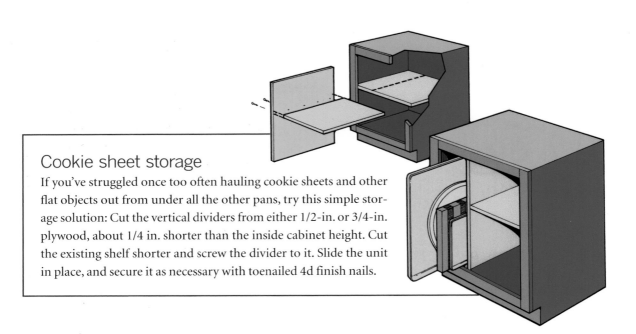

Cookie sheet storage

If you've struggled once too often hauling cookie sheets and other flat objects out from under all the other pans, try this simple storage solution: Cut the vertical dividers from either 1/2-in. or 3/4-in. plywood, about 1/4 in. shorter than the inside cabinet height. Cut the existing shelf shorter and screw the divider to it. Slide the unit in place, and secure it as necessary with toenailed 4d finish nails.

Mobile stacking totes

Make these stacking totes from 1/2-in. birch veneer plywood. The dimensions we give allow each tote to interlock snugly with the one above and below it. You can cut four totes from one full sheet of plywood—five from about a sheet and a third. Cut all the plywood parts to size, cut out the hand grips, and sand all edges smooth. Then glue and assemble the totes with 4d finishing nails. Leave them unfinished or apply paint or stain. Mount 2-in. casters on the bottom tote to make the stack mobile.

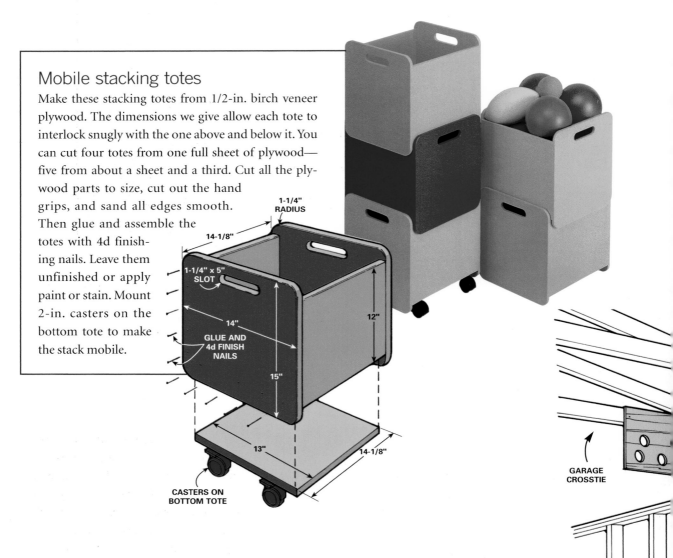

1-1/4" RADIUS

14-1/8"

1-1/4" x 5" SLOT

14"

GLUE AND 4d FINISH NAILS

12"

15"

13"

14-1/8"

CASTERS ON BOTTOM TOTE

GARAGE CROSSTIE

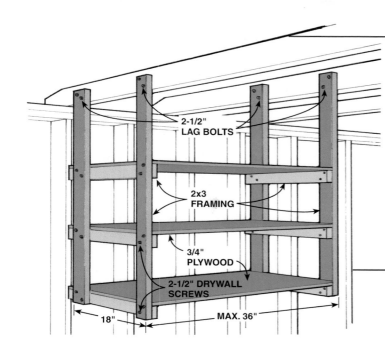

Hanging garage rack

This hold-anything rack mounts over the hood of your car and takes up no valuable garage floor space. Build the two 2x3 end support frames first, determining shelf width and spacing to suit your needs. Hang the frames from overhead beams with 2-1/2 in. lag bolts. If you build the rack in a corner, you can mount the shelf supports for one side directly to the side wall of the garage.

2-1/2"
LAG BOLTS

2x3
FRAMING

3/4"
PLYWOOD

2-1/2" DRYWALL
SCREWS

18"

MAX. 36"

Utility shelves

This sturdy, freestanding shelf unit is made from any inexpensive 1-by lumber (3/4 in. thick) for the legs, and plywood or particleboard for the shelves. Glue and nail the four L-shaped legs together with 6d finish nails. Clamp the shelves in place, getting them evenly spaced and level, then secure each shelf with eight 2-in. screws through the legs.

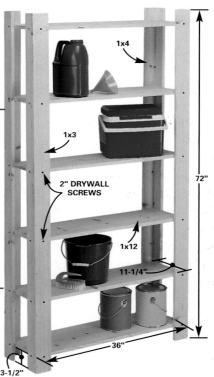

1x4

1x3

2" DRYWALL
SCREWS

1x12

11-1/4"

72"

36"

3-1/2"

PLYWOOD

DRYWALL
SCREWS

6"

2" DIA. HOLES

Overhead storage
for garden tools

Rakes, shovels, brooms and other long-handled tools seem to be in the way no matter how they're stored in the garage. Here's a rack that works: Cut two pieces of plywood about 12 in. x 48 in. and drill matching 2-in. holes in each, spaced about 6 in. apart. Mount the racks on crossties below your garage roof rafters.

Shel

ving

Rotating garage shelves

Easy access for all your small stuff

Set aside a Saturday to build this handy bin, and you'll clean up all those loose boxes of screws, bolts and other small stuff that clutter your garage or workshop. This bin rotates on a pair of lazy Susan rings to maximize corner space and provide quick, easy access. A stationary upper shelf secured to the wall steadies the bin so it'll spin easily and won't tip over. You can add as many shelves as you need, or leave one bay open top to bottom for storing tall things like levels and straightedges. You won't need special joints or fasteners to construct it; simple butt joints and screws hold it all together. You need only basic carpentry tools to cut and fasten the pieces.

Materials and cost

This project costs about $100. This project was constructed from one and a half 4x8 sheets of birch plywood (about $40 per sheet, $25 per half sheet). Birch plywood is easy to work with because it's smooth and flat, but you can cut your costs by about half if you use 3/4-in. CDX-grade plywood. Buy two lazy Susan rings, 12-in. round and 3-in. square diameters, from a woodworkers' store if your home center doesn't carry them. You can find all of the other materials at most home centers, including the 3-in. vinyl base we used for the shelf edging. See the Materials List, p. 48, for a complete rundown of what you'll need.

project at a glance

skill level
beginner to intermediate

special tools
jigsaw
drill

approximate cost
$100

Careful cutting and layout make assembly a snap

Cut all the pieces to size from Figure B, p. 49. Accurate cuts will result in tight, clean joints. Clamp a straightedge to the plywood to guide your circular saw when making the straight cuts. Use a carbide blade with at least 36 teeth to minimize splintering.

Photo 1 shows you how to mark the circle for the plywood bottom. Substitute a narrow strip of 1/4-in.-thick wood for the compass arm if you don't have peg board. Use the bottom as a template to mark the arcs on the quarter-circle shelves (Figure B). Use a bucket to mark the arcs on the tops of the dividers.

Before assembling the pieces, lay out the shelf locations on the dividers. Make the shelves any height you want, but making them different heights in adjacent sections simplifies the screwing process.

Fasten the shelves to the two narrow dividers first (Photo 2), then set them upright and attach them to the wide center divider (Photo 3).

Drilling an access hole is the trick to mounting the lazy Susan

At first glance, attaching the 12-in. lazy Susan is a bit mysterious. The lazy Susan rotates on ball bearings with the top ring secured to the bin bottom and the bottom ring secured to the base. Securing it to the base is straightforward—you center it and screw it down. Once it's fastened, you have to drive screws upward to fasten the top ring to the bin bottom. The bottom ring

Electrical

Tapes

Auto

Stains

Spray Paint

Plants

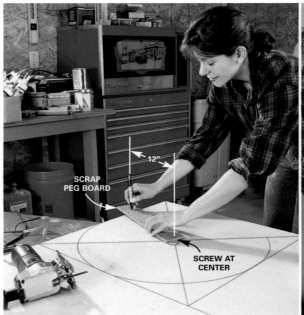

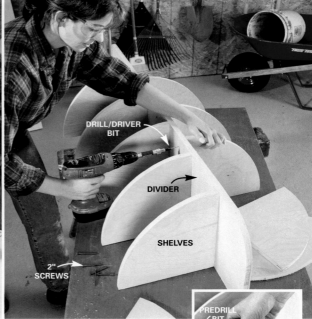

1 Cut all the pieces with a circular saw and jigsaw, using the dimensions in Figure A, p. 49, and our Cutting List. Mark the circle cut for the bottom with a 12-in. compass made from a scrap of peg board. Cut it out with a jigsaw. Then trace the arcs of the shelves using the bottom as a template. (*NOTE:* The shelf sides are 11-5/8 inches.)

2 Measure and mark the shelf locations on the dividers, spacing them anywhere from 10 to 14 in. apart. Align the shelves with these marks, then predrill and screw the shelves to the two narrow dividers with 2-in. drywall screws. A drill/driver bit speeds this process.

Handy Hints®

Use a magnetic screwdriver tip to keep from dropping the screws. It's a hassle to retrieve them!

of the lazy Susan has a special 3/4-in. access hole to help here. Drill a 3/4-in. hole in the plywood base at the access hole point (Photo 4). Then poke your screws through the access hole to fasten the top ring to the bin base (Photo 5).

The 3-in. lazy Susan rotates on square plates. You won't need an access hole to fasten them. Just screw through the holes in the corners (Photos 6 and 7).

Putting the unit in place

If you're placing the base on a concrete floor, rest it on treated 1x2s to avoid rot. Level it with shims, if needed, for smooth rotation. Fasten the support shelf to the walls (Photo 8).

Anchor the base to the floor with masonry screws set in the exposed corners. Predrill the holes into the concrete with a 5/32-in. masonry bit or the size the screw package recommends.

materials list

- One and a half 4x8 sheets of (birch) plywood
- One 12" round lazy Susan ring
- One 3" square lazy Susan ring
- 1 lb. of 2" No. 8 screws
- Sixteen 3/4" No. 6 flat head screws
- Ten 4' strips of 3" vinyl base
- 1 lb. of 1" tacks
- One tube of vinyl base adhesive
- Two 2' treated 1x2s
- Three 2-1/2" x 3/16" masonry screws
- Eight 2-1/2" screws

figure a
bin details

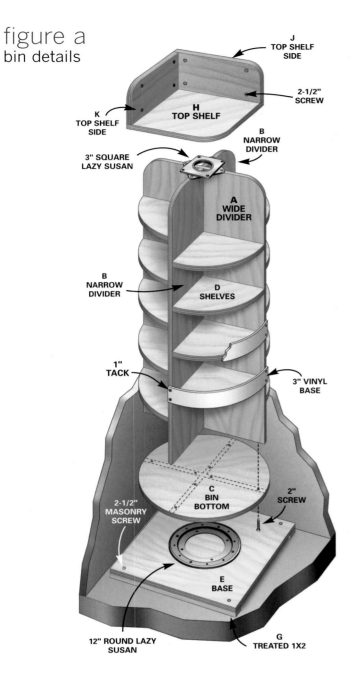

J
TOP SHELF
SIDE

2-1/2"
SCREW

K
TOP SHELF
SIDE

H
TOP SHELF

3" SQUARE
LAZY SUSAN

B
NARROW
DIVIDER

A
WIDE
DIVIDER

B
NARROW
DIVIDER

D
SHELVES

1"
TACK

3" VINYL
BASE

2-1/2"
MASONRY
SCREW

C
BIN
BOTTOM

2"
SCREW

12" ROUND LAZY
SUSAN

E
BASE

G
TREATED 1X2

cutting list

A   Wide divider, 3/4" x 24" x 54"

B   Two narrow dividers, 3/4" x
     11-5/8" x 54"

C   Bin bottom, 3/4" x 24" diameter

D   Up to 16 shelves, 3/4" x 11-5/8"
     x 11-5/8"

E   Base, 3/4" x 24" x 24"

G   Two treated 1x2s, 1" x 2" x 24"

H   Top shelf, 3/4" x 18" x 18"

J   Shelf side, 3/4" x 7-1/2" x 18"

K   Shelf side, 3/4" x 7-1/2" x 17-1/4"

figure b
cutting layout

**Space shelves according to your
storage needs, typically, 8 to 14 in.
apart.**

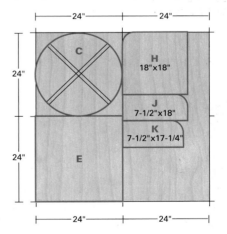

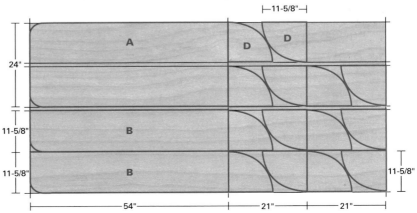

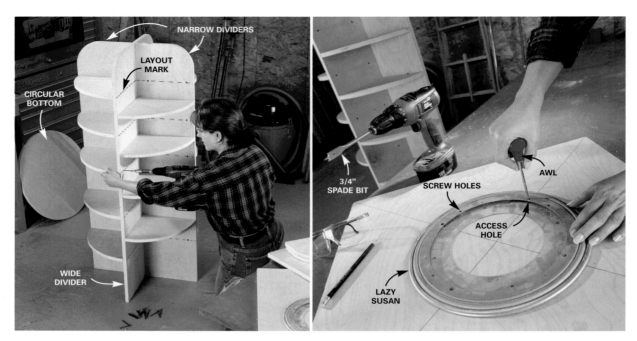

NARROW DIVIDERS

LAYOUT MARK

CIRCULAR BOTTOM

WIDE DIVIDER

3 Connect the two shelf assemblies to the wide center divider with 2-in. drywall screws. Center and screw the circular bottom to the dividers.

3/4" SPADE BIT

SCREW HOLES

AWL

ACCESS HOLE

LAZY SUSAN

4 Center the 12-in. lazy Susan on the base. Align the screw holes on the top and bottom rings. Locate the access hole in the lazy Susan and mark its location on the plywood with an awl or nail. Remove the lazy Susan and drill a 3/4-in. hole at the mark. Center the lazy Susan again, aligning the access hole to the hole drilled in the plywood, and fasten the bottom ring to the base with 3/4-in. No. 6 flat head screws.

Handy Hints®

Mark the center line of each shelf on the opposite side of the dividers to help position the screws (Photo 3).

The vinyl base provides an edge for the shelves. Buy the type that's not preglued. The 4-in.-wide type is most common, but buy the 3-in.-wide type if you can. Otherwise, use a sharp utility knife to trim an inch off the 4-in. one. Secure it to the edges of the curved plywood shelves using cove base adhesive and 1-in. tacks, as shown in Photo 9. Then load up your shelves and take them for a spin.

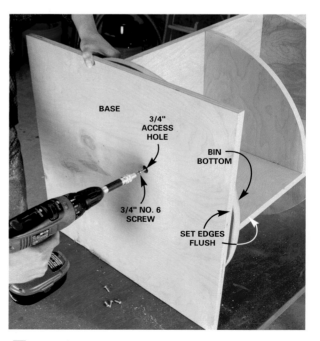

BASE

3/4" ACCESS HOLE

BIN BOTTOM

3/4" NO. 6 SCREW

SET EDGES FLUSH

5 Center the base on the bin bottom and align a screw hole in the top ring of the lazy Susan with the access hole. Fasten the top ring of the lazy Susan to the bin bottom with a 3/4-in. No. 6 flat head screw driven through the access hole. Turn the bin bottom to align the remaining screw holes in the top ring with the access hole, and fasten with additional screws.

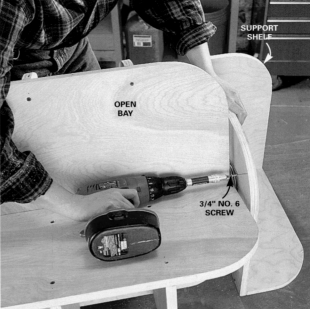

6 Screw the bottom ring of the 3-in. lazy Susan to the dividers on top of the bin with 3/4-in. screws. Assemble the support shelf (Figure A). Mark the bin rotation center on its bottom (about 13 in. from each wall) so the bin will clear the wall by about an inch when it rotates.

7 Center the 3-in. lazy Susan at the rotation center on the support shelf. Screw the top ring of the lazy Susan to the support shelf with the 3/4-in. screws.

8 Set the bin on treated 1x2s with the base about 1 in. from the walls. Shim to level if needed. Level the support shelf and screw it to the wall studs with 2-1/2-in. screws. Spin the bin to test for smooth operation. If it runs rough, shim the base or slide it side to side slightly until it spins smoothly. Predrill and fasten the base to the floor with 2-1/2-in. masonry screws.

9 Squeeze a 3/8-in. bead of cove base adhesive along the shelf edges. Position the vinyl base with the lip to the top, curling out. Secure the ends with 1-in. tacks. Trim the ends flush with a utility knife.

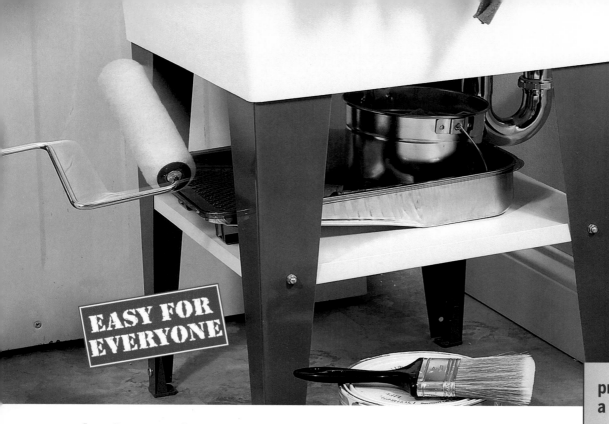

EASY FOR EVERYONE

Under-sink shelf

Make every square inch count.

project at a glance

skill level
beginner

special tools
aviation snips
drill
circular saw

approximate cost
$5

Tired of moving all that stuff under the sink every time you mop the floor? Just buy a Melamine closet shelf ($5) from a home center and a length of suspended-ceiling wall angle (sorry, it only comes in 10-ft. lengths, but it's cheap and you can have it cut for transport). Also pick up four 1/2-in. No. 8-24 bolts, washers and nuts. Follow Photos 1 – 3.

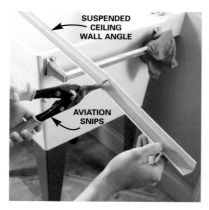

1 Using an aviation snips, cut two lengths of suspended ceiling channel to support the undersink shelf.

2 Clamp pieces of ceiling angle or aluminum angle to your sink legs (about 11 in. from the floor) and drill through with a 3/16-in. bit. Insert 1/2-in. long No. 8-24 bolts from the inside and thread on acorn nuts to cover sharp bolt edges.

3 Cut a shelf from 3/4-in. Melamine board and drop it onto the angle braces. You may need to notch your shelf if the sink trap is in your way. Paint the raw edges of the board to protect them from moisture.

Coat & mitten rack

Build this handsome project in just a few hours—you won't believe you got along without it!

This simple coat rack is designed to be easy to build with butt joints connected by screws that get hidden by wooden screw-hole buttons and wood plugs. The rack mounts easily to the wall with screws driven through the hidden hanging strip on the back. The five large Shaker pegs are great for holding hats, umbrellas and coats, and the hinged-hatch door at the top keeps the clutter of gloves and scarves from view.

You can build this project in a few hours, with an additional hour to apply a finish. Maple is an ideal wood for Shaker-style pieces, but any hardwood will do. Figure on spending about $65 for wood, hardware and varnish.

tip*

Be sure this project is screwed to the wall studs. Drill two holes into the hanging strip at stud locations and use 2-1/2 in. or longer wood screws.

project at a glance

skill level
beginner

special tools
jigsaw
drill
clamps

approximate cost
$65

figure a
shaker rack details

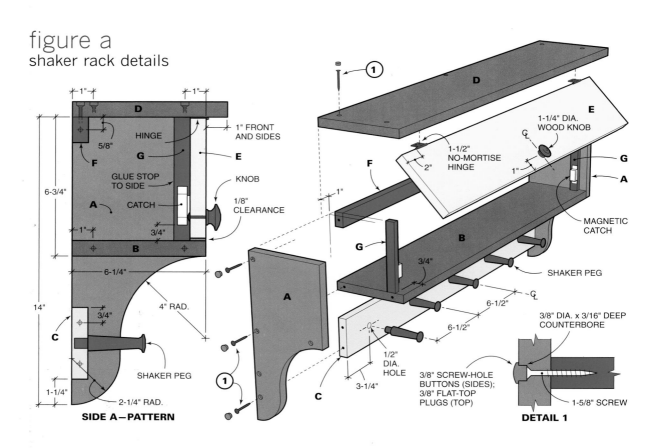

SIDE A—PATTERN

1" FRONT AND SIDES

HINGE

GLUE STOP TO SIDE

CATCH

KNOB

1/8" CLEARANCE

6-3/4"

5/8"

6-1/4"

14"

4" RAD.

SHAKER PEG

3/4"

1-1/4"

2-1/4" RAD.

3/4"

1-1/2" NO-MORTISE HINGE

2"

1"

1-1/4" DIA. WOOD KNOB

MAGNETIC CATCH

SHAKER PEG

6-1/2"

6-1/2"

3/4"

1/2" DIA. HOLE

3-1/4"

3/8" SCREW-HOLE BUTTONS (SIDES); 3/8" FLAT-TOP PLUGS (TOP)

3/8" DIA. x 3/16" DEEP COUNTERBORE

1-5/8" SCREW

DETAIL 1

Cutting the pieces

Using a compass, transfer the pattern measurements in Figure A, above, and then cut the sides (A) with a jigsaw (Photo 1). Next cut the top (D) to length and rip the shelf (B) to the width given in the Cutting List, at right. Cut the hanging strip (F) and the peg strip (C) to the same length as the shelf (B). Now, using your spade bit, drill the 3/8-in. counterbore holes for the screw-hole buttons 3/16 in. deep into the outside of parts A (Figure A and Photo 2). Also drill the 3/8-in. counterbore holes in the top. These holes must be 3/8 in. deep.

Mark and drill the 1/2-in. holes for the Shaker pegs in the peg strip. Drill the holes for the Shaker pegs perfectly perpendicular to the peg strip to ensure they all project evenly when glued in place.

materials list

ITEM	QTY.
1x8 x 12' maple (A, B, D, E)	1
1x4 x 6' maple (C, F, G)	1
1-1/2" no-mortise hinges*	1 pair
1-1/4" beech knob*	1
Narrow magnetic catch*	2
3-3/8" long Shaker pegs*	5
3/8" screw-hole buttons*	10
3/8" plugs*	5
3/8" spade bit	1
1/2" spade bit	1
1-5/8" wood screws	15
Carpenter's glue	1 pint
Danish oil	1 pint
150- and 220-grit sandpaper	

*Available from home centers or Rockler Woodworking and Hardware, (800) 279-4441, www.rockler.com.

cutting list

KEY	PCS.	SIZE & DESCRIPTION
A	2	3/4" x 6-1/4" x 14" maple sides
B	1	3/4" x 6-1/4" x 32-1/2" maple shelf
C	1	3/4" x 3-1/2" x 32-1/2" maple peg strip
D	1	3/4" x 7-1/4" x 36" maple top
E	1	3/4" x 5-13/16" x 32-5/16" maple hatch
F	1	3/4" x 1-1/4" x 32-1/2" maple hanging strip
G	2	3/4" x 1/2" x 6" maple hatch stops

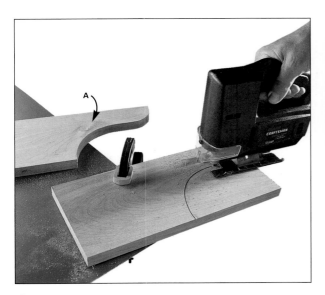

1 Cut the side pieces (A) using a jigsaw or band saw. Sand the curved edges smooth with a 1-1/2 in. drum sander attached to your drill.

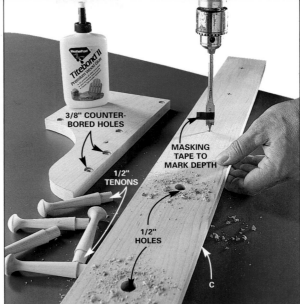

2 Drill the 1/2-in. holes 5/8 in. deep for the 3-3/8 in. Shaker pegs and the 3/8-in. counterbore holes 3/16 in. deep for the screw-hole buttons in parts A.

Assembly

Lay the pieces on your workbench, as shown in Photo 3. Align the hanging strip (F), the shelf (B), and the peg strip (C) as shown and clamp the sides (A) to these parts. Predrill the holes with a combination pilot hole/countersink bit using the center of the counterbore holes as a guide. Next, screw the sides to B, C and F. Mark and drill hinge mounting holes in the top (D), then fasten the top to the sides in the same manner.

tip Sight down the edge of the peg strip to perfectly align each peg as the glue sets.

Glue and clamp the hatch stops to the inside of parts A, as shown in Figure A, p. 54. To finish the assembly, cut the hatch (E) to size and install the hinges on the underside of part D and the top of the hatch. Now glue the buttons and plugs into their corresponding holes. Use only a small drop of glue for the buttons but be sure to apply a thin layer of glue completely around the plugs. This will swell the plugs for a tight fit. After the glue is dry, trim the wood plugs flush with the top.

Finishing

After assembly, lightly sand the entire piece with 220-grit sandpaper. Apply two coats of clear Danish oil or polyurethane to all the surfaces (remove the hinges and knobs). Once the finish is dry, add magnetic catches to the hatch stops (G).

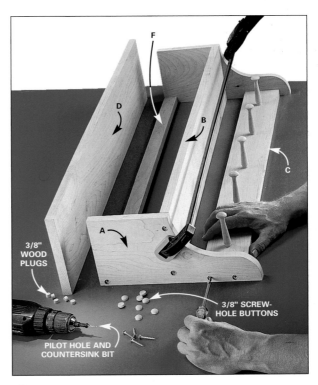

3 Assemble the shelf by clamping parts C, F and B to the sides. Drill pilot holes and screw the pieces together. The screws will be covered by the buttons and plugs.

Open kitchen shelves

Converting a few of your wall cabinets to open shelving is a great way to create display space for dishes or to keep cookbooks and cooking supplies within easy reach. Anyone handy with a paintbrush can complete this project in a leisurely weekend. Don't forget to order the glass shelves about a week before you need them.

You'll need a screwdriver, hammer and tape measure as well as basic painting equipment like a paintbrush, putty knife, masking tape and sandpaper or a sanding sponge. Use a drill with a 9/32-in. bit to drill holes for the metal sleeves (Photo 3).

Some cabinets are easy to convert by simply removing the doors and ordering glass shelves. Others may require a little carpentry work, like removing a fixed shelf. Take a close look inside the cabinet to see whether there are hidden challenges. If it looks good, remove the doors and carefully measure for shelves. Measure from one side of the cabinet to the other and from front to back. Deduct 1/8 in. from these meas-

urements to arrive at the glass size. Look in the Yellow Pages under "Glass" to find a company that will cut the glass and polish all of the edges. About $30 was spent for the three 1/4-in.-thick glass shelves in this kitchen. Ask the glass salesperson what thickness you need for strength and safety. Longer spans require thicker glass.

While you're waiting for the glass to arrive, paint the cabinet interiors. Choose a color that matches or complements a floor or wall color. Preparation is the key to a long-lasting, perfectly smooth paint job. Photos 1 and 2 show the painting steps. If you're painting over Melamine or another hard, shiny surface, make sure to thoroughly roughen the surface with 80-grit sandpaper and prime with shellac before brushing or spraying on the coats of paint.

Photo 3 shows the hardware used to support the glass shelves. If you don't have holes for the shelf pins, use a tape measure and square to mark the hole locations and bore 9/32-in. holes to accept the metal reinforcing sleeves.

1 Remove the cabinet doors and hinges. Fill all extra shelf bracket or hinge holes with a hardening-type wood filler. Allow this to harden, sand it smooth and apply a coat of lightweight surfacing compound to fill low spots left after the wood filler shrinks. Let the second coat dry. Then sand the entire cabinet interior with 80-grit sandpaper to provide a rough surface for the paint to grab.

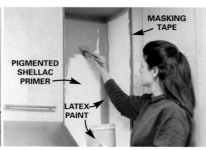

2 Use masking tape to protect unpainted areas. Prime the interior with white pigmented shellac (BIN is one brand) to keep the filler from showing through and to provide a binder for the final coats of paint. Sand the primer lightly with a fine sanding sponge after it dries. Remove the dust with a vacuum cleaner and brush on the final coats of latex or oil paint.

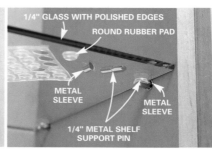

3 Support glass shelves with metal shelf pins inserted into holes drilled in the cabinet sides. To prevent the pins from enlarging the holes, drill 9/32-in. holes and tap in metal sleeves. Then insert the metal shelf support pins in the sleeves and apply a self-adhesive round rubber pad to each pin to keep the glass shelves from sliding off.

Glass shelves

Most bathrooms have one space you can count on for additional storage, and that's over the toilet. Open glass shelving is a great place to display decorative bathroom bottles or knick-knacks. There are zillions of glass shelving systems on the market. Follow the directions that come with the system for the installation details, but read on for help anchoring them to the wall because you probably won't have studs exactly where you need them. Use masking tape to avoid marking the walls.

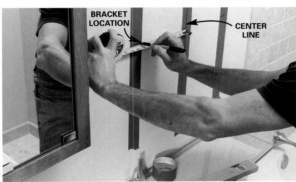

BRACKET LOCATION

CENTER LINE

1 Apply a strip of 2-in.-wide masking tape above the center of the toilet and on both sides where the shelf brackets will be mounted. Draw a center line with a level and mark the heights of the shelves on the center tape. Transfer the heights to the bracket tape with a 2-ft. level. Then measure from the center line to mark the exact left and right locations for the brackets.

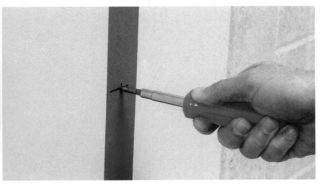

2 Indent the drywall at the marks with a Phillips head screwdriver and remove the tape.

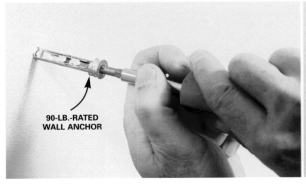

90-LB.-RATED WALL ANCHOR

3 Select hollow wall anchors based on wall thickness and weight rating, and install them.

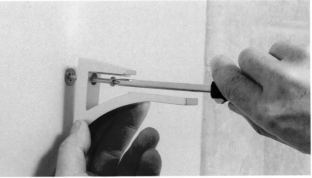

4 Screw the brackets to the wall using the screws included with the anchors.

Modular closet organizer

Expert planning advice and step-by-step instructions for making every inch of storage count

I f you find yourself rummaging in your closet every morning mumbling to yourself, "One of these days I've got to get organized," then read on, because here's the solution.

For about the price of a dresser, you can install modular closet organizers that practically double your storage space and look great, too. The units are constructed of particleboard with a durable Melamine coating. Although wire shelves are more economical, the modular systems offer several advantages: They look like built-in units, offer adjustable shelves and closet rods, and allow you to add drawers or shelves in the future.

Installing a modular closet system is a great weekend project. The Melamine units shown here assemble easily with special locking hardware. If you're familiar with basic leveling, drilling and sawing, you'll have no problem assembling and installing the units in an average-sized closet in half a day. But don't get too excited yet; first you have to measure and plan the closet, round up the parts, and prepare the

project at a glance

skill level
beginner

special tools
drill
circular saw
level
basic hand tools

approximate cost
$600

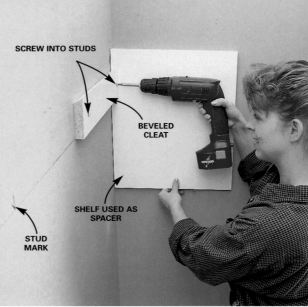

1 Draw a level line on the back wall of the closet to indicate the bottom of the hanging cleats. Refer to the
instructions for the height of this line. Locate the studs
along this line and mark the wall.

2 Drill 3/16-in. screw clearance holes through the cleat
at the stud locations. Then screw the cleat to the
wall with 3-in. pan head screws, leaving them a little
loose. Use a shelf to space the cleat from the end wall to
allow room for the side panel of the storage unit.

making it fit
your budget

**The biggest difference among brands
is in the quality of the drawer slides,
closet poles and mounting system
and in the range of unit sizes and
available options. Better-quality units
also have a more durable surface.**

bits, a circular saw with a 140-tooth plywood blade
and a hacksaw with a 24-tooth-per-inch blade. An
electronic stud finder would be handy, but rapping on
the wall with your knuckle or looking for nails in the
baseboard are great low-tech methods. Once you find
the first stud, the others should be spaced at 16- or 24-in.
intervals.

Sketch out a master plan

Start by carefully measuring the closet's width, depth
and height. Use graph paper to make scaled drawings
of the floor plan and each wall where you plan to hang
old closet for
the new shelves.
    For this
project, you'll
need a tape
measure, a level,
a No. 3 Phillips
screwdriver, an
electric drill
with a No. 2
Phillips bit and
3/16-in. wood
and 1/2-in. pade

shelves. Include the width and position of the door on
your plan. Let each square equal 6 inches. This allows
you to sketch in and try out different storage unit
options.

The knock-down storage units are available in standard widths, with 12, 18 and 24 in. being the most
common. Depths range from 12 to 18 in. depending on
the manufacturer. Some units rest on the floor and
reach a height of about 84 in.; others, like the ones
shown above, hang from a cleat or are rail-mounted to
the wall.

Each storage unit consists of two side panels drilled
for shelf pins and connecting bolts, one or two hanging cleats and some fixed shelves (Photo 4). The parts
are connected with ingenious two-part knock-down
fasteners consisting of a connecting bolt that screws
into the side panels and a cam mechanism mounted in
each fixed shelf and cleat. To assemble, just screw the
connecting bolts in the right holes, slide the parts
together, and turn the cam clockwise to lock the parts
together. There are systems available at home centers
and discount stores that simply screw together, but
they're harder to assemble and not nearly as sturdy.

The basic units are essentially boxes with a lot of
holes drilled in the sides. Complete the system by

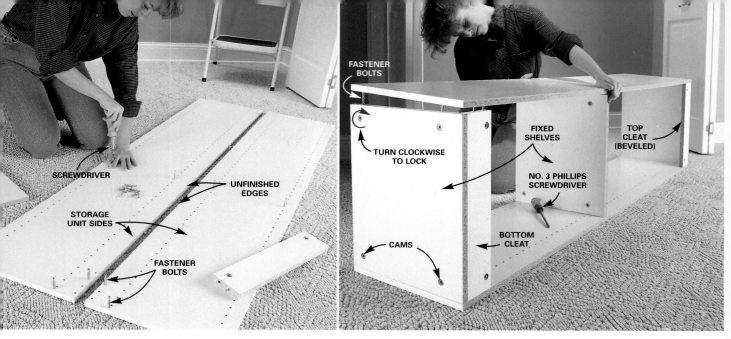

3 Lay the sides of the first storage unit on a carpet or dropcloth with unfinished edges together. Screw fastener bolts for the fixed shelves and cleats into the predrilled holes. Your instruction sheet will show which holes to use.

4 Assemble the cabinet by aligning the holes in the fixed shelves and cleats with the fastener bolts. Lock them together by turning the cams clockwise. Then position the second side and lock it in. Face the cams where they'll be least visible when the cabinet is hung.

adding adjustable shelves, drawers and closet rods. All the components are designed to fit into or attach to the predrilled holes, so very little additional drilling is required.

Check the Yellow Pages under "Closet Accessories" and make a few calls to see who sells modular closet systems in your area, or use the Internet to locate local suppliers. Some closet specialists insist on installing the systems, while others will help with the design and provide the storage units, hardware and instructions you need to do your own installation. Take your sketch along and get estimates on a couple of different systems.

The closet system shown above cost about $600. You could save about $150 by using standard-sized, floor- standing, modular storage units, but that would require settling for a less efficient plan and doing more assembly work. Also, hanging the units on the wall avoids the extra work of cutting around or removing baseboards or dealing with uneven floors and keeps your floor clear for cleaning.

Although Melamine-coated shelving is a great product for an affordable, prefinished storage unit, it does have some limitations. The particleboard core will not stand up to moisture. Wire shelving may be a better choice in damp places. The Melamine coating is more durable than paint but not as tough as the plastic laminate used on countertops, so don't expect this stuff to tolerate the same abuse you give your kitchen counters. Storing books or heavy objects may cause the particleboard to sag over time; consider a stronger material like plywood or metal shelves.

Get your closet ready to go

If your closet is anything like the one shown above, the biggest part of this project will be clearing it out. When that's done, remove the rod, shelf and everything except the baseboard from the walls. Place a scrap of wood under your hammer or pry bar to avoid crushing the drywall or plaster when you pry off the shelf support boards. Patch the holes with a lightweight surfacing compound. Then sand and repaint the walls and you're ready to hang shelves.

Once your design is complete and the closet walls are patched and painted, it's all coasting downhill. The storage unit systems are so well engineered that even if you can't pound a nail, you'll feel like a master cabinetmaker when you're done. Photos 1 through 10 show the basic steps involved. Consult the instruction sheet provided with your system for exact procedures and placement of connecting bolts and other hardware.

ASSEMBLED
STORAGE UNIT

TOP CLEAT

WALL CLEAT

5 Hang the storage unit by pushing it tight to the wall and sliding it down onto the interlocking cleat.

LEVEL

SCREW TO
CORNER STUD

6 Check the side panel to make sure the cabinet is plumb and screw through the bottom cleat into a stud to secure it.

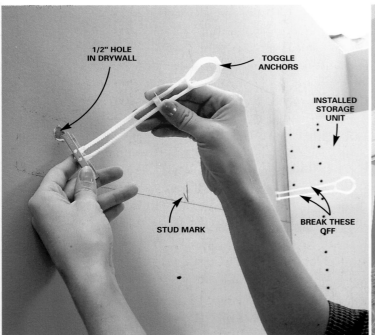

1/2" HOLE
IN DRYWALL

TOGGLE
ANCHORS

INSTALLED
STORAGE
UNIT

STUD MARK

BREAK THESE
OFF

7 Install toggle anchors for additional support if cleats land on only one stud. Hold the cleat in position and drill a 3/16-in. hole through the cleat and the drywall or plaster to mark the location of the toggle anchor. Remove the cleat and enlarge the hole in the wall to 1/2 inch. Then install the anchor and attach the cleat, making sure to leave a space for the side panel of the next storage unit.

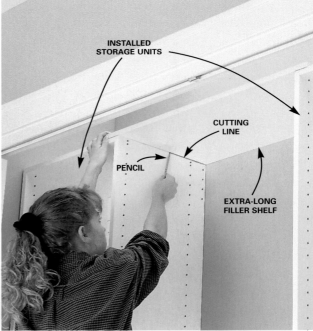

INSTALLED
STORAGE UNITS

CUTTING
LINE

PENCIL

EXTRA-LONG
FILLER SHELF

8 Mark the oversized filler shelf for cutting by laying it on top of the storage units and drawing lines along each side panel onto the shelf.

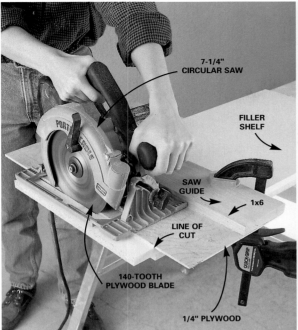

7-1/4"
CIRCULAR SAW

FILLER
SHELF

SAW
GUIDE

1x6

LINE OF
CUT

140-TOOTH
PLYWOOD BLADE

1/4" PLYWOOD

BOTTOM
FILLER
SHELF

SHELF
PINS

CLOSET
PLAN

HACKSAW

METAL
CLOTHES
ROD

DRAWER
SLIDES

DRAWER

DRAWER
FRONT

ADJUSTABLE
SHELVES

9 Cut the filler shelf with a 140-tooth plywood blade in a circular saw. Clamp a cutting guide so it just covers the line, and run the saw against it to provide a straight cut with a minimal amount of chipping. Construct the cutting guide by screwing a straight 1x6 to an oversized piece of 1/4-in. plywood. Run the saw against the 1x6 fence to cut the plywood at the exact blade location.

10 Tilt in the filler shelves, resting them on shelf support pins. Cut the metal closet rods with a 24-tooth-per-inch hacksaw. Tighten all of the mounting screws after adjacent units are connected. Install drawers, drawer fronts and adjustable shelves.

Here are a few assembly tips and things to watch out for:

● Take off the closet doors if they're in your way during construction.

● Extend the level line (Photo 1) only as far as necessary to line up the cleats. Find the studs and mark them above the line, where the marks will be hidden by the cleats. Double-check the stud locations by probing with a nail to be certain the hanging screws will hit solid wood.

● Get help setting the units in place. Avoid twisting the assembled storage units out of shape; the thin area of particleboard near the connectors might break.

Handy Hints®

Check the end walls of your closet with a level to see if they're plumb. If they slant inward on the bottom, you'll have to mount the first cleat farther from the wall to allow the storage unit to hang plumb.

● Don't tighten the mounting screws until you've joined the units with the special two-part connectors. You'll need the "slack" to align the holes properly. If the closet walls are wavy or crooked, slide shims behind the units to get them lined up.

● Install all of the full-size units. Then cut the filler shelves to complete the system (Photos 8 and 9). Tilt the top filler shelf in from below, and then install the shelf clips under it. A snug-fitting shelf is hard to install from the top.

● Some systems have adjustable drawer fronts. Loosen the screws just enough to move the fronts into alignment, with even spacing between the drawers. Then tighten the screws and drill for the knobs.

Simple shelves
Strong, quick to build and no visible supports.

Made from only two parts:

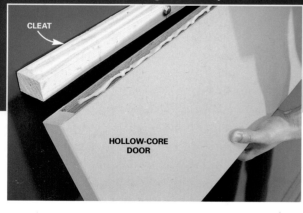

CLEAT

HOLLOW-CORE
DOOR

These "floating" shelves are perfect for displaying your collectibles, photos, travel mementos or just about anything. Without the brackets and clunky hardware you'd find with store-bought shelves or kits, they seem to be suspended in midair.

These shelves are strong, too. While they're not designed to hold your old set of *Encyclopaedia Britannicas,* they're certainly capable of it. No one would believe that they're made from plain, old lightweight and inexpensive hollow-core doors.

In this article, we'll show you how to install these shelves (and shorter ones) securely with basic tools. Even if you think you have no DIY skills, you can tackle this project.

Surprise—a low-cost project that requires only basic tools
Each shelf is made from half of an 18-in. hollow-core door, which costs $18. That's only about $9 a shelf, plus the minimal cost of the lag screws (Photo 4) and cleat

that hold the shelf to the wall. You can buy new hollow-core interior doors at a home center or lumberyard (just be sure the door doesn't have predrilled holes for locksets). You may find only 24-in. wide doors, but the door can be any width; just try to minimize the waste. And you might be able to get doors free from yard sales or other sources.

As far as tools go, you can get by with just a circular saw and edge guide (Photo 2) to cut the door. Use a table saw to cut the cleat because a clean, straight cut is impor-

tant for a good-looking shelf. (If you don't own a table saw, use a friend's or have the cleat cut at a full-service lumberyard.) You'll also need a stud finder, a chisel, a hammer, a wrench, 1-in. brads, 3-1/2 in. lag screws, carpenter's glue and a level. Simply follow photos 1 – 9 for information on building these simple shelves.

Want a different look?

We chose to paint our shelves, but if you want the beauty of real wood, you can buy

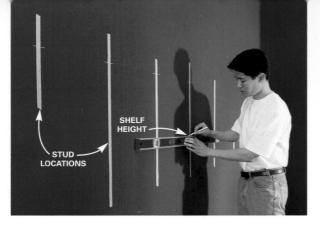

1 Trace the horizontal location for each shelf using a 4-ft. level as your guide. Use a stud finder to mark the locations of the studs and lightly press masking tape over each one. If you don't have a string line, use a long straightedge and mark the wall with a pencil. Check your marks with the 4-ft. level.

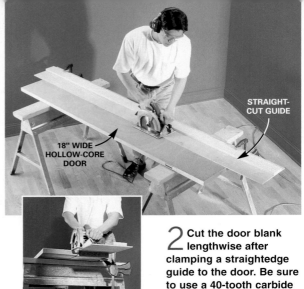

2 Cut the door blank lengthwise after clamping a straightedge guide to the door. Be sure to use a 40-tooth carbide blade for a smooth cut.

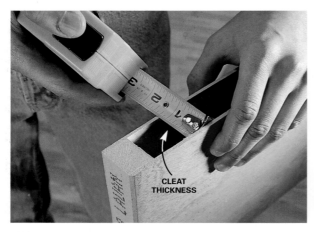

3 Measure the space between the outer veneers of the door and cut cleats from a 2x4 to this thickness. Our measurement was 1-3/32 in. Use straight, dry lumber for the cleats.

4 Predrill 1/4-in. dia. holes at the stud locations after you cut the cleats to length (the measurement between the end blocks of the door half). Hold the cleat to your line on the wall and drill into the stud with a 1/8-in. bit. Using a wrench, install one lag screw into each stud until it's tight. Use 1/4-in. x 3-1/2 in. lag screws. Each cleat must be straight as an arrow.

tip* If you intend to paint the room, do so before you install the shelves because it's a drag to cut around each shelf with a paintbrush.

the door in wood veneers like oak or maple (ours was lauan). If you decide on a natural wood finish, you'll need to cover the exposed edges with a matching wood trim. If you go this route, first shave off 1/8 in. from the front and side edges with a table saw to eliminate the slight bevel on each edge, then apply the matching trim. You can also cover the entire shelf with plastic laminate if you want a tough, hard-surfaced shelf.

You may want to change the depth of your shelves as well. Don't exceed 9 in. or you'll start to weaken the cantilever strength of the shelf. Feel free to make narrower or shorter shelves, as shown in Photo 9.

Create a rock-hard finish with a low-gloss enamel paint

The whole job will go a lot smoother if you paint the shelves before you install them. Just be sure to sand your wood door with 150-grit sandpaper before you paint. If the surface is still rough and porous after sanding, fill the pores by applying a paste wood filler (like

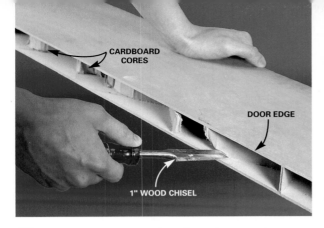

5 Cut away the corrugated cardboard cores at least 1-1/2 in. from the cut edge. Scrape away the glue carefully without gouging the wood surface.

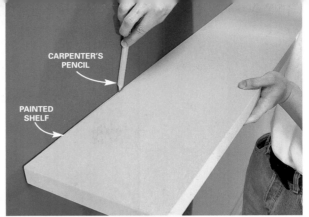

6 Dry-fit the shelf to make sure the blank fits over the cleat. Check the back side of the shelf and scribe it to the wall if necessary. Use a block plane or sander to remove material from the back edge for a tight fit.

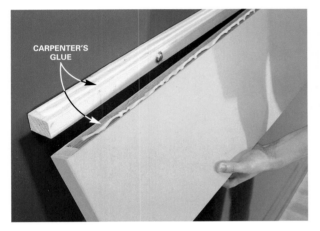

7 Apply glue to the top of the cleat and the inside bottom edge of the door blank. Slide the shelf over the wood cleat.

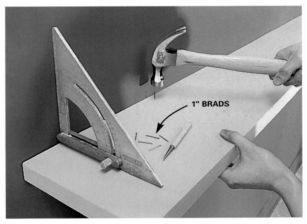

8 Nail the shelf to the cleat using a square as your guide. Start at the middle and work your way to each end. Use 1-in. brad nails spaced 8 in. apart.

Elmer's wood filler) with a 3-in. drywall knife. Let it dry and sand the surface again.

These shelves are permanent— they're tough to remove!

The glue not only makes the shelves strong but also impossible to remove without ruining them. You'll have to cut them in place 2 in. away from the wall with a circular saw to expose the lag screws and then remove the cleats with a wrench. That's unfortunate, but you can always make another set cheaply and easily.

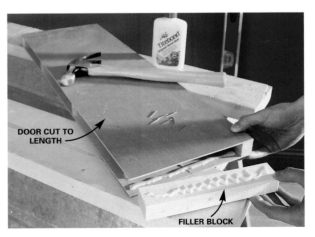

9 Build shorter shelves by cutting the shelf to length. Glue a filler block flush with the end and nail each side with small brad nails.

Leaning tower of shelves

This stylish but sturdy shelf unit will neatly hold your stuff—and you can build it in a day.

This shelf unit may look lightweight and easy to topple. But don't be fooled. It's a real workhorse. The 33-1/2 in. x 82-3/4 in. tower features five unique, tray-like shelves of different depths to hold a wide variety of items up to 13-1/4 in. tall. Despite its 10-degree lean, the unit is surprisingly sturdy, and its open design won't overpower a room.

project at a glance

skill level
intermediate

special tools
miter saw
finish nailer
iron

approximate cost
$60–$80

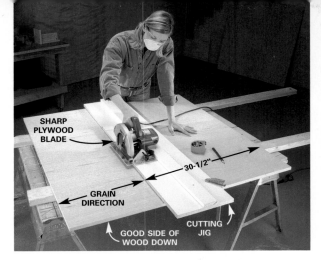

1 Cut 3/4-in. shelf plywood to width first, using a circular saw and a homemade jig for exact cuts. Use a sharp plywood blade and cut with the best side of the wood facing down to minimize splintering.

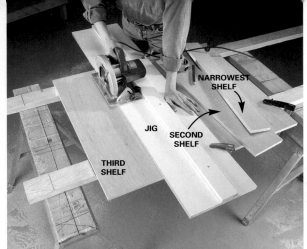

2 Cut the individual shelves, beginning with the narrowest, using the jig for perfectly straight cuts.

3 Cut both shelf uprights to length with a miter saw. Clamp to sawhorses. Mark the 10-degree angle at the top (dimensions in Figure B), then cut with a circular saw.

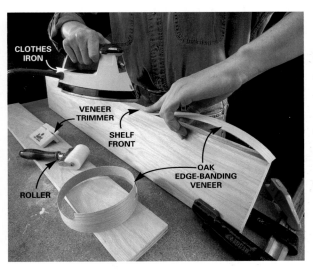

4 Iron edge-banding veneer to the front edge of all five shelves. Roll the entire surface to ensure a solid bond, and trim the edges.

Whether you choose to make this piece more functional, as in this office setting, or place it in a family room to showcase treasures, the basic construction is the same. You select the type of wood and stain or paint to dress it up or down to fit the look of any room.

All the materials can be purchased in home centers or lumberyards. The only special tools you'll need are a power miter box for crisp angle cuts and an air-powered brad nailer for quick assembly and almost invisible joints. And you'll have to rustle up an old clothes iron for applying oak edge-banding material. Once you've gathered all the material, you can build the shelf unit in one afternoon.

Buying the wood

We built our unit with red oak and oak veneer plywood and finished it with two coats of red oak stain.

One note when buying boards: Use a tape measure to check the "standard" dimensions of 1x3s and 1x4s. They sometimes vary in width and thickness. Also check the two full-length 1x4s you plan to use as the uprights to be sure they're straight, without warps or twists. And always examine the ends, edges and surface for blemishes or rough areas that won't easily sand out.

Cut plywood shelves first

Lay a couple of 2x4s across sawhorses (Photo 1) to cut the half sheet of 3/4-in. plywood cleanly and without

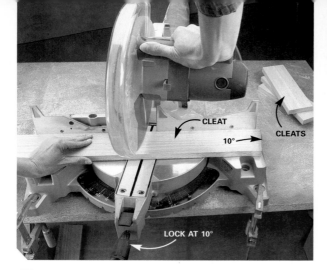

5 To maintain accuracy, lock the miter box at 10 degrees, then cut all angled pieces—uprights, cleats and one end of shelf sides—without changing the table.

6 Glue and nail the shelf cleats to the uprights using a 1x3 spacer. Hold each cleat tight to the spacer.

pinching the saw blade. Since all five shelves are 30-1/2 in. wide, cut this width first, making sure the grain will run the long way across the shelves. Remember to wear safety glasses, earplugs and a dust mask. Make a homemade jig to fit your circular saw and clamp it to the plywood.

Next, cut all five shelf depths, starting with the smallest shelf (3-3/8 in.) first. Cut smallest to largest so you'll have enough wood to clamp the jig. Make sure you account for the width of your saw blade when you cut each shelf.

tip *The beauty of this project is that any wood species will work. If you plan to paint it, select alder or aspen for the solid parts and birch for the plywood.*

Now mark and cut the top of all four 1x4 uprights (the end that rests against the wall), according to Photo 3 and the two dimensions provided in Figure B. Use a sharp blade in your circular saw to prevent splintering. Then stow the sawhorses and move to the workbench.

Select the best front of each plywood shelf, clamp it to the bench on edge and sand it smooth with 150-grit paper on a sanding block. Then preheat a clothes iron to the "cotton" setting and run it over the top of the edge-banding veneer, making sure the veneer extends beyond all edges (Photo 4). Roll it smooth immediately after heating. Let each shelf edge cool for a couple of minutes before trimming and sanding the edges.

Cut the uprights and shelf frame next

Now enter the miter saw, which you use to make all the 90-degree straight cuts first (five shelf backs and 10 shelf sides; see Cutting List). Remember that one end of each shelf side has a 10-degree cut, so we recommend first cutting them square at their exact length, then cutting the angle carefully so the long edge of each piece remains the same.

Next, rotate the miter saw table to the 10-degree mark and cut all the angle pieces. First cut the bottom of both uprights so each upright rests flat against the floor and wall (see Figure A). Then trim the top of the upright to match the bottom, being careful to maintain the 84-in. total length. Next, cut the cleats based on the Cutting List dimensions, which are measured edge to edge (Photo 5 and Figure A). Leave the top cleats long and cut them to exact fit during assembly. Then, to speed finishing, use an orbital sander with 150-grit sandpaper to smooth all pieces before assembly.

materials list

- One half sheet (4' x 4') of 3/4" oak plywood
- Three 8' oak 1x3s
- Four 8' oak 1x4s
- One package (25') of 7/8" oak iron-on veneer (Band-It brand, The Cloverdale Co., (800) 782-9731, www.band-itproducts.com, purchased at Home Depot)
- Veneer edge trimmer (Band-It brand; see above and click "Retail," "Related Products")
- Wood glue
- 1-1/4" brad nails
- Foam pads (1 pkg. of Ace brand 3/4" round, self-adhesive non-skid pads from Ace Hardware)

figure a
modular shelf assembly

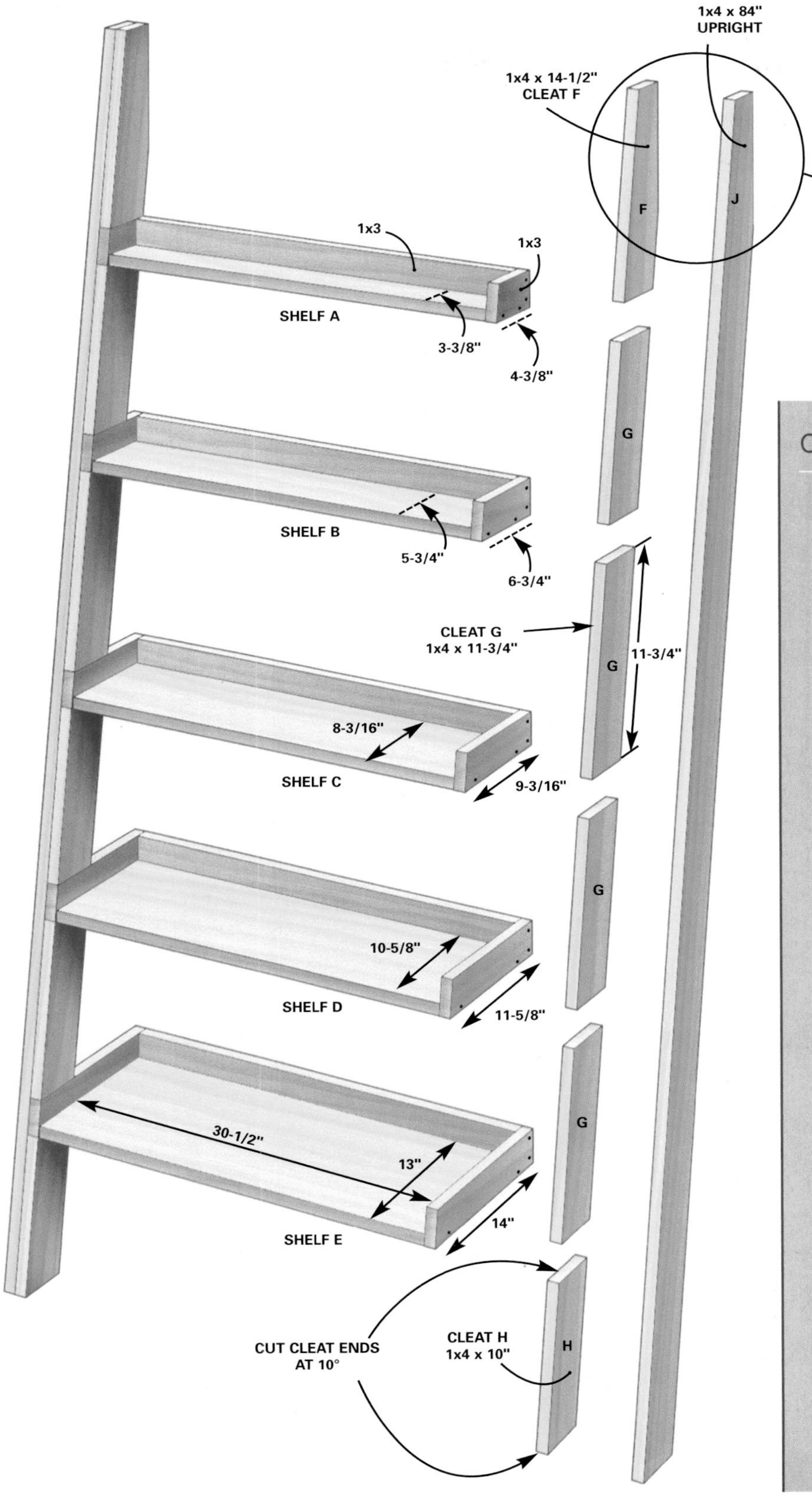

1x4 x 84"
UPRIGHT

1x4 x 14-1/2"
CLEAT F

2-1/32"

8-3/8"

F
AND
J

10° ANGLE

1x3

1x3

SHELF A

3-3/8"

4-3/8"

F

J

G

SHELF B

5-3/4"

6-3/4"

CLEAT G
1x4 x 11-3/4"

G

11-3/4"

8-3/16"

SHELF C

9-3/16"

G

10-5/8"

SHELF D

11-5/8"

G

30-1/2"

13"

14"

SHELF E

CUT CLEAT ENDS
AT 10°

CLEAT H
1x4 x 10"

H

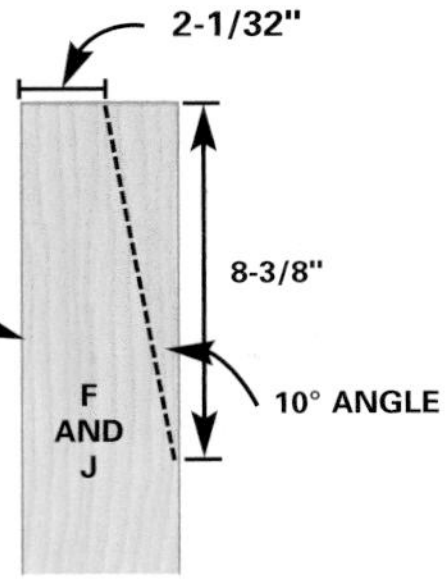

cutting list

PCS.	SIZE & DESCRIPTION
1	3/4" x 3-3/8" x 30-1/2" oak plywood (shelf A base)
1	3/4" x 5-3/4" x 30-1/2" oak plywood (shelf B base)
1	3/4" x 8-3/16" x 30-1/2" oak plywood (shelf C base)
1	3/4" x 10-5/8" x 30-1/2" oak plywood (shelf D base)
1	3/4" x 13" x 30-1/2" oak plywood (shelf E base)
2	3/4" x 2-1/2" x 4-3/8" oak (shelf A sides)*
2	3/4" x 2-1/2" x 6-3/4" oak (shelf B sides)*
2	3/4" x 2-1/2" x 9-3/16" oak (shelf C sides)*
2	3/4" x 2-1/2" x 11-5/8" oak (shelf D sides)*
2	3/4" x 2-1/2" x 14" oak (shelf E sides)*
5	3/4" x 2-1/2" x 30-1/2" oak A - E (shelf backs)
2	3/4" x 3-1/2" x 14-1/2" oak shelf cleats F (cut with 10-degree angles)
8	3/4" x 3-1/2" x 11-3/4" oak shelf cleats G (cut with 10-degree angles)
2	3/4" x 3-1/2" x 10" oak shelf cleats H (cut with 10-degree angles)
2	3/4" x 3-1/2" x 84" oak uprights J (cut with 10-degree angles)

*Front part of side cut at 10 degrees

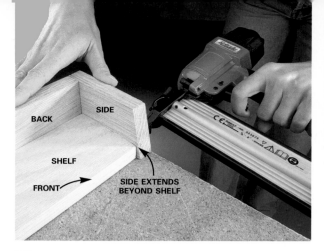

BACK
SIDE
SHELF
FRONT
SIDE EXTENDS
BEYOND SHELF

7 Glue and nail the shelf backs, then attach the sides to the plywood shelves. Position the sides to overlap the shelf base as shown.

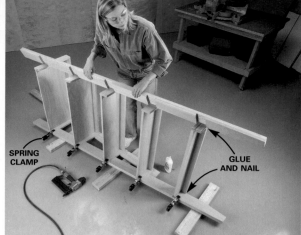

SPRING CLAMP
GLUE AND NAIL

8 Clamp the shelves into one upright. Spread glue in the shelf notches of the other upright, position it flush with the front of the shelves and nail. Flip the unit over and attach the other upright.

Assemble uprights first, then the shelves

To begin assembly, lay out both uprights and all cleats to ensure that the angles are correct so the shelves will be level when the unit is against the wall. Then glue and nail the first cleat flush with the base of each upright (using five or six 1-1/4 in. brads) on each cleat. Work your way upward using 1x3 spacers (Photo 6). Make sure the spacer is the exact same width as the shelf sides! Set these aside to dry.

For shelf assembly, first glue and nail on the shelf backs. Next, apply the sides with glue and nails (Photo 7).

For final assembly, lay one upright on 2x4s, then clamp on the shelves as shown in Photo 8. Apply the glue, position the second upright on top flush with the front edge of the shelves, then sink four 1-1/4 in. brads into each shelf from the upright side. Carefully turn the unit over and repeat the process to attach the second upright. Work quickly so the glue doesn't set. Lift the ladder shelf and place it upright against a straight wall. Check it with a framing square and flex it if necessary to square it up and to make sure that the uprights rest flat against the floor and wall (assuming your floor is level). Attach three bar clamps as shown in Photo 9 while the glue dries.

The shelf is highly stable as designed, but once you've stained or painted it, you can add self-adhesive foam gripping pads to the bottom of the uprights. And if you don't feel secure having it on a slippery floor, the unit's width is perfect for screwing the top of the uprights into wall studs.

BAR CLAMP
1/2" GAP

9 Set the shelf unit against a straight wall, check for squareness and apply three bar clamps until the glue dries.

NON-SKID FOAM PAD

Entryway pocket screw coat locker

Intimidated by cabinet work? Even a novice can make fine joints with pocket screws.

If you've ever seen a pocket screw jig being demonstrated at a woodworking show, you'll know how this simple tool will enable you to quickly and painlessly assemble tight-fitting joints without investing in a bunch of expensive clamps or special tools.

Pocket screw joints are best described as a screw version of toenailing, where boards are joined by angling a fastener through the edge of one into the other. The concept is simple, but the precisely engineered drill guide (the jig), drill bit and pocket screws make the system so easy and foolproof.

project at a glance

skill level
intermediate

special tools
pocket screw jig kit
power miter box
drill
power sanders
circular saw
basic hand tools

approximate cost
$400–$450

Buy a good pocket screw jig

You can purchase a $65 kit that contains the Kreg "Rocket" jig shown on p. 77, the special clamp and the stepped drill bit with a stop collar and square driver bit. Avoid the temptation to buy an inexpensive jig; you'll never experience the real benefits of pocket screws if you're frustrated by a poorly designed tool. Less-expensive jigs lack the self-aligning lip and built-in clamp found on this and other high-quality models. You can get higher-priced pocket hole jigs that have more elaborate clamping systems and built-in motors to speed up the operation, but the end result is essentially the same.

The joinery system is incomplete without the specially designed pocket screws. These screws have a narrow shank with a thread-cutting tip to avoid splitting hardwoods, and a strong head with a square recess for slip-proof driving. The most common length is 1-1/4 in., the best size for joining 3/4-in.-thick material. Corrosion-resistant exterior screws, washer head screws for joining particleboard, and hi-lo thread screws for softwood are also available. To check out the various types, order an assortment for about $20 from the Kreg Tool Company.

Building the coat locker

The coat locker we built is constructed of 3/4-in. birch plywood with 3/4-in. solid-birch boards for the face frame, drawer sides and front, baseboard and top edge. The back and drawer bottoms are 1/4-in. birch plywood. The plywood and boards shown here were purchased from a local hardwood lumber supplier. This is usually the best source for good-quality hardwood boards, and you can have them cut to the right width and planed smooth on all four edges. You can also get your materials at home centers and full-service lumberyards.

Even though this coat locker is built with simple pocket screw joints, many of the parts must be cut to precise dimensions. You can use a circular saw guided by a clamped straightedge to cut the plywood. You'll need a power miter box ($25 a day to rent) for cutting the face frame, edge band, drawer sides and moldings.

Cut out the plywood parts and drill pocket holes in the horizontal fixed shelves (A) and top and bottom pieces (also A). See Photo 1. For this project, the pocket holes will either be hidden from view or filled,

so there's no need to precisely locate the holes.

Join all of the horizontal panels (A) to the sides and uprights (B1 and B2) with pocket screws, making sure to face the screw holes to the hidden or least conspicuous side (Photo 2). Check the cabinet box for square by measuring diagonally across the corners. Now you can use the box as a pattern for cutting out and joining the face-frame parts.

Cut the 3/4-in. solid-birch face frame parts to length using a power miter box. For tight-fitting joints, the edges of the boards must be square to the face and the end joints cut perfectly square. Bore the pocket screw holes (Photo 3). Now assemble the frame without glue and set it onto the box to check the fit. Take the frame apart, adjust the size if necessary, reassemble it using glue, and attach it to the box (Photos 4 and 5).

Photos 6 and 7 show how to assemble the drawer box and attach the slides. You can use the inexpensive epoxy-coated drawer slides, as shown, but for better access to the drawer interior, you could install full-extension slides instead. Use whatever shimming material you have around to build out the sides of the drawer compartments flush with the edge of the face frame. Then you can mount the slide as shown in Photo 7.

Attaching the drawer front (T) so it's perfectly aligned is a little tricky. Start by drilling four 5/16-in. holes in the front of the drawer box. Place the drawer in the opening. Use double-faced carpet tape or hot-melt glue to temporarily secure the drawer front to the drawer box. Gently open the drawer and clamp the front to the box. Attach it with four No. 8 x 1-1/4-in. pan head screws with No. 10 finish washers under the heads. Snug the

materials list

ITEM	QTY.
3/4" x 4' x 8' birch plywood	2
1/4" x 4' x 8' birch plywood	1
1x2 x 12' birch or maple board	2
1x3 x 6' birch or maple board	2
1x4 x 6' birch or maple board	2
1x6 x 8' birch or maple board	1
1x6 x 5' birch or maple board	1
1x8 x 3' birch or maple board	1
11/16" x 1-3/8" x 6' birch base cap	1
9/16" x 2" x 6' birch cove molding	1
2x4 x 3' scrap for fillers	
1-1/4" pocket screws	130
1-1/4" drywall screws	8
No. 8 x 1-1/4" pan head screws	8
No. 10 finish washers	8
6d finish nails	1 lb.
1" x 17-gauge brads	1 pkg.
1" paneling nails	1 pkg.
Carpenter's glue	8 oz.
Blum B230M 12" drawer slides	2 pair
Coat hooks	6
Drawer knobs	2
Benjamin Moore No. 241 Colonial Maple stain	1 qt.
Black stain	1 pt.
Sanding sealer	1 qt.
Satin finish varnish	1 qt.
Interior wood primer and paint	

cutting list

KEY	QTY.	SIZE & DESCRIPTION
PLYWOOD BOX		
A	8	3/4" x 13-3/4" x 16-7/8" horizontals
B1	2	3/4" x 14" x 72" sides
B2	1	3/4" x 13-3/4" x 72" upright
C	1	3/4" x 14-7/8" x 36-1/4" top
D	1	1/4" x 35-1/2" x 72" back
FACE FRAME PARTS		
E	1	3/4" x 5-1/2" x 31" bottom rail
F	1	3/4" x 3" x 31" top rail
G	4	3/4" x 1-1/2" x 14-3/4" intermediate rails
H	2	3/4" x 2-1/2" x 72" side rails
J	1	3/4" x 1-1/2" x 62-7/8" middle rail
TRIM AND EDGE BAND		
K1	2	3/4" x 1-1/2" x 17" edge band*
K2	1	3/4" x 1-1/2" x 40" edge band*
L1	2	3/4" x 3" x 16" base*
L2	1	3/4" x 3" x 40" base*
M1	2	11/16" x 1-3/8" x 16" base cap*
M2	1	11/16" x 1-3/8" x 40" base cap*
N1	2	9/16" x 2" x 17" cove molding*
N2	1	9/16" x 2" x 40" cove molding*
P	2	3/4" x 3-1/2" x 16-7/8" hook strips
*Miter-cut to finished lengths during assembly		
DRAWER PARTS		
Q	4	3/4" x 12-1/4" x 4-3/4" ends
R	4	3/4" x 13" x 4-3/4" sides
S	2	1/4" x 13-3/4" x 13" plywood bottom
T	2	3/4" x 5-13/16" x 14-9/16" fronts
U	4	1" x 2" x 6-3/4" fillers
V	2	3/4" x 6-3/4" x 13-3/4" filler panels
W	2	3/8" x 1-1/2" x 13-3/4" filler strips

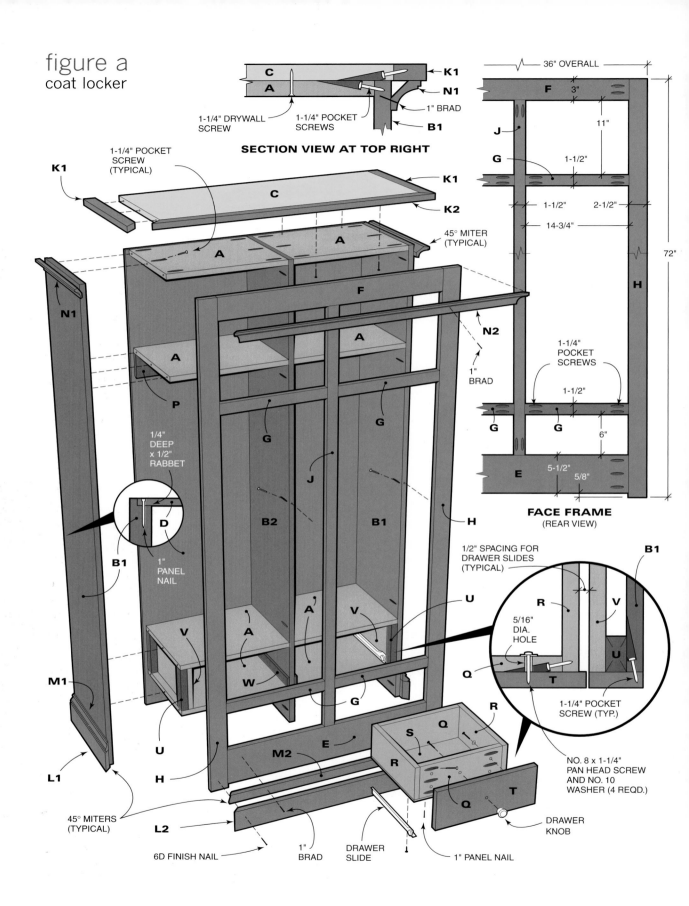

figure a
coat locker

SECTION VIEW AT TOP RIGHT

1-1/4" DRYWALL SCREW

1-1/4" POCKET SCREWS

1" BRAD

K1

N1

B1

C

A

1-1/4" POCKET SCREW (TYPICAL)

K1

C

K1

K2

45° MITER (TYPICAL)

A

A

A

F

N2

1" BRAD

P

A

N1

G

G

J

1/4" DEEP x 1/2" RABBET

D

1" PANEL NAIL

B2

B1

H

B1

M1

V

A

W

U

V

A

G

U

H

L1

45° MITERS (TYPICAL)

L2

M2

E

6D FINISH NAIL

1" BRAD

DRAWER SLIDE

1" PANEL NAIL

36" OVERALL

F

3"

J

11"

G

1-1/2"

1-1/2"

2-1/2"

14-3/4"

H

72"

1-1/4" POCKET SCREWS

1-1/2"

G

G

6"

E

5-1/2"

5/8"

FACE FRAME
(REAR VIEW)

1/2" SPACING FOR DRAWER SLIDES (TYPICAL)

B1

R

V

5/16" DIA. HOLE

Q

T

U

1-1/4" POCKET SCREW (TYP.)

S

Q

R

R

Q

T

NO. 8 x 1-1/4" PAN HEAD SCREW AND NO. 10 WASHER (4 REQD.)

DRAWER KNOB

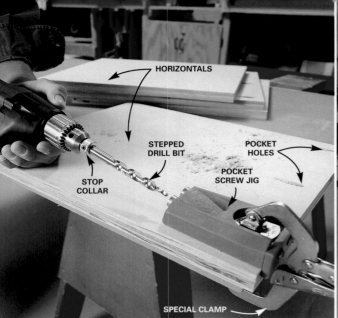

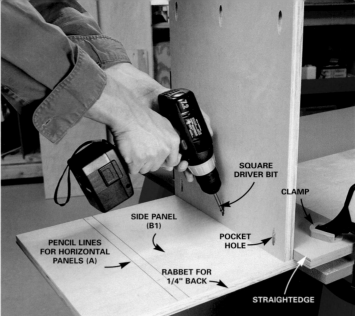

1 Clamp the pocket hole jig to the horizontal panel (A) and workbench. Follow the manufacturer's instructions for setting the stop collar on the special bit to the correct depth. Insert the bit into the jig's metal sleeve before you turn on the drill. Start the drill so the bit is turning at full speed (2,000 rpm is recommended). Then bore the clearance and pilot hole in one step by pushing the bit into the workpiece until the stop collar contacts the metal sleeve. Bore three holes on both ends of the eight horizontal panels.

2 Lay out the horizontal panel (A) locations with a framing square. Then clamp a straightedge along the line to hold the panels in position while you drive in the 1-1/4-in. pocket screws. Attach all eight panels (A) to the uprights (B1 and B2).

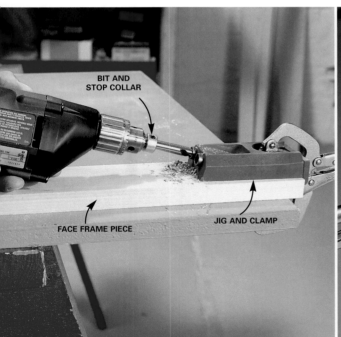

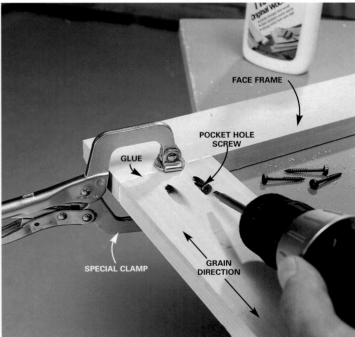

3 Clamp the jig to the end of a face frame board and bore holes for two pocket screws. Drill the opposite end, and all other face-frame parts that need pocket screw holes. Remember that only one half of each joint needs pocket screw holes. Drill parallel to the grain, as shown.

4 Spread wood glue on both pieces to be joined. Clamp the joint together to hold the faces flush, and drive in the 1-1/4-in. pocket screws. We used a special locking pliers–type clamp provided by the jig manufacturer.

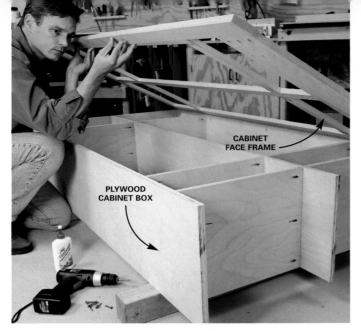

CABINET
FACE FRAME

PLYWOOD
CABINET BOX

5 Attach the face frame to the box. First bore pocket screw holes every 16 in. along the inside front edge of the box, placing them in concealed locations when possible. After checking the alignment, spread an even layer of wood glue on the edge of the plywood and use a clamp to hold the frame in position while you attach it to the box with pocket screws. Remove excess glue with a damp rag. When the glue is dry, sand the outside edge of the face frame flush with the box, being careful not to sand through the thin veneer on the plywood.

screws but don't tighten them. The extra-large holes will allow you to tap the drawer front into exact alignment before you fully tighten the screws.

Construct the cabinet top by attaching edging strips (K1 and K2) to the plywood (C) with pocket screws (Photo 8). Use this same procedure for edge-gluing boards for a tabletop or attaching wood nosing to a counter.

Complete the cabinet as shown in Photo 9. Glue wood plugs, available from the Kreg Company, into the exposed pocket holes on the cabinet interior and sand them flush.

Now you know how to use pocket screws in some of

Handy Hints®

Since screws enter the center upright panel from opposite sides, be sure to offset the pocket holes so the screws don't collide.

pros and cons of pocket screws

Pocket screw joints have many advantages over more traditional joinery:
● **You can assemble large frames without needing an arsenal of expensive clamps because the screws provide the clamping action while the glue dries.**
● **No fancy cutting is required; joints are simply butted together, saving time and reducing tool costs.**
● **The use of an alignment clamp during assembly ensures flush joints without any tricky measuring.**

Pocket screw joints aren't perfect:
● **Every joint leaves behind a long, oblong hole that looks bad when it's prominent, like on cabinet doors. Luckily, you can order wood plugs in just about any species to fill these odd holes—you just glue them in and sand them flush. Dowels, biscuits or mortise-and-tenon joints would be a better choice if the backside of a joint will be highly visible.**

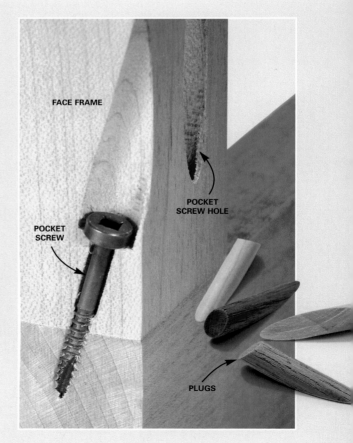

FACE FRAME

POCKET SCREW HOLE

POCKET SCREW

PLUGS

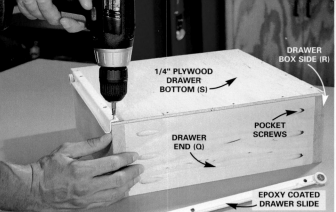

1/4" PLYWOOD
DRAWER
BOTTOM (S)

DRAWER
BOX SIDE (R)

DRAWER
END (Q)

POCKET
SCREWS

EPOXY COATED
DRAWER SLIDE

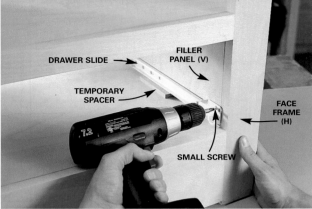

DRAWER SLIDE

FILLER
PANEL (V)

TEMPORARY
SPACER

FACE
FRAME
(H)

7.2

SMALL SCREW

6 Cut 1x6 boards to form a box that is 13 in. long and exactly 1 in. narrower than the drawer opening in the face frame. Bore pocket holes on the end drawer pieces (Q) as shown and screw the box together. Use a framing square to square up the drawer. Then nail on the 1/4-in. plywood bottom with 1-in. paneling nails. Attach the 12-in. epoxy-coated slides to the drawer with the screws provided, aligning the front (the end without the wheel) of the slide with the front of the drawer box.

7 Shim the sides of the drawer compartments flush to the face frame with scraps of plywood and shims ripped to the proper thickness. Then attach the other half of the drawer slides, holding the front edge of the slide even with the front edge of the face frame. (Check the manufacturer's specifications for exact placement.) Use a spacer to hold the drawer slide parallel to the cabinet bottom while you screw it in.

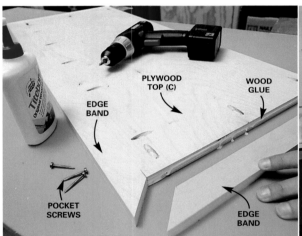

PLYWOOD
TOP (C)

WOOD
GLUE

EDGE
BAND

POCKET
SCREWS

EDGE
BAND

COVE (N1)

EDGE-
BANDED TOP

COAT
HANGING
STRIPS (P)

BASE
(L2)

BASE
CAP
(M2)

8 Band the edge of the plywood top with 1-1/2-in. strips of birch (K1 and K2), mitered to fit. Spread wood glue on both edges and secure the 1x2 band to the plywood (C) with pocket screws as shown. Wipe off the excess glue with a damp rag. Use an orbital sander to sand the 1x2 flush with the plywood. Position the top on the cabinet so that an equal amount hangs over both sides and the front. Hold the top in place with a clamp while you attach it through the top of the cabinet box with 1-1/4-in. drywall screws.

9 Mark, miter and nail on the 2-in. cove (N1 and N2), the 3/4-in. x 3-in. base (L1, L2) and the 1-5/8-in. base cap (M1 and M2). Use 6d finish nails for the base, and 1-in. brads to attach the moldings. Attach the hook strips with pocket screws. Then cut a piece of 1/4-in. plywood (D) to fit the back and attach it with 1-in. paneling nails. Draw lines to indicate dividers to help in placing the nails accurately.

the more common cabinetmaking applications, but don't ignore other possibilities. Once you get the pocket screw joining bug, you can come up with your own innovative uses for this ingenious little connector.

Traditional maple bookcase

Create your own classic bookcase with simple tools in these easy-to-follow steps

When you're ready to display your literary favorites, don't go to a furniture store and settle for a poorly constructed bookcase with zippo for detail. For about the cost of a cheap bookcase, you can build this handsome and solid heirloom-quality piece.

This project is too challenging for a beginner. Don't tackle it unless you've used a router and a doweling jig and feel confident with your circular saw. The project is broken into easy-to-follow steps and you have the option of selecting your own trim and finish.

The bookcase construction is straightforward and basic, so it's easy to cut and fit the pieces. The fixed shelves add stability and are designed to hold a variety of average-sized books, but you can customize the shelf heights to suit your collection.

The grooved vertical front pieces on each side (fluted casing) may look challenging, but with a shop-made jig and a router, you'll get perfect results. For details, see "Make your own fluted casing—the easy way," p. 86. Figure on about a day and a half for cutting and assembling, plus a couple of evenings for sanding and finishing.

1 Rip 3/4-in. hardwood plywood into 11-1/4-in.-wide pieces for the sides and the shelves. Cut these pieces to length to make the two sides and the six shelves. Also cut the 1/4-in. plywood back to width and length while you have the edge guide set up.

2 Mark and cut the 1/4-in. dadoes in the sides. Use a special 23/32-in.-wide straight-cut router bit for a tight fit for the thinner-than-3/4-in. plywood.

Labels on image 1: TOP PIECE OF RIP GUIDE; RIP GUIDE; SAW BASE; LOWER EDGE OF RIP GUIDE; FACTORY EDGE; ALIGN YOUR MARK WITH THIS EDGE; PIECE BEING CUT FROM SHEET

Labels on image 2: EDGE GUIDE; 23/32" GROOVES; A

All you need are simple hand and power tools

The only power tools you'll need are a 7/8-hp router, a circular saw (Photo 1) with a fine-toothed plywood blade, a drill, a power miter saw and an orbital sander. (And you could substitute a hand miter saw for the power one.) You'll also need other woodworking tools like C-clamps, bar clamps, spring clamps, a screwdriver, drill bits and a doweling jig (Photo 5) with a 3/8-in. brad point bit. Although you could get by without it, a 24-in. Clamp & Tool edge guide (Photo 2) is great for routing perfectly straight grooves (dadoes) to support the shelves. This tool clamps firmly to the edges of the plywood and leaves an unobstructed path to push your router from one side to the next. It's not a tool you'll get and use only once. The Clamp & Tool guide has dozens of uses, such as helping you make super-straight crosscuts (perpendicular cuts to the wood grain) on lumber and plywood.

making it fit your style

Our bookcase is made primarily from maple plywood and detailed with solid maple boards and regular lumberyard maple colonial stop molding (Figure A). If maple isn't your favorite wood, you could opt for birch and oak plywood and moldings. They, too, are commonly stocked in full-service lumberyards and good home centers.

Get straight rip cuts with a homemade jig

If you've got a fancy setup for achieving perfectly straight cuts (rips) from a sheet of plywood on a table saw or something else, all the better. If you don't, this simple jig (Photo 1) is what you need.

Construct the jig by screwing together two scraps of either 1/2- or 3/4-in. plywood. The top narrow piece (2-1/2 in. wide) must have one factory straightedge. Leave the bottom piece a few inches wider than your saw base (in most cases, that will make the bottom piece about 10 in.). Screw the top piece to the bottom with drywall screws every 5 inches. Now you need to trim the lower piece perfectly straight.

Now, clamp the jig to the entire piece of 3/4-in. maple plywood, setting it to the correct width. Rip-cut (lengthwise) the two bookcase sides (A), then cut them to length (crosscut). Rip two additional lengths and crosscut them (outer sides "A" facing up) into 31-7/8-

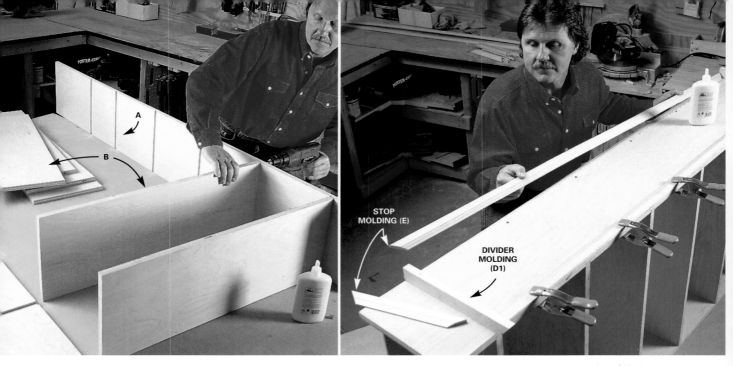

3 Glue and screw the shelves to the sides with 1-5/8-in. wood screws. Drill pilot and countersink holes no more than 3/4 in. from the front and back to accept the screws. The screws will be covered by molding later. Align the 1/4-in. plywood back (C) and square the assembly by nailing into the back of the sides and shelves.

4 Apply the divider and stop molding to the sides. Glue, then nail the divider molding to the sides with 6d finish nails (two per piece). Glue the stop molding to the sides as shown in Figure A. Further secure the molding with 7/8-in. brads spaced every 12 inches. Set the brads with a nail set. You'll fill the holes later with wood putty.

in. lengths for the shelves. Cut the 1/4-in. plywood back (C) to the dimensions in the Cutting List, p. 84.

Rout the 1/4-in.-deep shelf slots into the sides

The shelves (B) lock into 1/4-in.-deep slots (dadoes) in the upright sides (A). To make the dadoes, install a 23/32-in. straight-cut router bit in your router and set the depth of cut to 1/4 inch. The special 23/32-in. router bit is the same width as 3/4-in. plywood, so the slots it cuts will make a nice snug fit for the shelves. Don't substitute a 3/4-in. bit; you'll be unhappy with the sloppy fit.

Clamp your edge guide (Photo 2) to a scrap piece of plywood and rout a test dado. Then measure the distance from the edge guide to the near edge of the dado. This will give you the distance you'll need for setting up each dado groove. Mark and cut (see Figure A, p. 95) all the 1/4-in.- deep dadoes on the inside face of each part A. Tip: When you cut dadoes with a router and straightedge, clamp the edge guide to the left of your intended groove, then push the router base away from you as you rout the groove. This keeps the router tight against the edge guide as the bit rotates through

the cut. Finish-sand all the plywood pieces now with 150-grit sandpaper; otherwise, you'll struggle with sanding in tight spaces after assembly.

Glue and screw the shelf ends into the slotted sides

It's essential to have a flat surface for assembly so you can align the shelves squarely to the sides. The shelves (B) should fit tightly into the grooves. Test the fit. If the shelf won't slip into the dado, wrap some fine sandpaper (150-grit) around a 1/2-in.-square block about 3 in. long and sand the sides of the grooves until you get a snug fit.

Once you're sure everything fits, you'll have to work fast to complete the assembly. You'll need to get the shelves glued into the dadoes and the 1/4-in. plywood back nailed into place before the glue sets (about 15 minutes). This means you need to get your drill, countersink bit and a power screwdriver and screws ready to go.

Spread a light coat of glue on one shelf side and into the dado, then fit each shelf into its dado. Have a moist cotton rag handy to wipe away any oozing glue. Next, screw the shelf to the side as shown in Figure A. The screw holes for each shelf side must be predrilled within 3/4 in. of the front and the back. The screwheads will be covered later by the molding. Follow this procedure for each shelf.

Now, before the glue sets, grab the 1/4-in. plywood back (C) to square the assembly. There's no need to glue the plywood back to the shelves or sides. First nail the back along one entire side using a 1-in. panel nail every 5 inches. Then align the top of the other side flush with the top edge of the plywood; this will square the assembly. Nail along this side, then nail the rest of the back into the backside of the shelves. Let the glue dry for at least two hours before continuing.

personally speaking

Don't make the same mistake I made when I moved into my new house. I left my books stacked in boxes for two years before I finally got around to building bookcases. I can't tell you how many times I rummaged through those boxes looking for reference books or that mystery novel I wanted to revisit.

–Dave Radtke, editor
The Family Handyman

Detail the sides of the box with molding

Now it's time to detail the sides with the divider moldings (D1 and the lower D2; Figure A) and the colonial stop moldings. The divider molding, with the stop molding (Photo 4), breaks the strong vertical line to give the bookcase a distinct architectural look. It has a base section, a main vertical section and a top section similar to the cornice of a building.

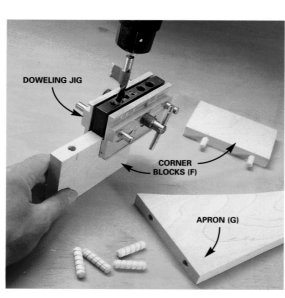

5 Drill 3/8-in. dowel holes in the corner blocks and corresponding holes in the aprons. Glue and clamp this assembly after you glue the stop moldings to the front of the blocks.

DOWELING JIG

CORNER BLOCKS (F)

APRON (G)

materials list

ITEM	QTY.
3/4" x 4' x 8' maple plywood	1-1/4 sheets
1/4" x 4' x 8' maple plywood	1 sheet
1x4 x 7' maple	2
1x6 x 5' maple	4
Colonial stop molding	80 ln. ft.
7/8" brad nails	1 pkg.
1" panel nails (for plywood back)	1 pkg.
Carpenter's glue	1/2 pint
1-5/8" wood screws	1 lb.
6d finish nails	1 lb.
4d finish nails	1 lb.
Colored wood putty sticks	2
Router bits	

cutting list

KEY	PCS.	SIZE & DESCRIPTION
A	2	3/4" x 11-1/4" x 78" maple plywood sides
B	6	3/4" x 11-1/4" x 31-7/8" maple plywood shelves
C	1	1/4" x 32-3/4" x 76" maple plywood back
D1	6	3/4" x 1-1/2" x 13" maple divider molding*
D2	2	3/4" x 1-1/2" x 35-7/8" maple divider molding*
D3	2	3/4" x 1-1/2" x 4-5/8" maple divider caps*
E	80 ln. ft.	7/16" x 1-1/4" colonial stop molding (allows for waste)
F	4	3/4" x 3-1/2" x 5-1/2" maple corner blocks
G	2	3/4" x 5-1/2" x 26-3/4" maple curved aprons
H	2	3/4" x 3-1/2" x 64-3/4" maple fluted casing
J1	1	3/4" x 12-15/16" x 35-3/4" maple plywood top
J2	5-1/2 ln. ft.	3/4" x 3/4" maple edge banding*
K1	2	3/4" x 1-1/2" x 4" maple front feet*
K2	2	3/4" x 1-1/2" x 2" maple back feet*
L	2	3/4" x 5-1/2" x 11-1/4" support strips

*Have the lumberyard cut these pieces to width from a 1x6.

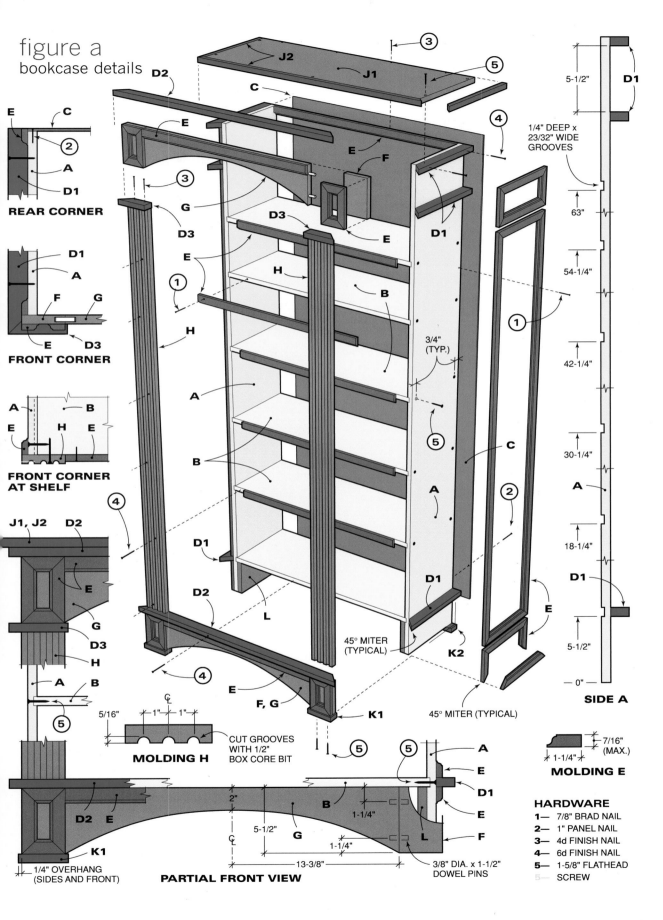

figure a
bookcase details

REAR CORNER
E C
2
A
D1

FRONT CORNER
D1
A
F G
E D3

FRONT CORNER AT SHELF
A B
E H E

J1, J2 D2
E
G
D3
H
A B
5

D2 J2 J1
C 3
5
4
E
E F
E
D3
D1
H
B
1
H
A
B
D1
D2
L
G
E
F, G
K1
K2
45° MITER (TYPICAL)
45° MITER (TYPICAL)
3/4" (TYP.)
5
C
A
2
E

MOLDING H
5/16" 1" 1"
CUT GROOVES WITH 1/2" BOX CORE BIT

PARTIAL FRONT VIEW
5
5
A
E
D1
E
B
L
F
G
2"
5-1/2"
1-1/4"
1-1/4"
13-3/8"
3/8" DIA. x 1-1/2" DOWEL PINS
1/4" OVERHANG (SIDES AND FRONT)

SIDE A
D1
1/4" DEEP x 23/32" WIDE GROOVES
5-1/2"
63"
54-1/4"
1
42-1/4"
30-1/4"
A
18-1/4"
D1
5-1/2"
— 0"

MOLDING E
7/16" (MAX.)
1-1/4"

HARDWARE
1— 7/8" BRAD NAIL
2— 1" PANEL NAIL
3— 4d FINISH NAIL
4— 6d FINISH NAIL
5— 1-5/8" FLATHEAD
5— SCREW

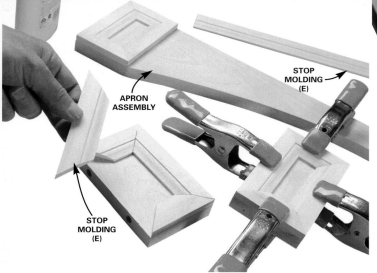

APRON ASSEMBLY

STOP MOLDING (E)

STOP MOLDING (E)

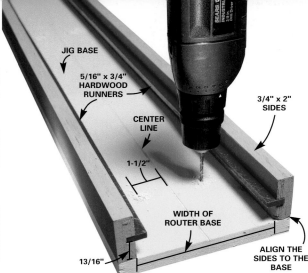

JIG BASE

5/16" x 3/4" HARDWOOD RUNNERS

CENTER LINE

1-1/2"

3/4" x 2" SIDES

WIDTH OF ROUTER BASE

13/16"

ALIGN THE SIDES TO THE BASE

6 Glue the stop molding to the front of the corner blocks. Be very precise about the miter cuts. A simple wooden handsaw miter box works great for these small, hard-to-hold pieces. After the glue is set, sand the edges of the block with 100-grit, then 150-grit, sandpaper. Glue the dowel joints and clamp the corner blocks to the apron to complete the apron assemblies.

7 Drill holes 1-1/2 in. on both sides of the center line of your jig. Keep the holes about 4 in. back from each end and spaced about 2 ft. apart toward the middle. The holes are spaced 1-1/2 in. from the center to avoid having screw holes show through your flutes. If you rout a different width or number of flutes, you may need to change the hold-down screw locations. After drilling the holes, flip the jig over and countersink them to accept screws for holding the workpiece.

To begin detailing the sides, first cut the divider molding, then glue and nail it (use 6d finish nails) to the sides (Photo 4). Drill pilot holes through the molding to prevent splitting. The colonial stop molding (E) and the backside of the divider molding must be applied so they align flush with the 1/4-in. plywood back. Glue and clamp this molding to the side. Drive 7/8-in. wire brads through the stop molding into the sides every 12 in., then set them.

Cut the corner blocks and apron

The decorative upper and lower corner blocks (Photo 6) are simple to make from 3/4-in.-wide x 5-1/2-in.-long pieces of solid maple. The detail on the front of the corner blocks is made by gluing mitered colonial stop molding to each block face. First cut the four corner blocks (F) and the two curved aprons (G). Use a 27-1/2-in. radius to mark the curve onto the aprons. A nail, a wire and a pencil will work fine. Drill the dowel holes into the inside edge of the blocks and corresponding holes into the end of each apron. Don't glue these parts together yet. Mark the backside of each block and apron so you know which piece goes where.

Now to detail the corner blocks, miter the stop molding to fit the perimeter of each block. You can use

a wooden handsaw miter box for control. Avoid cutting small pieces with the power miter saw. Once you've cut all the pieces, glue them to the blocks and clamp them with spring clamps (Photo 6). When the glue is dry, sand the edges of each block clean and glue the doweled joints for each upper and lower apron assembly. Clamp each assembly for at least two hours.

Make your own fluted casing— the easy way

There are a variety of ways to make decorative flutes for cabinet trim.

You can attach an edge guide to a router and run them down the length of the board three times. But if the router wanders even once, the piece is ruined.

You can run the board through a router table, but there's a risk of creating burn marks while pausing to reposition your hands.

The jig shown here will help you churn out perfectly fluted pieces.

Build the fluting jig

Use one-third of a sheet (lengthwise) of 3/4-in. cabinet-grade plywood for the base and sides of the jig and two strips of hardwood for the runners (Photo 1).

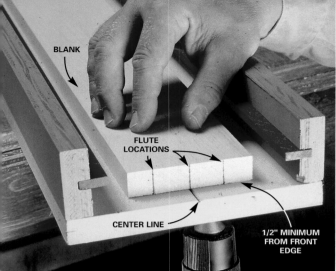

BLANK

FLUTE LOCATIONS

CENTER LINE

1/2" MINIMUM FROM FRONT EDGE

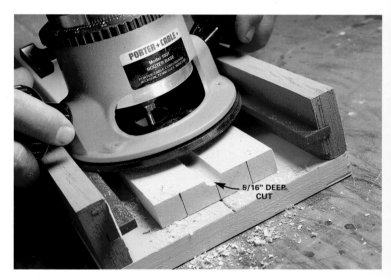

5/32" DEEP CUT

8 Mark your flute locations 1 in. apart on each end of your 1x4 blank. Align the center mark of the workpiece with the center line of the jig and screw the blank to the jig from underneath. Do the same on the opposite end and be sure to install the hold-down screws toward the middle as well. If your blank has a slight bow or crook, the hold-down screws will hold it straight and flat as you rout.

9 Rout the first pass of the first flute 5/32 in. deep. Don't try to take the whole depth at once, because you may get some tear-out and chatter. For a smooth cut, keep the router moving all the way to the other end in one continuous pass.

5/16" DEEP CUT

10 Rout a second pass with the router bit set at 5/16-in. depth. Be sure to check your router depth gauge so you can repeat the exact depth for the final pass on the next flutes.

Here's how to measure, cut and assemble the jig:

- Measure the base of your router plus two thicknesses of your plywood sides (usually 23/32 in. each, or 1-7/16 in. total) to get the right width for the jig base.
- Rip the measured jig base width lengthwise (8 ft.) from your plywood sheet. Accuracy is critical; use your cutting guide for your circular saw or a table saw.
- Rip the two plywood sides 2 in. wide.
- Rip two runners 5/16 in. wide from a 3/4-in.-thick hardwood board.
- Cut the 5/16-in.-wide dadoes into the two sides using either a dado blade or multiple passes with a standard table saw blade. The dadoes must be 3/8 in. deep.
- Glue (carpenter's glue works best) and screw the jig sides to the jig base (Photo 7). The sides must be flush with the base on each side. Drill pilot and countersink holes for the screws. Use a 1-1/4-in. screw every 8 in. along each side.
- Secure the hardwood runners into the dadoes using carpenter's glue and spring clamps. Set the jig aside to dry.

Once the jig is assembled, test the fit of your router base. Move it along the chute from end to end. It must glide freely along the runners without binding on the sides. You may have to sand the sides a bit if the router is too tight in the chute. Conversely, if there's play between the router and the sides, install a strip of veneer on one side.

Now that you've made the jig, follow the instructions in Photos 7 – 11 and practice on some scrap pieces. To ensure consistent depth (you'll make two progressively deeper passes for each flute), familiarize yourself with the depth gauge on your router. It's usually a dial or ring on the housing.

FLUTED
CASING (H)

FINAL
FLUTE

CENTER LINE

DIVIDER MOLDING
(FRONT) (D2)

APRON
ASSEMBLY
(BOTTOM)

11 Rout each side flute using the same two-pass method as with the center flute. When the blank is positioned to the side of the jig, only one row of hold-down screws is necessary.

12 Align the bottoms of the fluted side casing with the corner blocks. Glue, clamp and nail the casing to the bookcase sides. Use six 6d finish nails per side. Set the nails and fill the nail holes.

safety smarts

Although stable on hard flooring, tall narrow cabinets like this bookcase can be unsteady when set on wall-to-wall carpeting. The 1/4-in.-thick tackless wood strip below the carpeting and near the wall can slightly elevate the back of the cabinet and make the bookcase tippy. You can remedy this problem by reducing the thickness of the back feet by 1/4 in. and attaching an 18-gauge steel safety wire, as shown below, near the center back of the cabinet. Fasten the other end of the wire to a stud.

Mark your bookcase height on the wall. Screw in a 2-1/2-in. drywall screw with a finish washer halfway into the wall stud, wrap the wire around the screw, then tighten the screw to the drywall. Drive a 1-in. screw and finish washer near the back of the bookcase into the plywood top. Position the bookcase and wind the wire tight around the screw. Tighten the screw and finish wire down and cut the excess wire. Now you can pile on the books.

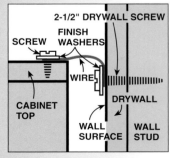

2-1/2" DRYWALL SCREW

FINISH
WASHERS

SCREW

WIRE

DRYWALL

CABINET
TOP

WALL
SURFACE

WALL
STUD

Glue and nail your detail moldings to the bookcase front

Turn the bookcase on its back to glue the front trim pieces in place. Start by aligning the bottom edge of the lower apron assembly even with the bottom edge of the sides (A). Let the apron overhang the sides an equal amount. Mark this location. Next, glue and clamp the assembly (Photo 12) in place. Then, cut and glue the fluted casing pieces in place. Be sure they overhang the same distance as the lower apron assembly. For added insurance, nail the casing to the plywood sides with six 6d finish nails (Figure A) spaced evenly along the length.

Now glue and nail (Photo 13) the divider caps (D3) to the top of the fluted casing and to the side pieces of the divider molding (D1) with 4d finish nails. The caps are a continuation of the divider molding and establish an end point for the fluted columns. After the upper apron assembly is glued in place, glue the upper full-length divider molding (Figure A) to the top of the apron assembly and then nail the miter joints together with 4d nails.

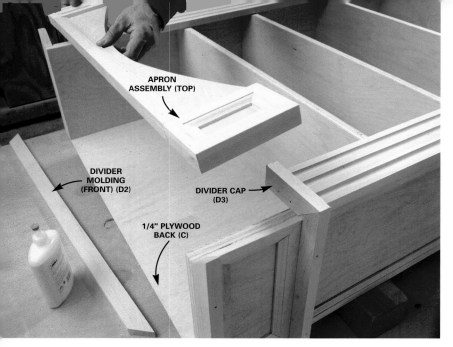

APRON
ASSEMBLY (TOP)

DIVIDER
MOLDING
(FRONT) (D2)

DIVIDER CAP
(D3)

1/4" PLYWOOD
BACK (C)

13 Glue the upper apron assembly to the sides after nailing the divider cap molding to the top of the casing. Once the apron assembly is glued, the next step is to glue, nail and clamp the top center section of the divider molding in place.

Cut the plywood top and glue solid maple strips to the edge

Now cut and glue the stop molding (E) to the top of the plywood back. Use spring clamps to hold it in place. While the glue is drying, cut the plywood top (J1) and the 3/4 x 3/4-in. edge banding (J2) to length. Glue the molding around the front and sides of the plywood top. Use masking tape to hold the edging in place until the glue dries. Once the glue has dried, sand the edging flush to the plywood on the top and bottom. Screw the top assembly to the sides (A). Use 4d finish nails to secure the top to the stop molding in the back. Now cut the stop molding strips to cover the cut-edge shelf fronts. Secure the molding with glue and 7/8-in. brads. Set the brads and fill the holes with wood putty.

Screw the feet to the bottom

To complete the assembly, cut the front and back feet and secure each with two 1-5/8-in. wood screws. Be sure the support strips (L) are glued to the underside (Figure A) first to help support the feet. Cut the front and back feet and screw them to the bottom with 1-5/8-in. wood screws.

Wipe on a beautiful Danish oil finish

Bookcase projects like this are really tough to finish with a brush-on varnish after assembly, so use a wipe-on oil/varnish commonly called Danish oil. You can select colored oil/varnish or clear. The combination oil/varnish is as easy to apply as an oil and buffs to a nice luster like a brushed-on varnish. Apply the finish according to the manufacturer's instructions, using a cotton rag and keeping a brush on hand to get into the corners. Fill all the nail holes after the first coat of finish is dry. Use colored putty sticks to match the surrounding wood tone. Two coats of finish will be adequate but a third will give you a bit more luster and depth. Note: Hang the oil-soaked rags outside to dry to prevent combustion.

Portable bookshelf

Here's a cool knock-down shelf for a dorm room or den. You just slide the shelves between the dowels, and they pinch the shelves to stiffen the bookshelf. It works great if you're careful about two things:

- Make the space between the dowel holes exactly 1/16 in. wider than the thickness of the shelf board.
- Be sure the shelf thickness is the same from end to end and side to side.

After test-fitting a dowel in a trial hole (you want a tight fit), drill holes in a jig board so the space between the holes is your shelf thickness plus 1/16 inch. Clamp the jig board on the ends of the legs and drill the holes. Cut the dowels 1-3/4 in. longer than the shelf width, then dry assemble (no glue). Mark the angled ends of the legs parallel to the shelves and cut off the tips to make the legs sit flat. Disassemble and glue the dowels in the leg holes. When the glue dries, slide the shelves in and load them up.

Cutting List
Perfectly flat 1x12 lumber or plywood
2 shelves: 11-1/4 in. wide x 3 ft. long
4 risers: 2-1/4 in. wide x 24 in. long
8 dowels: 3/4 in. dia. x 13 in. long

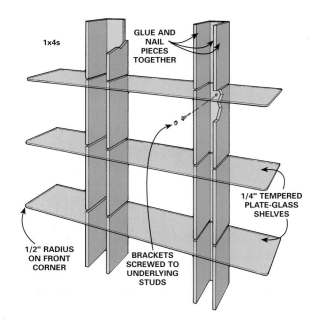

Easy-to-build display shelving

Assemble this simple shelf from 1x4s and tempered glass. Fasten the side boards to the 4-ft. back sections with carpenter's glue and 6d finish nails. Paint the brackets and screw them to wall studs. Buy round-cornered tempered glass shelves and slide them into place.

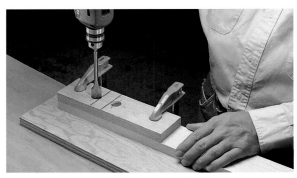

1x4s

GLUE AND NAIL PIECES TOGETHER

1/4" TEMPERED PLATE-GLASS SHELVES

1/2" RADIUS ON FRONT CORNER

BRACKETS SCREWED TO UNDERLYING STUDS

Closet rod and shelf

This project will save you hours of ironing and organizing. Now you can hang up your shirts and jackets as soon as they're out of the dryer—no more wrinkled shirts at the bottom of the basket. You'll also gain an out-of-the-way upper shelf to store all sorts of supplies and other odds and ends.

Just go to your home center and get standard closet rod brackets, a closet rod and a precut 12-in.-deep Melamine shelf (all for about $25). Also pick up some drywall anchors, or if you have concrete, some plastic anchors and a corresponding masonry bit. Follow the instructions in Photos 1 and 2.

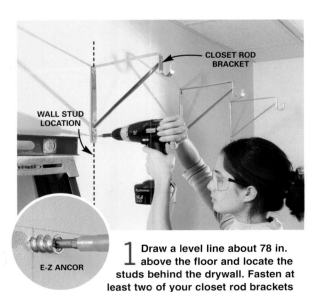

1 Draw a level line about 78 in. above the floor and locate the studs behind the drywall. Fasten at least two of your closet rod brackets into wall studs (4 ft. apart) and then center the middle bracket with two 2-in.-long screws into wall anchors (inset).

2 Fasten your 12-in.-deep Melamine shelf onto the tops of the brackets with 1/2-in. screws. Next, insert your closet rod, drill 1/8-in. holes into the rod, and secure it to the brackets with No. 6 x 1/2-in. sheet metal screws.

Household Improvements

Hang a ceiling fan

It's easier than you think, even on an angled ceiling.

You don't have to be a *Casablanca* aficionado to appreciate the elegance a ceiling fan can bring to your home. And you can enjoy a fan all year long as it creates a welcome breeze in the summer and circulates warm air in the winter.

Ceiling fans (technically called paddle fans) used to be frustrating to install, to say the least. Most of the time you had to wing it because specialty hanging systems were poorly developed or nonexistent. Now most manufacturers have designed versatile mounting systems that take the hassle out of installation. When you add in the improved, stronger ceiling boxes, you'll find that just about any ceiling fan can go up quick and easy on any ceiling, sloped or flat.

In this section, we'll illustrate crystal-clear instructions that go beyond the basic set included with the fan. We'll also show you how to avoid common pitfalls like putting on parts in the wrong order and forgetting to slip shrouds on ahead of time. Some mistakes are more serious than these. Standard electrical boxes or blades hung too low can be downright dangerous.

Expect to spend at least $150 for a high-quality fan (see "Buying a Ceiling Fan," p. 97) and a bit more for accessories like electronic controls, fancy light packages and furniture-grade paddles.

Put up a new fan in a leisurely Saturday afternoon

If everything goes well, you can put up a ceiling fan in a couple of hours, including cleanup. In most cases, the whole job will take only a hammer, a screwdriver, a 3/8-in. nut driver and a wire stripper.

Most of the time, the wires that fed a previous ceiling light fixture are adequate for hooking up a new fan. If you have a wiring arrangement that's different from ours and you are unfamiliar with wiring techniques, consult an electrician or building inspector for help.

project at a glance

skill level
intermediate

special tools
wire stripper
basic hand tools

approximate cost
$100–$300

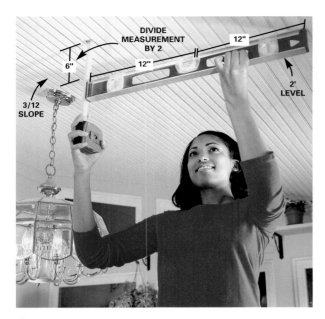

1 Determine the ceiling slope by holding a 2-ft. level against the ceiling and measuring the vertical distance from the level to the ceiling. Divide that number by 2 to get the drop over 12 in. of horizontal run, 3/12 slope in our case. See the chart on p. 98 to determine the minimum downrod length for the blade diameter you'd like.

2 Shut off the power at the main panel and remove the light fixture. Knock the existing electrical box free of the framing with a hammer and a block of wood, then pull the electrical cable free of the old box and through the ceiling hole. Leave the old box in the ceiling cavity unless you can easily remove it through the hole.

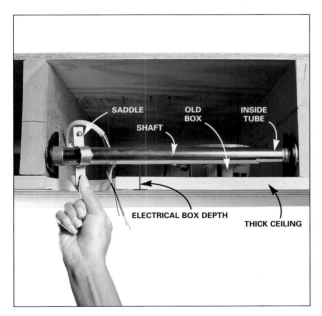

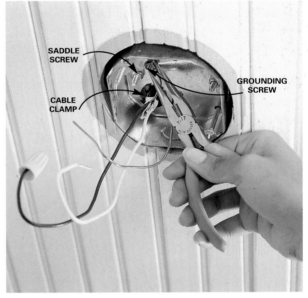

3 Feed the fan brace up into the hole, rest the flat edge of the feet against the ceiling and center the shaft over the hole. If your ceiling is more than 1/2 in. thick, as ours was, rotate the feet and position the rod the depth of the box from the ceiling. Rotate the shaft to secure the brace to the framing. Snap the metal saddle over the shaft so it's centered over the hole.

4 Feed the existing wire through the cable clamp in the top of the new metal box, slip the box over the saddle screws, and tighten the nuts to clamp the box to the shaft with a nut driver or a deep-well socket. Crimp a loop of grounding wire three-quarters around the grounding screw and tighten the screw.

HANGER BRACKET

5 Position the hanger bracket so that the opening in the bracket is on the uphill side of the sloped ceiling. Then screw it into the box with the special screws provided with the fan brace.

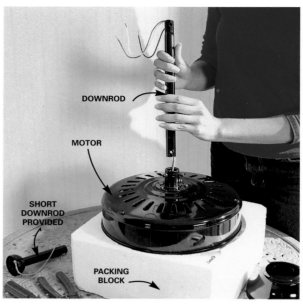

DOWNROD

MOTOR

SHORT DOWNROD PROVIDED

PACKING BLOCK

6 Place the motor right side up, thread the wire through the downrod and insert the downrod into the mounting collar.

Follow the photo series for basic installation steps that apply to more than 95 percent of all fans. There may be small variations, particularly when it comes to the light and blade mountings, so you'll still need to consult the instructions provided with your fan. As with any other electrical work, you may need an electrical permit from your local building department before starting the job. The inspector will tell you when to call for an inspection.

Replace electrical boxes with specially designed paddle fan braces

Before starting any work, shut off the circuit breaker that feeds the switch and light fixture. If there's a working bulb in the fixture, turn it on. Then you'll know you have the right breaker when the bulb goes out. Check the wires with a voltage tester to make sure they're off after removing the fixture and when changing the wall switch.

The next step is to remove the existing plastic or metal electrical box and install a "fan brace" that's designed to hold ceiling fans. Few conventional boxes are strong enough to support a ceiling fan, so don't even think about trying to hang your fan from an existing box. Instead, buy a fan brace (about $15) when you purchase your fan. You can choose braces that fasten

with screws if the framing is accessible from the attic or if it's new construction. Otherwise, pick a brace that's designed to slip through the ceiling hole and through the electrical box. These braces (Photo 3) adjust to fit between the framing members in your ceiling; you simply rotate the shaft to anchor them to the framing.

Most existing electrical boxes are fastened to the framing with nails, making them easy to pound out with a hammer and a block of wood (Photo 2). After you free the cable, just leave the old box in the cavity (Photo 3) rather than struggling to work the box through the ceiling hole. Then pull the cable through the hole and slip the fan brace through the opening and secure it, following the directions that came with the brace. Little feet on the ends of braces keep them the correct distance from the back side of 1/2-in. thick ceilings so the new electrical box will be flush with the surface. If you have a thicker ceiling (like ours), rotate the ends to achieve the correct spacing.

tip Before you blast out the box, bend back the plastic clamps or loosen the metal cable clamps so it'll be easier to pull the electrical cable free after the box is loosened.

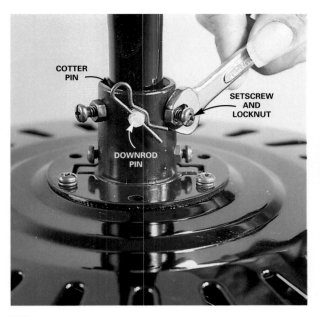

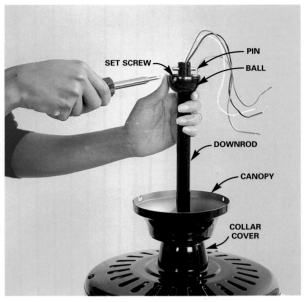

7 Slip the downrod pin through the collar and tube, lock it into place with the cotter pin, and tighten the screws and locknuts.

8 Slip the collar cover, then the canopy over the downrod. Slide the ball over the downrod and push the pin through both sets of holes, then lift the ball over the pin and tighten the set screw.

Buying a ceiling fan

If you haven't walked under a large fan display yet, hold onto your hat. You'll be overwhelmed by the selection of colors, styles and accessories, especially if you visit a ceiling fan store. If you intend to use your fan regularly, invest in a model in the $150-plus category. You'll get a quieter, more efficient, more durable unit. If you spend beyond that amount, you're usually paying for light packages, radio-actuated remote and wall controls, style, and design (fancier motor castings, inlays, blade adornments or glasswork). If you spend less, you're likely to get a less efficient, less durable, noisier unit with fewer color, blade and electronic choices.

Choose the blade diameter that best suits the room visually and make sure the unit will fit under the ceiling without jeopardizing beehive hairdos. (See p. 99 for height requirements.) Bigger rooms call for wider fan blade diameters. The bigger fan will not only look better but also move more air.

Most ceiling fans are designed for heated, enclosed spaces. If you're putting a fan in a screen room, a gazebo or other damp area, the building code requires you to use a "damp-rated" fan. These fans have corrosion-resistant stainless steel or plastic parts that can stand up to high humidity and condensation. If you live in a coastal area with corrosive sea air, or if you're putting a fan in a particularly wet environment like a greenhouse or an enclosed pool area, you should choose a "wet-rated" fan.

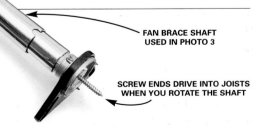

FLAT FOOT FOR 1/2" THICK CEILING

FAN BRACE SHAFT USED IN PHOTO 3

SCREW ENDS DRIVE INTO JOISTS WHEN YOU ROTATE THE SHAFT

Buyer's Guide

- Hampton Bay Fan and Lighting Co., 2455 Paces Ferry Road N.W., Atlanta, GA 30339; (770) 433-8211, www.homedepot.com

- Hunter Fan Co., 2500 Frisco Ave., Memphis, TN 38114; (800) 448-6837, www.hunterfan.com

- Regency Ceiling Fans, www.regencyfan.com.

9 Lift the assembly over the open side of the bracket and lower it into place. Rotate the motor until the ball slot locks into place over the tab on the bracket.

10 Connect the bare ground wire from the box to the green ground wire on the bracket with a wire connector. Connect the white neutral wire from the motor to the neutral wire from the box. Connect the blue and black wire from the motor to the black hot wire from the box and neatly fold them into the box.

New electronic controls save you from running additional wiring

Since most fan installations are retrofits into existing electrical boxes, there's usually a single electrical cable connecting the fixture to a single wall switch. You can leave the switch and use it to turn the fan on and off, then use the pull chains on the fan to control fan speed and lights. A second option is to install electronic controls. Higher-quality fans give you the option of adding a radio receiver kit for about $75. The receiver accepts signals from a special wall switch (included in the kit) to control the fan and light separately without additional wiring. The receiver also accepts signals from a handheld remote, so you can operate multiple fans and fine-tune fan speed and light intensity from your La-Z-Boy. Electronic switches are matched to fans by flipping code toggles in the controls and the fan, just like with your garage door opener. Installing an electronic switch (Photo 12) is

tip

Tighten the locknuts firmly. Loose nuts are the most common cause of wobbly fans.

a snap. The receiver drops right into the fan housing and plugs into the bottom of the motor.

If the old light is fed by two three-way switches instead of a single switch, the control options are a little more complicated. You have three choices:

1. Leave the existing switches in place and turn one of them on. Then use a remote to control the fan and lights.
2. Use the existing switches and control the fan and lights independently with pull chains.
3. Disable one of the three-way switches and rewire the other one to receive a wall-mounted electronic control. Sorting out all the wires is complex. You'll need an electrician's help for this.

Minimum downrod length (in inches) for angled ceilings

Blade Dia.	Ceiling Slope						
	3/12	4/12	5/12	6/12	8/12*	10/12*	12/12*
27 in.	6	6	6	12	18	24	36
36 in.	6	6	6	12	18	24	36
44 in.	6	6	12	12	24	30	42
52 in.	6	12	18	18	24	30	42
56 in.	12	12	18	24	30	36	48

* Also requires slope adapting kit.

BRACKET · BLADE

11 Screw the fan blades to their brackets and screw the brackets to the bottom of the motor. It's easiest to hold the screw in the bracket with the screwdriver while you lift the blade assembly into position. Then drive in the screw.

Fan height requirements

Manufacturers generally require that fan blades be at least 7 ft. above the floor. Since most fan and motor assemblies are less than 12 in. high, they'll fit under a standard 8-ft. ceiling with the proper clearance.

Angled ceilings require that you install downrods (also called extension tubes or downtubes) that will lower the motor and fan blades so they'll clear a sloped ceiling surface. The more space between the ceiling and the fan, the better. The fan will have more air to draw from, and you'll feel more air movement because the blades are closer to you.

Most fans come with a short downrod designed for mounting on 8-ft. ceilings. If your ceiling's less than 8 ft., you'll need to remove the rod provided and flush-mount the fan. But if you have a higher or sloped ceiling, purchase a longer downrod.

OPTIONAL REMOTE CONTROL

SWITCH HOUSING HUB

MOTOR WIRING

RADIO RECEIVER

SWITCH HOUSING

LIGHT POD

CODE SWITCHES

12 Place the radio receiver into the switch housing/light pod assembly and connect the light pod wires according to the manufacturer's instructions. Note the settings on the receiver's code toggles so you can dial in the same settings on the electronic controls at the wall switch. Now loosen the screws in the switch-housing hub halfway. Plug the motor wiring into the receptacle on the receiver and twist the switch housing into place on the hub. Retighten the screws.

13 Check and reset (if necessary) the code toggles on the wall-mounted electronic switch to match the ones on the receiver. Remove the existing wall switch and connect the two black wires on the new switch to the ones that were connected to the old switch with wire connectors. Screw the switch into the box and install the cover plate.

Chair rail

Attractive, lightweight and easy to install.

Urethane moldings are both lightweight and easy to apply, making them a great alternative to wood molding. In this story, we used them for chair rail and window trim.

One manufacturer recommends cutting the molding about 1/4 in. overlong for long runs (12 to 16 ft.) to help make up for seasonal wall expansion. It'll compress slightly and snap into place. Shorter lengths to 8 ft. should be cut about 1/8 in. overlong and anything less than 4 ft. should be cut to fit. The company also recommends butting crosscut ends together when splicing long lengths instead of bevel-cutting moldings at mid-wall joints. The molding is applied just like wood molding

tip*

To widen your miter box as shown in Photo 1 on p. 101, use a hammer to tap the sides free of the original base. Drill pilot holes and screw the sides to the new base. With the wider base, you'll be able to crosscut and bevel-cut the moldings. However, the other miter operations won't be possible, since the precut slots will no longer line up. This won't be a problem for cutting the moldings we show here.

except that it cuts and nails easier.

Set the molding into your miter box (screw the miter box down to your sawhorse or worktable) and cut it on your mark with slow, steady strokes as you hold the molding firmly with your other hand. Support long ends with additional sawhorses. Don't bother coping joints in corners; just lay the molding on its back side and cut at 45 degrees for inside and outside corners. Nails alone won't do—you must use the polyurethane adhesive caulk to bond it to the wall surface to make up for its low density.

Fill nail holes with spackling compound and then wipe the surface clean with a damp rag (Photo 4). This process will take two coats. Sand urethane molding as little as possible because unlike wood, the factory finish on the urethane molding is thin. Because you'll be painting the molding, you can touch up joints with acrylic caulk and wipe the excess away with a damp rag. You can save yourself a lot of time by prepainting the molding and then touching it up after you've cut and installed it.

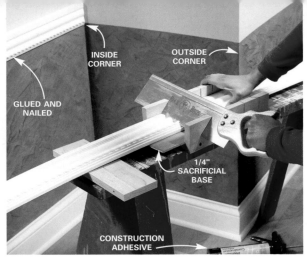

1 Hand miter boxes and fine-tooth hand saws are best for cutting urethane moldings. The moldings, however, are often wider than the miter box bed. Widen the bed by removing the screws on the side of the box and adding a wider base.

2 Measure the length, then cut the moldings with 45-degree bevel cuts in the corners and glue the back sides and joints with polyurethane molding adhesive.

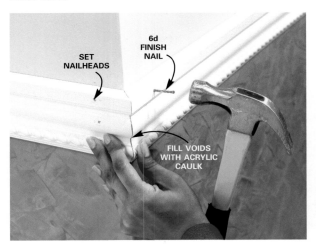

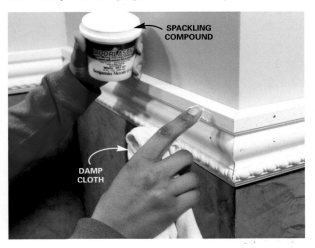

3 Glue and nail the moldings to the wall. Make small reference marks along the wall with your level to make sure you keep the molding straight as you nail. Set the nails with a nail set.

4 Fill the nail holes with spackling compound and the joints with acrylic caulk, then wipe with a slightly damp cloth. You'll need a second application once the spackling compound and caulk are dry. Wipe smooth or lightly sand, then paint.

Buying urethane moldings

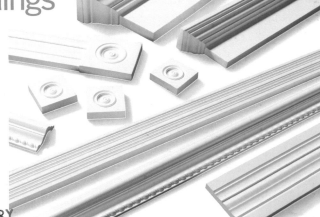

Home centers and lumberyards carry a limited selection of urethane moldings. They come in a wide variety of preprimed profiles and sizes for windows, doors, crown moldings and decorative panels. They're expensive but cost less than decorative wood moldings with the same profiles. To see all your options, go to the help desk. There you can order moldings to suit your taste. The moldings shown here are only a small sample.

For more information on urethane molding options, call (800) 446-3040, or go to www.fypon.com. Also, visit www.focalpointap.com or call (800) 662-5550 to find a dealer in your area.

Snap-together wood flooring

No glue, no nails, and you can do it in a weekend.

Here's a wood floor that's so easy to install you can complete an average-size room in a weekend. The joints just snap together. Simple carpentry skills and a few basic tools are all you need to cut the floorboards and notch them around corners.

In this article, we'll show you how to prepare your room and lay the snap-together flooring. The flooring we're using is similar to snap-together laminate floors except that it has a surface layer of real wood. The 5/16-in. thick flooring has specially shaped tongues and grooves

that interlock to form a strong tight joint without glue or nails. Once assembled, the entire floor "floats" in one large sheet. You leave a small expansion space all around the edges so the floor can expand and contract with humidity changes.

Wood veneer floors cost $6 to $15 per sq. ft., depending on the species and thickness of the top wood layer. Most home centers sell a few types of snap-together floors, but you'll find a better selection and expert advice

at your local flooring retailer. You can also buy flooring online.

Before you go shopping, draw a sketch of your room with dimensions. Make note of transitions to other types of flooring and other features like stair landings and exterior doors. Ask your salesperson for help choosing the right transition moldings for these areas.

You'll need a few special tools in addition to basic hand tools like a tape measure, square and utility knife. We purchased an installation kit from the manufacturer ($40) that included plastic shims, a tapping block and a last-board puller, but if you're handy you could fabricate these tools. You'll also need a circular saw and a jigsaw to cut the flooring, and a miter box to cut the shoe molding. A table saw and power miter saw would make your job easier but aren't necessary.

project at a glance

skill level
intermediate

special tools
circular saw
jigsaw
installation kit
basic hand tools

approximate cost
$6–$15 per sq. ft.

tip*   A pull saw works great to undercut doorjambs and casing (Photo 3). It's difficult to get close enough to the floor with a standard handsaw.

DUCT TAPE

4-MIL PLASTIC

CONCRETE FLOOR

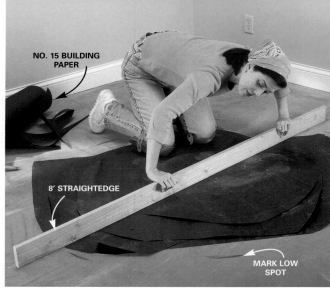

NO. 15 BUILDING PAPER

8' STRAIGHTEDGE

MARK LOW SPOT

1 Test for excess moisture in concrete floors by sealing the edges of a 3-ft. square of plastic sheeting to the floor with duct tape. Wait 24 hours before you peel back the plastic to check for moisture. Water droplets on the plastic or darkened concrete indicate a possible problem with excess moisture. Ask your flooring supplier for advice before installing a wood floor.

2 Check for low spots in the floor with an 8-ft. straightedge and mark their perimeter with a pencil. Fill depressions less than 1/4 in. deep with layers of building paper. Fill deeper depressions with a hardening-type floor filler available from flooring stores.

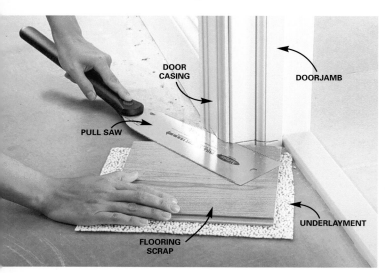

DOOR CASING

DOORJAMB

PULL SAW

UNDERLAYMENT

FLOORING SCRAP

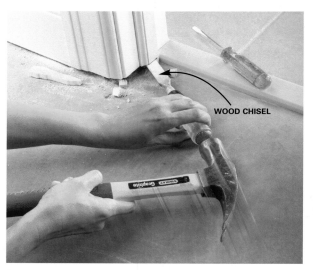

WOOD CHISEL

3 Undercut doorjambs and casings (door moldings) to make space for the flooring to slip underneath. Guide the saw with a scrap of flooring stacked on a piece of underlayment.

4 Break and pry out the cutoff chunks of jamb and casing with a screwdriver. Use a sharp chisel or utility knife to complete the cut in areas the saw couldn't reach.

Make sure your floor is dry

Don't lay this type of floor over damp concrete or damp crawlspaces. Check all concrete for excess moisture. As a starting point, use the plastic mat test shown in Photo 1. Even though some manufacturers allow it, most professional installers advise against installing floating floors in kitchens, full or three-quarter baths, or entryways, all areas where they might be subjected to standing water.

Prepare your room for new flooring

You have to make sure the existing floor is smooth and flat before installing a floating floor on top. Clear the old floor, then smooth it by scraping off lumps and sweeping it. Check the floor with an 8-ft. straightedge and mark high spots and depressions. Sand or grind down ridges and fill low spots (Photo 2). Most manufacturers recommend no more than 1/8-in. variation in flatness over an 8-ft. length.

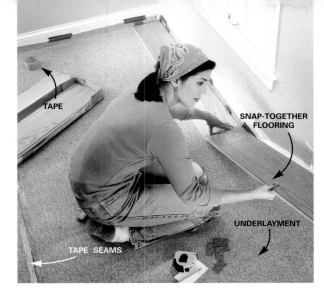

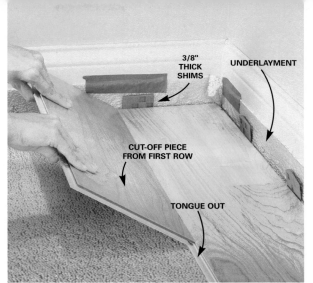

5 Unroll the underlayment and lap it up the baseboards or walls 2 in. Temporarily secure the edges with masking tape. Butt the sheets together and seal the seams with the tape recommended by the manufacturer. Cut the first row of boards narrower if necessary to ensure that the last row of flooring will be at least 2 in. wide. Then start the installation by locking the ends of the first row of flooring together. Measure and cut the last piece to fit, allowing the 3/8-in. expansion space.

6 Start the second row with the leftover cutoff piece from the first row, making sure the end joints are off-set at least 12 in. from the end joints in the first row. With the board held at about a 45-degree angle, engage the tongue in the groove. Push in while you rotate the starter piece down toward the floor. The click indicates the pieces have locked together. The joint between boards should draw tight.

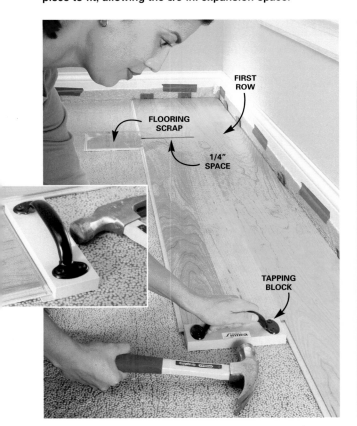

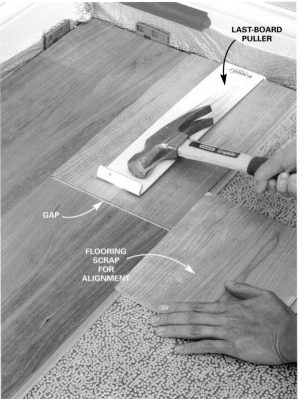

7 Leave a 1/4-in. space between the next full piece of flooring and the previous piece. Snap this piece into the first row. Snap a scrap of flooring across the ends being joined to hold them in alignment while you tap them together. Place the tapping block against the end of the floor piece and tap it with a hammer to close the gap.

8 Close a gap at the end of the row by hooking the last-board puller tool over the end of the plank and tapping it with a hammer to pull the end joints together.

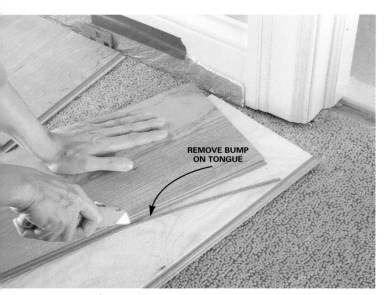

REMOVE BUMP ON TONGUE

9 Plan ahead when you get near a doorjamb. Usually you have to slide the next piece of flooring under the jamb rather than tilt and snap it into place. To accomplish this, you must slice off the locking section of the tongue from the preceding row with a sharp utility knife before installing it.

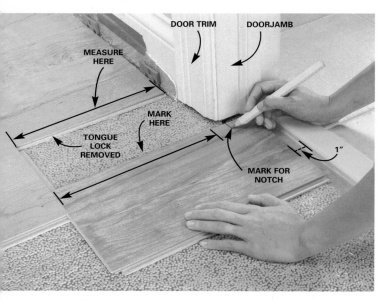

DOOR TRIM DOORJAMB

MEASURE HERE

MARK HERE

TONGUE LOCK REMOVED

MARK FOR NOTCH

1"

10 Cut the plank to be notched to length, allowing a 1-in. space for the future transition piece. Align the end with the end of the last plank laid and mark 3/8 in. inside the jamb to make sure the flooring extends under the door trim.

tip* If you have wood floors, fix squeaks and tighten loose boards by screwing them to the joists with deck screws before you install your new flooring.

Allowing the floor to expand and contract freely is critical. Leave at least a 3/8-in. expansion space along the edges. You can hide the gap under the baseboards or leave the baseboards in place and cover the gap with shoe molding or quarter round as we did. Cover the expansion space at openings or transitions to other types of flooring with special transition moldings (Photo 13). Buy these from the dealer.

Finally, saw off the bottoms of doorjambs and trim to allow for the flooring to slide underneath (Photo 3). Leaving an expansion gap at exterior doors presents a unique challenge. In older houses, you could carefully remove the threshold and notch it to allow the flooring to slide underneath. For most newer exterior doors, you can butt a square-nosed transition piece against the threshold.

Floating floors must be installed over a thin cushioning pad called underlayment (Photo 5). Underlayment is usually sold in rolls and costs 25¢ to 50¢ per sq. ft. Ask your flooring dealer to suggest the best one for your situation. Some types combine a vapor barrier and padding. Install this type over concrete or other floors where moisture might be a problem. Others reduce sound transmission.

Take extra care when installing underlayment that includes a vapor barrier. Lap the edges up the wall and carefully seal all the seams as recommended by the manufacturer. Keep a roll of tape handy to patch accidental rips and tears as you install the floor.

After the first few rows, installing the floor is a snap

You may have to cut your first row of flooring narrower to make sure the last row is at least 2 in. wide. To figure this, measure across the room and divide by the width of the exposed face on the flooring. The number remaining is the width of the last row. If the remainder is less than 2, cut the first row narrower to make this last row wider. Then continue the installation as shown in Photos 6 – 8.

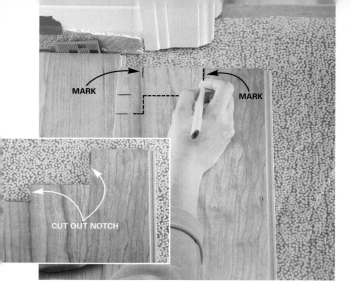

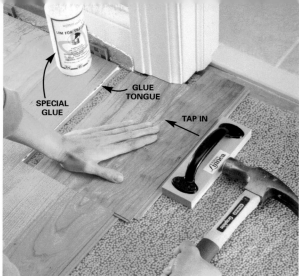

11 Align the flooring lengthwise and mark for the notches in the other direction, allowing for the floor to slide under the doorjamb about 3/8 in. Connect the marks with a square and cut out the notch with a jigsaw.

12 Apply a thin bead of the manufacturer's recommended glue along the edge where the portion of the tongue was removed. Slide the notched piece of flooring into place and tighten the glued edge by pounding on the special tapping block.

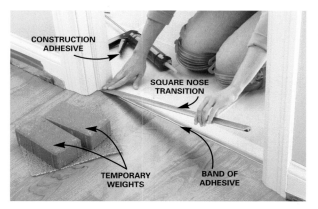

13 Cut a transition molding, in this case a square nose transition, to fit between the doorstops or jambs. Spread a bead of construction adhesive only on the area of the floor that will be in contact with the transition piece. Set the transition in place and weight it down overnight.

14 Complete the flooring project by trimming off the protruding underlayment with a utility knife and installing shoe molding. Predrill 1/16-in. holes through the shoe. Then nail the shoe molding to the baseboard with 4d finish nails. Set and fill the nails. Do not nail the shoe molding down into the flooring.

You can't use the same tilt-and-snap installation technique where the flooring fits under doorjambs. You have to slide the flooring together instead. Photos 9 – 12 show how. If the opening requires a transition molding, cut the flooring short to leave space for it (Photo 13).

Complete the floor by cutting the last row to the correct width to fit against the wall. Make sure to leave the required expansion space. Finally, reinstall the baseboards if you removed them, or install new quarter-round or shoe molding to cover the expansion space (Photo 14).

Buyer's Guide

Here are some of the manufacturers that currently offer snap-together wood veneer floors. Many others are in the process of converting their glue-together floating floors to the snap-together system. Check with your local flooring supplier for current offerings.

● Alloc: (800) 362-5562, www.alloc.com
● Award: (888) 862-9273, www.awardfloors.com
● BHK: (800) 663-4176, www.BHKuniclic.com
● Kahrs: (800) 800-KAHR, www.kahrs.com
● wicanders: (410) 553-6062, www.wicanders.com

Fast & easy lamp fixes

You can fix almost any lamp—and make it safe as well.

When a lamp flickers or doesn't light up at all, chances are that one of the parts has gone bad. In the next few pages, we'll show you how to replace all the key parts. But don't overlook the obvious: no power or a bad bulb. Try a new bulb and plug the lamp into a different outlet before taking things apart.

If that doesn't work, operate the switch. It should turn on and off without flickering. Next, unplug the lamp and inspect the cord and plug. If you can't find any obvious problems, replace all the electrical parts. It only takes a few more minutes than replacing just one, and the parts usually cost less than $10.

EASY FOR EVERYONE

project at a glance

skill level
beginner

special tools
wire stripper
pliers
screwdrivers

approximate cost
$10 or less

Replace a faulty socket

A lamp socket itself can go bad, but more often it's the switch inside the socket. Either way, the solution is replacement. A new socket costs about $5. Regardless of the existing switch type, you can choose a push-through switch, a pull chain, a turn knob or a three-way turn knob that provides two brightness levels. You can also choose a socket without a switch and install a switched cord instead.

The old socket shell is supposed to pop out of its base with a squeeze and a tug, but you might have to pry it out with a screwdriver (Photo 1). The socket base can be stubborn too. It's screwed onto a threaded tube that runs down through the lamp's body. When you try to unscrew it, you might unscrew the nut at the other end of the tube instead. This will allow the parts of the lamp body to come apart, but that isn't a big problem. Just use a pliers to twist the base off the tube (Photo 2), reassemble the lamp body and screw on the new socket base to hold it all together.

When you connect the new socket, don't reuse the bare ends of the wires. Some of the tiny strands of wire are probably broken. Cut them off and strip away 1/2 in. of insulation with a wire stripper (Photo 3). Using a wire stripper is almost foolproof, as long as you choose the correct pair of notches to bite through the wire's insulation. Most wire strippers are sized for solid wire, rather than the slightly larger stranded wire used in lamp cords. You can get around this problem by using the next larger pair of notches. Since most lamp wires are 18 gauge, start with the notches labeled 16. If the stripper won't remove the insulation, use smaller notches. If the stripper removes strands of wire, cut off an inch of cord and start over using larger notches.

When you connect the wires to the new socket, the neutral wire must connect to the silver screw (Photo 4). To identify the neutral wire, start at the plug. The wider

1 Pry the socket shell out of its base. Cut the wires to remove the socket. Then loosen the setscrew so you can unscrew the socket base.

2 Unscrew the socket base from the threaded tube. If the base won't spin off by hand, grab the tube and the base with a pliers to spin it free. Then screw on the new base and tighten the setscrew.

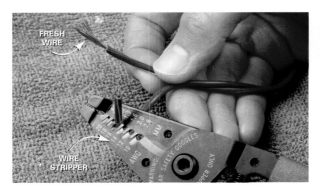

3 Strip off 1/2 in. of insulation with a wire stripper and twist the wire strands together. If you pull off any wire strands while stripping, cut back the cord and start over.

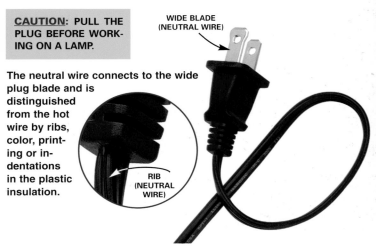

CAUTION: PULL THE PLUG BEFORE WORKING ON A LAMP.

The neutral wire connects to the wide plug blade and is distinguished from the hot wire by ribs, color, printing or indentations in the plastic insulation.

4 Tie an underwriter's knot in the cord. Then connect the wires by wrapping them clockwise around the screws and tightening. Connect the neutral wire to the silver screw.

5 Pull the excess cord down through the lamp. Slip the insulation sleeve and socket shell over the socket and snap the shell into the base.

plug blade is connected to the neutral wire, and you'll find that the neutral wire is distinguished from the "hot" wire (photo, p. 109). The two wires may be different colors, there may be printing on one

or the other, or there may be tiny ribs or indentations in the plastic covering the neutral wire. If your old plug blades are of equal width, replace the plug and cord along with the socket.

An underwriter's knot prevents the wires from pulling out of the screw terminals when the cord is tugged.

Replace a cracked cord

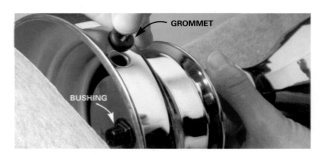

1 Cut the old cord at the socket and pull it out. Push a grommet into the cord hole and screw a bushing onto the tube, if they're missing.

2 Feed the new cord through the threaded tube and socket base. Connect the cord to the socket as shown on p. 163.

The insulation on cords becomes stiff and brittle as it ages. Eventually, it cracks and might even flake off the wire, creating a shock and fire hazard. Don't try to solve this problem with electrical tape. Replace the cord. Cord replacement is also the best fix for a bad cord-mounted switch. You can buy a cord that has a switch attached.

GROMMETS

Save yourself some time by buying a cord that's already connected to a plug ($3). Lamp cord sold at home centers and hardware stores is usually 18 gauge. That's large enough to handle 840 watts of lighting. If you have one of those rare lamps that uses bulbs totaling more than 840 watts, have it fixed at a lamp repair shop.

Make sure the cord is protected by a screw-on bushing where it enters the threaded tube and by a plastic or rubber grommet through the lamp body (Photo 1). Without a bushing or grommet, sharp edges can cut into the cord's insulation. If you can't find a bushing or grommet the right size at a home center or hardware store, see "Lamp Part Sources," p. 111.

To replace the cord, you'll take most of the socket replacement steps shown in the first part of this article. Remove the socket from its base, cut the old cord and pull it out. Feed the cord up through the threaded tube in the lamp's body (Photo 2). Then connect the new cord to the socket. Most cords come with the ends already stripped, so you won't even need a wire stripper.

Replace a problem plug

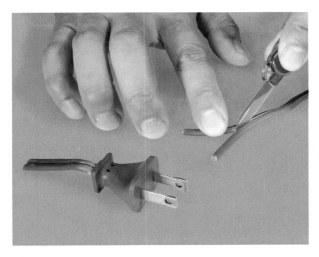

1 Cut the cord a couple of inches from the plug. Then split about an inch of cord with a pocketknife and strip off 3/4 in. of insulation.

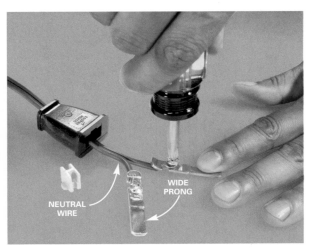

NEUTRAL WIRE

WIDE PRONG

2 Wrap the wires clockwise around the terminal screws of the new plug and tighten. The neutral wire must connect to the wider prong.

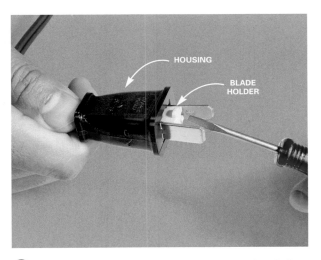

HOUSING

BLADE HOLDER

3 Slip the blades into the housing and push the blade holder into place.

Lamp part sources

Home centers and hardware stores carry basic lamp parts like sockets, cords and plugs. For hard-to-find parts and a wider selection of basic parts, visit a lamp repair shop (in the Yellow Pages under "Lamps & Shades, Repair") or these Web sites:

- www.grandbrass.com. Shop online and order online or by phone: (212) 226-2567

- www.paxtonhardware.com. Shop online and order by phone: (800) 241-9741

Plugs on lamp cords often have a weak point where the cord enters the plug. Pulling and flexing can break the wires at this point, leaving you with a lamp that flickers when you jiggle the cord. The cure is to replace the plug. To do this safely, choose a polarized plug ($5). A polarized plug has one blade that's wider than the other so it fits into an outlet only one way (photo, p. 109). Before you buy a plug, take a close look at the cord. Along with other labeling, you should find "SPT-1" or "SPT-2." This refers to the thickness of the cord's sheathing, and the plug you buy must have the same listing so it will fit over the sheathing. If you can't find the SPT listing, replace the entire cord as shown on p. 110.

The plug you buy may not look exactly like the one shown here, but installing it will be similar. Be sure to read the manufacturer's instructions. When you split the two halves of the cord (Photo 1), be careful not to expose any wire. If you do, cut back the cord and start over. Strip the wire ends (see Photo 3, p. 109) and make connections (Photo 2). The neutral wire must connect to the wider blade. See p. 109 for help in identifying the neutral wire. If you're not able to identify it, replace the entire cord.

Fast furniture fixes

Make those nicks and scratches go away with just a few minutes' work.

Furniture looking a little shabby with all those little scratches and dings? You know, the vacuum cleaner bumps here and there, and the Hot Wheels hit-and-runs? Not to worry. We'll show you simple touch-up techniques that will make these minor eyesores disappear quickly and painlessly.

We're not talking about refinishing or even repairing here, which are different games altogether. This is about hiding flaws so only you will know they're there.

The procedures and materials shown in this article won't damage the original finish on your furniture if it was made in the last 50 years.

However, if the piece of furniture you're touching up is very old, or an antique, it may have a shellac finish. With shellac, you shouldn't attempt the scratch-removal process shown on p. 114. And if the piece is an antique, think twice about doing any touch-up, which could actually devalue it.

You can test for a shellac finish with a few drops of alcohol in an out-of-sight spot. Alcohol will dissolve shellac.

Think safety: Even though all the fluids and sprays we show here are everyday hardware-store products, most are both flammable and toxic. Read and follow the directions on the label. Don't use them in a room where there's a pilot light, or near open flames or in an unventilated space. If you'll be doing anything more than a few quick passes with the sprays shown here, work outdoors and wear a respirator mask with organic cartridges. And if you're pregnant, stay away from these materials altogether.

project at a glance

skill level
beginner

special tools
felt-tip markers
putty sticks

approximate cost
$5–$10

touch up scratches

1 **Hide scratches with permanent-ink felt-tip markers.** You can either use the furniture touch-up markers available at hardware stores and home centers, or, to get an exact match, buy markers at an art supply store that carries an array of colors (check the Yellow Pages). For thorough coverage, you may need to dab the ink onto the scratch, let it dry, then even out the color by stroking lightly across it with the tip. Keep in mind that colors tend to darken when they soak into wood fibers.

2 **Touch up thin scratches with a fine-tip permanent marker.** When filling in scratches, steady your hand against the furniture for accuracy; as much as possible, flow the ink only onto the scratch.

FINE-TIP MARKER

patch gouges

Fill in gouges with colored putty sticks, sold at most hardware stores and home centers. This putty works well for small holes and nicks but is somewhat trickier to use as a fill for larger damage, as shown here. Unlike hardening putties, it remains soft and somewhat flexible, so you have to shape it carefully. And it won't hold up under heavy wear.

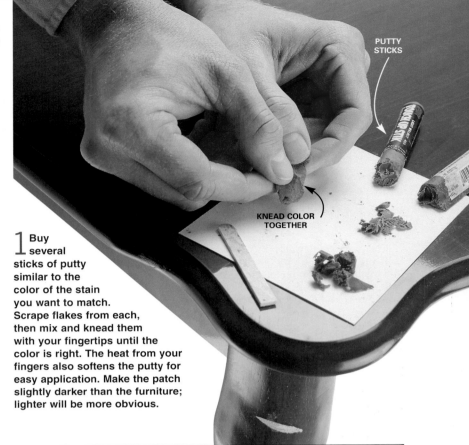

PUTTY STICKS

KNEAD COLOR TOGETHER

1 Buy several sticks of putty similar to the color of the stain you want to match. Scrape flakes from each, then mix and knead them with your fingertips until the color is right. The heat from your fingers also softens the putty for easy application. Make the patch slightly darker than the furniture; lighter will be more obvious.

2 Press putty tightly into the gouge with a small flat stick, then flatten it and scrape away the excess with the stick's long edge. Round the end of the stick with sandpaper.

3 Wipe away any putty adhering to the wood around the gouge, and smooth the surface of the putty with a clean cloth. A thin, light-colored line will usually appear around the perimeter of the patch. Use a matching marker to color this line, as shown in Photo 2 on p. 112.

4 Spray the patch with two or three quick passes of shellac, then after it dries, a few quick passes of spray lacquer—either high gloss or satin, depending on your furniture's finish. Never apply lacquer or polyurethane/varnish directly over a putty patch; it will leave a permanently soft mess. Shellac will harden; however, the patch will remain somewhat pliable under the finish, so don't attempt this on a heavy-wear surface.

wipe away scratches and recoat the surface

You can buff out fine scratches using very fine (0000) steel wool saturated with clear Danish oil. (You can also use ultra-fine automotive rubbing compound.) The process shown here only works for scratches in the finish itself, not scratches that are all the way into the stain or the wood.

1 Pour a generous amount of clear or neutral Danish oil onto a very fine steel wool pad. Rub the surface with the oil-saturated pad using your flat hand. Rub *with* the grain, never against it or at an angle to it. Continue rubbing until you remove enough of the clear surface finish to eliminate the scratches, *but be careful not to remove any of the stain below the clear finish.* Rub not only the scratched area but also the area around it in gradually decreasing amounts. Be careful not to rub edges or corners excessively; they wear through quickly.

2 Wipe away all the Danish oil with rags or paper towels, then thoroughly clean the entire surface with mineral spirits several times to make sure all the oil is removed. If any oil remains, the lacquer (Photo 3) won't adhere. Allow the surface to dry overnight before applying lacquer.

3 Spray the entire surface with clear lacquer. Move the spray can in one continuous, straight stroke, allowing the spray to extend beyond the edges in all directions. Wipe the nozzle with a rag after each stroke to prevent drips. Move with the grain, and make sure the angle of the spray remains the same all the way across. Keep the spray aimed away from other surfaces that you don't want coated, or mask them with newspaper.

CAUTION: RAGS AND STEEL WOOL SATURATED WITH DANISH OIL CAN SPONTANEOUSLY COMBUST IF LEFT BUNCHED UP. DRY THEM OUTDOORS, SPREAD OUT LOOSELY. WHEN THE OIL HAS DRIED, YOU CAN SAFELY THROW THE RAGS AND STEEL WOOL IN THE TRASH.

clean dirty, greasy, gummy surfaces

The results of a simple surface cleaning with mineral spirits may amaze you. Polish buildup and the dirt embedded in it muddy the finish but will wipe away. Don't use stronger solvents; they might dissolve the finish itself.

1 Soak a coarse, absorbent, clean cloth with mineral spirits and wipe the finish. Keep applying and wiping until the cloth no longer picks up dirt. Then do a final wipe with a fresh, clean rag.

2 Clean crevices, grooves and carved areas with cotton swabs dipped in mineral spirits.

5¢ sponge brushes

Need a quick touch-up brush? If you have any leftover self-adhering foam weatherstripping, you can save yourself a trip to the store. A short piece—1/2 in. thick x 3/4 in. wide—wrapped around the end of a thin strip of wood or a tongue depressor will work as well as store-bought foam brushes for small jobs. Foam weatherstripping is made from extra-porous foam, which holds a lot of paint and smoothly applies it to flat surfaces. It also smooshes down nicely when you're coating molding contours or painting in tight corners.

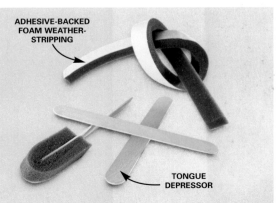

ADHESIVE-BACKED FOAM WEATHER-STRIPPING

TONGUE DEPRESSOR

Repair washing machine leaks

Fix the most common leaks yourself and avoid that $75 service call.

project at a glance

skill level
beginner to intermediate

special tools
basic hand tools
slip joint and
   hose clamp
   pliers
spanner wrench

approximate cost
$10–$50
   depending on
   repair

When the washing machine starts leaking water all over the floor, you face a tough choice. Either call a service technician to fix the problem or purchase a new machine. Both decisions are expensive. Most service technicians charge $50 to $100 just to walk in the door and diagnose the problem, and labor expenses can quickly accumulate. After receiving the final bill, you may even wish you'd replaced the machine!

This article will help you avoid the service call by showing you how to diagnose and fix the most common washing machine leaks. We cover hose, pump and tub leaks, but there may be additional problem areas specific to your brand of machine.

There are two types of washing machines: belt drive and direct drive. If you open up the cabinet and don't find any belts, then you've got a direct-drive machine. Repairs are similar for both machines, but generally easier on the direct-drive unit. The following photos are from a belt-drive washing machine. If you have a direct drive, refer to your owner's manual or diagrams (see "Buying Parts," p. 118) for brand-specific details.

figure a   common leak locations

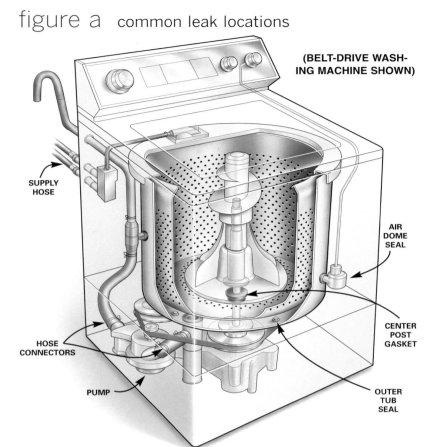

(BELT-DRIVE WASH-ING MACHINE SHOWN)

SUPPLY HOSE

AIR DOME SEAL

CENTER POST GASKET

HOSE CONNECTORS

PUMP

OUTER TUB SEAL

tip Make sure the water on the floor isn't the result of a plugged floor drain. It happens!

First, replace leaky supply hoses

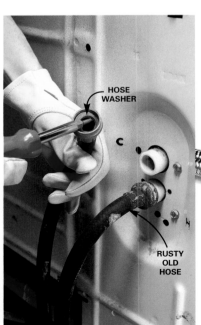

HOSE WASHER

RUSTY OLD HOSE

Turn off the water main or shutoff valve and unscrew the supply hoses from the back of the machine with an adjustable pliers. Pry out the old hose washers with a flat-blade screwdriver. Install new gaskets in both hoses and reconnect the supply lines.

NEW NO-BURST HOSE

NEW HOSE WASHER

The first step is to locate the source of the leak. Empty the washing machine, move it away from the wall and start the fill cycle. Look for drips around the water supply hose connection at the back of the machine while it fills with water. Shut off the water and replace any old, heavily corroded or rusted hoses with new ones (photo, left). If the hoses are in good shape, replace the internal washers only. Special no-burst hoses ($10), regular hoses ($6) and new hose washers ($2 per 10-pack) are available at home centers and hardware stores.

Second, replace leaky internal hoses

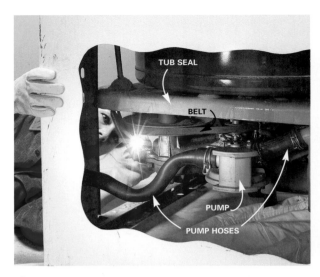

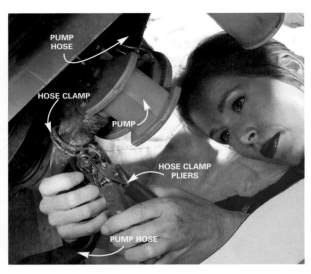

1 Unscrew the access panel from the back of the machine or open the cabinet. Look for leaks while the machine fills with water. If you don't see any, advance the machine to the agitate cycle and check again.

2 Squeeze the hose clamp together, slide it down the hose and pull off the hose. Keep a bucket or pan handy so you can catch any residual water left in the hoses. Replace the hose with an identical part and new worm-drive clamps (bottom of page).

Buying parts

Washing machine parts are available at appliance parts distributors. (Look in the Yellow Pages under "Appliance Parts.") Try to find a parts supplier with a well-informed staff, ideally ex–repair technicians, who can provide diagrams and help diagnose any problems specific to your brand of machine. A great Internet source is www.searspartsdirect.com. Enter your model number to access exploded-view diagrams and a thorough parts list for easy online ordering.

You'll need the brand and model number for proper part identification. Model numbers are usually stamped on a small metal plate (photo above) located under the tub lid or on the side or back of the machine. Copy down all the plate information and take it along to the parts distributor.

If the supply hoses aren't leaking, open the cabinet and inspect the internal components. Belt-drive machines typically have a rear access panel that unscrews. Access direct-drive machines by removing the two screws on the outside of the control panel and flipping up the lid. Then pry up the cabinet clips and pull off the entire cabinet. With the cabinet open, restart the fill cycle to check for internal leaks (Photo 1). Look for additional clues like rust and calcium deposits. Most often you'll find the leaks in the spots we show in Figure A.

Hoses tend to leak around a worn-out spring clamp. First try to remove the spring clamp with an adjustable

CAUTION: UNPLUG THE MACHINE BEFORE PERFORMING ANY REPAIRS.

pliers. If you can't get it, you'll need a special $15 hose clamp pliers (Photo 2) available from your local parts supplier. Replace the old spring clamp with a new worm-drive clamp (photo below). If the hose itself is cracked and leaking, remove it and take it to the appliance parts supplier for a replacement.

WORM-DRIVE CLAMP

Third, replace a leaky pump

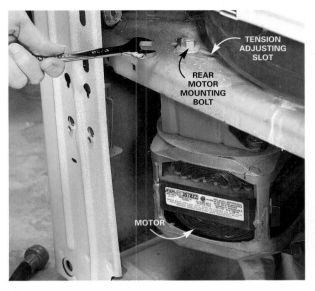

1 Loosen the two motor mounting bolts to relieve tension on the belt. One will be at the rear of the cabinet and the other is nearby.

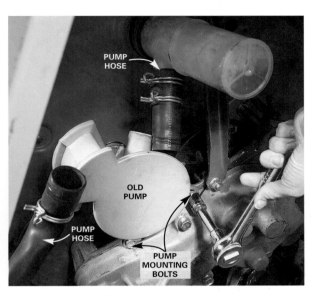

2 Disconnect the pump hoses. Then unscrew the pump mounting bolts, tip the pump pulley away from the belt and wiggle the pump loose. Direct-drive pumps will simply unscrew or unclip.

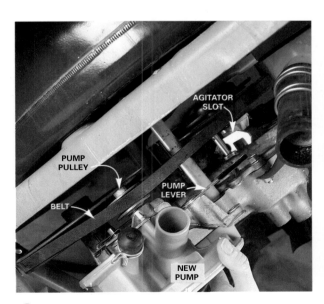

3 Install the new pump by sliding the pump lever into the agitator slot and aligning the belt with the pump pulley. Line up the bolt holes and firmly tighten the mounting bolts. Reconnect all hoses and clamps.

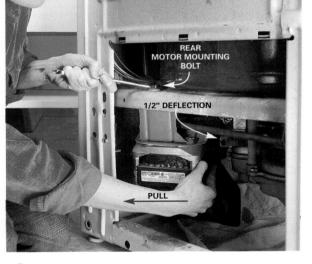

4 Pull against the motor to tension the belt and then tighten the rear motor mounting bolt. The belt should deflect about 1/2 in. when you push against it. Then tighten the mounting bolt located on the opposite side of the motor.

The pump usually leaks around the pulley seal. If you spot water leaking from this spot, the pump is shot and will have to be replaced. A new pump costs $35 to $45.

To replace the pump, work from underneath the machine. Unplug the machine and tip it up against the wall. Block up the front with a car jack or 2x4s so it can't tip over while you reach underneath. Replace the pump as shown in Photos 1 – 4. If the belt is darkened from burning or is worn down to the threads, replace it, too.

Fourth, replace worn-out tub fittings

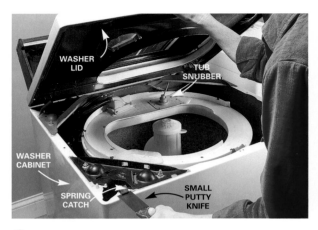

1 Slide a small putty knife between the washer lid and the cabinet. Push the putty knife against the spring catch while lifting up on the lid. Release both catches and fold the lid back.

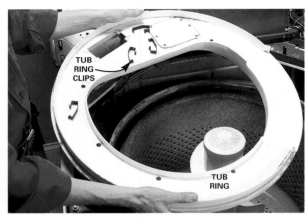

2 Pop off the tub ring clips, lift the tub ring out of the cabinet and set it aside.

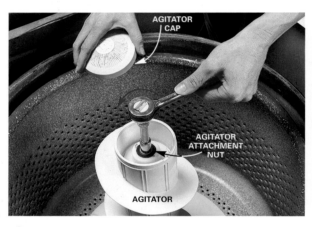

3 Twist or pry the cap off the agitator. Then unscrew the attachment nut and pull the agitator up and off the drive shaft.

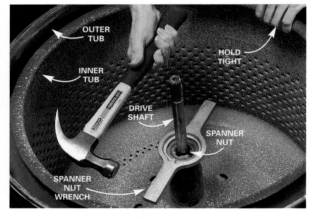

4 Hold the inner tub tight to the outer tub. Rap the special spanner wrench to break the spanner nut free. Remove the spanner nut.

5 Lift the inner tub up and off the drive shaft. You might have to wiggle it back and forth to help work it loose.

The most challenging repair is fixing a leaking tub fitting, whether it's the air dome seal ($5), the center post gasket ($8) or the tub seals ($15 to $20). (See Figure A and photos for locations.) Before proceeding, make sure that telltale drips are coming from around the tub. The details of this repair vary by brand and model. The details we show are for most Whirlpool and Kenmore belt drives. Study a schematic drawing or consult a parts specialist if your machine is different from what we show.

You'll need a special $15 spanner wrench (Photo 4) to remove the tub and replace the tub fittings on this type of machine. It's available at your local appliance parts supplier. Follow Photos 1 – 5 to access the tub fit-

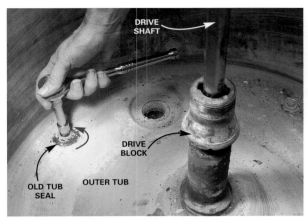

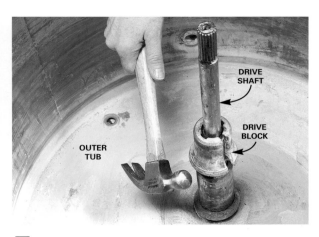

6 Unscrew the old leaky tub seals from the outer tub. Later, install the new tub seals, making sure the metal washer is on top of the rubber washer.

NEW TUB SEAL

7 Tap up on the drive block with a hammer to break it loose from the drive shaft. Pull off the drive block and set it aside. Lift the outer tub from the cabinet, twisting it back and forth to work it loose.

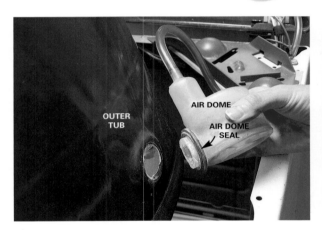

8 Twist the air dome a quarter turn and pull it free from the outer tub. Pry off the old air dome seal and replace it with a new one.

NEW AIR DOME SEAL

9 Squeeze the center post gasket together and pull it from the bottom of the outer tub. Install a new center post gasket and reassemble the machine.

NEW CENTER POST GASKET

tings. You can open the top of many machines by releasing the spring catches (Photo 1). However, on others you have to unscrew several screws and lift off the entire cabinet. Look in your owner's manual or at a parts diagram. (See the manufacturer's Web site or the site listed in "Buying Parts" on p. 118.) You'll have to unscrew the water inlet and the tub snubber (Photo 1) before unclipping the ring (Photo 2). Fastening systems for these vary by brand, as do attachment methods for the agitator (Photo 3) and inner tub (Photo 4).

There are four tub seals that secure the outer tub to the cabinet, each consisting of a bolt with a rubber and metal washer. Rust often develops around one of the tub seals, causing a tub leak. A new tub seal kit will come with four new bolts and oversized rubber and metal washers that will seal small leaks (Photo 6). But if the tub is completely rusted through around the bolt, it's time to buy a new washing machine. Replace all four tub seals as shown in Photo 6.

If the leaking occurs only when the machine is agitating, a bad center post gasket ("doughnut") is the culprit. Remove the outer tub to replace the center post gasket (Photos 8 and 9). While you're at it, replace the air dome seal as well (Photo 8). Reassemble the washing machine and run a test cycle.

Replace a
kitchen faucet

Just getting to it is the hard part.

Installing a new kitchen faucet isn't tough at all. Actually, the directions that come with your new faucet are probably all you'll need to do that part of the job. Barring unforeseen problems, you could be washing up under the new faucet in an hour or so.

But what the directions *don't* mention are the bugaboos that can pop up while you're trying to get the old faucet out. You may be faced with bushwhacking your way through a dark, dank jungle of drainpipes, water lines, a garbage disposer and maybe more, just to access the faucet. Then, you'll be called on to perform pretzel-like contortions inside the sink cabinet to pull an old faucet with connections that may be so badly corroded you'll swear they're welded together. Here's what you need to know to get through the tough parts.

The right stuff

Chances are, you'll need to make more than one trip to the hardware store for parts, but to give yourself a fighting shot at completing the job with one-stop shopping, consult this list.

project at a glance

skill level
beginner to intermediate

special tools
box end and specialty wrenches tubing cutter

approximate cost
$50 and up

tip*

Before disconnecting the drain lines, take a Polaroid or digital snapshot or make a sketch of the layout to help you put it all back together.

● **Shutoff valves:** Before you shop for your new faucet (see "Selecting a Faucet," p. 126), take a look under the sink and make sure that there are shutoff valves feeding the faucet. If you don't have shutoff valves, add them. If you have them, confirm that they're in working order by turning on the hot and cold water at the faucet and shutting off the valves. If the faucet still drips, install new ones. Most likely you have 1/2-in. copper supply pipes. If so, add easy-to-install solderless "compression fitting" valves (Photos 9 and 10) to your shopping list. But if not, buy whichever valve type is compatible with your pipes.

● **Supply tubes:** Next, measure the existing supply tubes and buy new stainless steel-sleeved ones (Photo 9). They're designed to give rupture-free service for years and can easily be routed around obstacles without kinking.

● **Basin wrench:** Also buy a basin wrench ($15; Photo 4). This weird little wrench is made specifically for removing and installing those hard-to-reach fasteners that clamp older faucet assemblies to the sink. (Newer faucets have plastic wing nuts that can usually be loosened and tightened by hand.) A basin wrench's spring-loaded jaws pivot so you can either loosen or tighten nuts in tight spaces. If you need to remove drain lines to access the faucet, get a pipe wrench or a slip-joint pliers (Photo 1). For cutting copper tubes, buy a conventional tubing cutter. But if your copper supply lines are within a few inches of the back of the cabinet, buy a

OLD STUCK FAUCET

NEED NEW SHUTOFF VALVES

MOP UP TRAP OVERFLOW

BACK-SAVING PLYWOOD LEDGE

DISPOSER IN THE WAY

OLD DRAIN LINES NEED REPLACEMENT

tip* If you're replacing the kitchen sink along with a new faucet, install the faucet before setting the sink into the countertop.

DISHWASHER DISCHARGE HOSE

P-TRAP

WATER SUPPLY LINES (SHUTOFF VALVES MISSING)

1 Disconnect the drain lines and P-traps if they block your access to the faucet and water supply pipes. (Place a bucket or coffee can under the P-trap to dump residual water after you pull it free.)

CUSHIONED PAINT CAN

RETAINING RING

2 Unplug the garbage disposer, or shut off the circuit breaker in the main service panel if the disposer is directly wired. Disconnect the dishwasher discharge line and place a 1-gal. paint can under the garbage disposer with some rags on top to cushion the disposer when it drops free. Release the disposer by tapping the retaining ring with a hammer in a counterclockwise direction.

special mini tube cutter (Photo 3). You'll also need a set of open-end wrenches for disconnecting and hooking up the water lines.

Getting at it

After you pull out all of the cleansers, buckets and old vases from under the sink, go ahead and lie under there and see if you can easily access the faucet. If so, go right to Photo 3. If not, it's time to start dismantling the things blocking your path.

Most likely, the main obstacles will be the pipes and P-traps that drain the sinks. Don't be afraid to pull them out, but more importantly, don't be afraid to replace them with new ones. If you have older, chrome-plated drain lines, the pipe walls may be so corroded that they'll

tip Prop up a scrap of plywood on some 1-qt. paint cans in front of the cabinet. You'll be much more comfortable lying under the sink. Otherwise, the edge of the cabinet would be digging into your back.

crush in the jaws of a pipe wrench or slip-joint pliers. After you remove them, throw all the parts in a box for matching them exactly at the store later. If you have plastic drain parts, be careful during removal—you'll probably be able to reuse them.

Sometimes a garbage disposer can be a 20-lb. roadblock. Don't be discouraged—it's easier than you think to remove it and then reinstall it after the faucet is in (Photo 2). Unplug it and pull it out of the cabinet to get it out of the way. If it's hard-wired, shut off the circuit breaker that controls the disposer, disconnect the disposer from the sink and set it aside inside the cabinet with the electrical cable still attached.

tip Plan on replacing your faucet during store hours. Chances are better than 50/50 you'll need at least one more part.

Disconnecting the old faucet

The first step in removing the old faucet is to disconnect the water supply lines (Photo 3). If there are no shutoff valves and the water pipes are hooked up directly to the

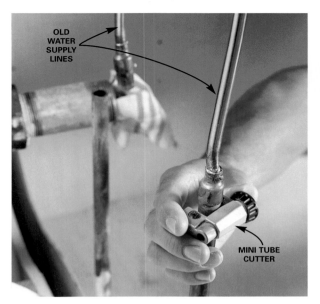

OLD WATER SUPPLY LINES

MINI TUBE CUTTER

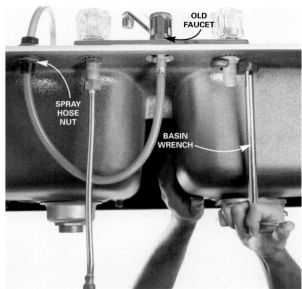

OLD FAUCET

SPRAY HOSE NUT

BASIN WRENCH

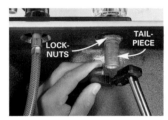

LOCK-NUTS

TAIL-PIECE

3 Shut off the water below the sink if you have valves, or shut off the main water supply valve if your old faucet is plumbed directly without valves. Open the kitchen faucet and another lower faucet to bleed off any pressure and to drain the water. If you're installing or replacing valves, cut the water lines directly below the fittings with a tube cutter or hacksaw.

4 Reach up behind the sink, fit the basin wrench jaws onto the tailpiece nuts and turn counterclockwise to loosen. Then disconnect the spray nozzle hose, remove the faucet and clean the sink area under the old faucet flange.

FLANGE

STUD, SPACER AND FLANGE NUT

5 Follow any manufacturer's preassembly instructions and place the optional flange (see Photo 8) over the faucet opening. Finger-tighten the flange nuts underneath the sink and check the alignment of the flange, faucet and sink hole from above.

6 Check the operation of the faucet and handle to confirm you're not putting it in backward, and thread the feeder lines through the flange and sink holes. Then slip on the faucet washer, and thread on and tighten the faucet-mounting nut from below, gently spreading the faucet supply tubes if necessary to gain tool clearance (sometimes manufacturers provide a special tool for this).

FLANGE NUT

7 Hand-tighten, then snug up the flange nuts with an open-end wrench. You can only turn the wrench about a one-sixth revolution at a time.

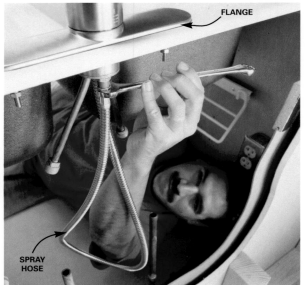

FLANGE

SPRAY HOSE

8 Thread the spray nozzle line through the faucet body, then thread the spray hose fitting onto the faucet supply tube and tighten it. Pull the nozzle out of the faucet to make sure the hose under the sink operates freely, then attach the counterweight following the manufacturer's instructions.

faucet supply lines, or if you're replacing defective valves, turn off the main water supply valve to the house and cut off the pipes (Photo 3) below the connections with a hacksaw or tube cutter. Make sure new valves are closed before turning the water back on to the house. Once the water lines are disconnected, use the basin wrench to loosen the old faucet and remove it (Photo 4).

When all else fails. . .

Sometimes, in spite of all your best efforts, it's simply impossible to loosen the old faucet nuts. Calm down! Try soaking the threads with penetrating oil and try again. If that doesn't do it, it's time to pull out all the stops and pull the sink so you can get at the nuts. It's not that tough to do. Loosen the screws on the bottom of the sink rim for a clamp-down sink, or cut the caulk between a drop-in sink and countertop with a utility knife and lift out the sink. Then you'll be able to go after those nuts with a locking pliers or a pipe wrench to free the old faucet.

Follow the manufacturer's directions to mount the new faucet, then remount the sink (with the new faucet) and hook up the water lines as we show.

Selecting a faucet

When you're buying a faucet (as with most other things), you get what you pay for. Faucets that cost less than $100 may be made of chrome-plated plastic parts with seals and valves that wear. They're OK for light-duty use but won't stand up long in a frequently used kitchen sink. Faucets that cost more than $100 generally have solid brass bodies with durable plating and washerless controls that'll give leak-free service for many, many years. Some even come with a lifetime warranty. Quality continues to improve up to about $200. Spend more than $200 and you're mostly paying for style and finish. Stick with brand name products so replacement parts will be easier to find—in the unlikely event you'll ever need them.

tip With most faucets, only three of the four holes are covered, so you'll either need to get a blank insert or use the extra hole for a liquid soap or instant hot water dispenser. Plan to do the installation while you're under the sink with everything torn apart.

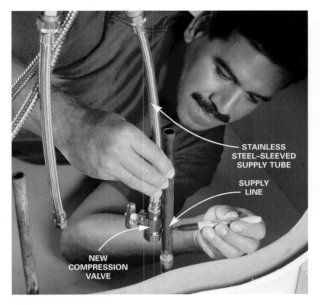

STAINLESS
STEEL–SLEEVED
SUPPLY TUBE

SUPPLY
LINE

NEW
COMPRESSION
VALVE

9 Tighten the new valves onto the supply tubes and mark the feeder lines just above the compression nuts on the valves for cut-off.

10 Clean the copper tubing with fine sandpaper, then slip the nut, compression ring and valve body over the pipe and tighten. Close the valve, turn on the main water valve and check for leaks. Place a bucket under the faucet and turn the faucet on to check for leaks. Re-assemble the garbage disposer, P-traps and drain lines.

Unclog a kitchen faucet aerator

If you get weak water flow when you turn on your faucet—whether it's brand new or ten years old—don't assume your water pressure has suddenly gone bad. You could simply have a filter screen, or aerator, that's clogged. Remove the aerator as shown in the photo, rinse it out and reinstall it. If it's corroded or worn, take it to a home center and pick up a new one ($3 to $5). Most stores have a slick gauge you can screw your old aerator onto to determine which replacement to buy. If you can't find a replacement for your aerator, soak the parts in vinegar overnight, scrub them with an old toothbrush and reinsert into the faucet (make sure to reassemble the parts in the same order you removed them).

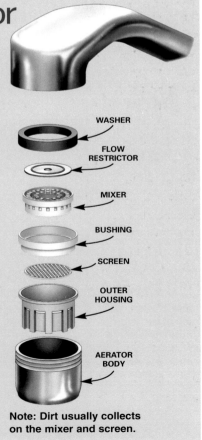

WASHER

FLOW
RESTRICTOR

MIXER

BUSHING

SCREEN

OUTER
HOUSING

AERATOR
BODY

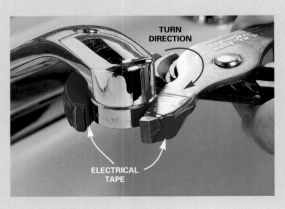

TURN
DIRECTION

ELECTRICAL
TAPE

Wrap the jaws of a pliers with tape to keep them from scratching the aerator. Unscrew the aerator body from the faucet and remove all the internal components. Clean and reassemble.

Note: Dirt usually collects on the mixer and screen.

Cabinet facelift

Simple, attractive kitchen upgrades you can do yourself—without replacing your cabinets.

Take a look, a really close look. At first glance it may be hard to recognize, but the kitchen on the right is the same as the one in the photo below. The cabinet "boxes," the countertop, the layout, the flooring, the sink and the window haven't changed a whit. Better yet, once the materials were in hand, this transformation took place in just a few days—without putting the kitchen out of commission. The frosting on the cake? The total cost for upgrading the cabinets was $2,200 (not including the wall tile). With the average full-scale kitchen remodeling project costing more than $30,000 (and about one-third of that amount spent on cabinetry), you can see we got a big impact for a small cost.

project at a glance

skill level
intermediate

special tools
power miter saw
drill
basic hand tools

approximate cost
$2,200 for
project shown
(not incl. tile)

Whether you tackle one or all of these cabinet upgrades, you'll increase the visual appeal of your kitchen quickly, inexpensively and with minimum hassle.

BEFORE

AFTER

If you're pleased with the basic layout and function of your kitchen but want to update the look—and add a few new features—read on. We'll show you how paint, new cabinet doors and drawer fronts, moldings and a few accessories can transform your kitchen.

Most of the projects require only a drill, basic hand tools and intermediate DIY savvy, although a power miter saw and pneumatic finish nailer allow you to cut and install the crown molding faster.

Bear in mind, these upgrades won't fix cabinets that are falling apart, create more storage space or make your kitchen easier to navigate. But if you want to give your kitchen an inexpensive yet dramatic facelift, here's how.

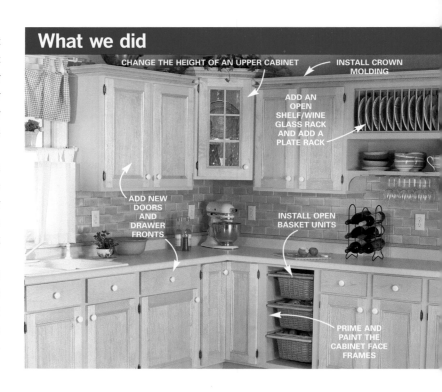

What we did

CHANGE THE HEIGHT OF AN UPPER CABINET

INSTALL CROWN MOLDING

ADD AN OPEN SHELF/WINE GLASS RACK AND ADD A PLATE RACK

ADD NEW DOORS AND DRAWER FRONTS

INSTALL OPEN BASKET UNITS

PRIME AND PAINT THE CABINET FACE FRAMES

Raise an upper cabinet

To break up the monotony of a row of cabinets, change the height of one or more upper cabinets. This provides more "headroom" for working and more space for lighting and appliances, while creating a more interesting and varied look.

In order to raise a cabinet, your cabinets must be the modular kind such that each cabinet is an independent "box" screwed to adjacent ones. Earlier "builder cabinets," with the entire row of cabinets built and installed as one unit, can't be easily

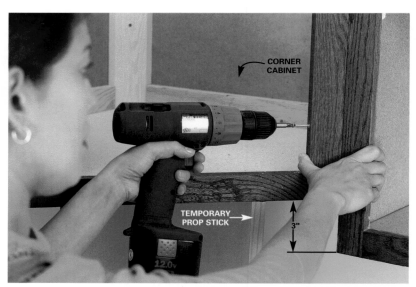

CORNER CABINET

TEMPORARY PROP STICK

3"

To raise a cabinet, remove the shelves and doors and then the screws securing it to the wall and cabinets on either side. Raise the cabinet, temporarily prop it in place, drill new pilot holes, then reinstall the screws.

separated. We elevated our corner cabinet 3 in., temporarily propped it up with scrap lumber, drilled pilot holes for new screws, then reattached it. A cabinet that's been in

place a long time may need a sharp rap with a hammer to free it from paint and grime that have "glued" it in place.

Paint your cabinet face frames

Proper preparation and sanding between coats are the keys to a smooth, durable paint job on your cabinet face frames.

Oil paints arguably create the smoothest surface, since they dry slowly and "self-level" as brush stroke marks fill in. However, this slow drying time means they're more vulnerable to dust. Cleanup is also more of a hassle. Latex paints dry quickly and may show brush strokes more, but additives like Floetrol (The Flood Co., 800-321-3444) improve "brushability."

After priming, paint the cabinets with a gloss or semigloss paint. Apply a thin first coat, let it dry, then lightly sand with 120- or 180-grit sandpaper. Wipe the surface, then apply a second coat. Two or three thin coats are better than one or two thick ones.

If you have a gas stove, turn off the gas for safety while using mineral spirits, shellac or oil paints, and provide plenty of ventilation.

Clean the cabinet face frames with mineral spirits, then scrub them with household ammonia and rinse. Fill holes with spackling compound, then sand with 120-grit sandpaper. Vacuum the cabinets, then prime them with a pigmented shellac. Lightly sand the dried primer.

Add new doors and drawer fronts

We had a local cabinet shop make our new doors and drawer fronts the exact same dimensions as the old ones. We used the same hinges and mounting holes in the face frames to ensure the right fit. You can have your components made locally or by one of the companies listed in the Buyer's Guide, p. 134.

Existing drawer fronts can be attached in a number of different ways. We were able to simply pry off the old and screw on the new. If yours can't be removed, you'll need to use a circular saw to cut all four edges of the drawer front even with the edges of the drawer box, then apply the new drawer front directly over the old. This will make your drawers 3/4 in. longer; make certain your drawer hardware and cabinets can accommodate the extra length. If not, you may need to install new drawer hardware or new drawer boxes.

Mount the hinges to the doors, then mount the doors to the face frames using the existing screw holes. Most hinges allow for some up-and-down movement and tilt so the doors can be adjusted evenly.

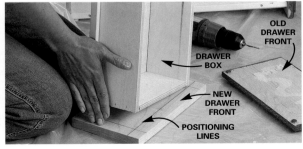

Replace the old drawer fronts. We pried off the old front using a chisel and a flat bar, marked the position of the drawer box on the back of the new drawer front, then joined the two using carpenter's glue and screws.

Add an open shelf, wine glass rack and plate rack

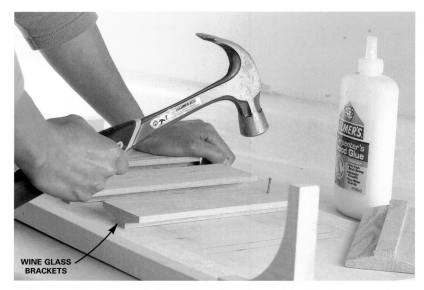

If you have a short cabinet flanked by two taller cabinets, you can add this combination shelf/wine rack.

We cut the shelf to length, then added mounting strips on each end. We cut four 9-in. sections of wine glass molding from a 3-ft. length (see Buyer's Guide, p. 134), then glued and nailed them to the bottom of the pine shelf. We also cut curved brackets from each end of a 1x6 maple board and cut the center 1 in. wide to serve as shelf edging. Finally, we installed the unit by driving screws through the mounting strips and into the cabinets on each side.

To display your plates and keep them accessible and chip-free, build and install this plate rack. The total cost of materials? Under $10.

To create the two plate rack "ladders," measure the cabinet, then build each ladder so the finished height equals the height of the inside of the cabinet. The finished width should be equal to the width of the face frame opening. Drill 3/8-in. holes, 3/8 in. deep in 3/4-in. x 3/4-in. square dowels and space them every 1-1/2 in. Cut the dowels to length, add a drop of glue in each hole, insert the dowels, then use elastic cords or clamps to hold things

WINE GLASS BRACKETS

Build a shelf to fit snugly between the cabinets on each side. We used a jigsaw to create curved brackets, nailed wine glass brackets to the bottom of the shelf, then installed the entire unit as one piece.

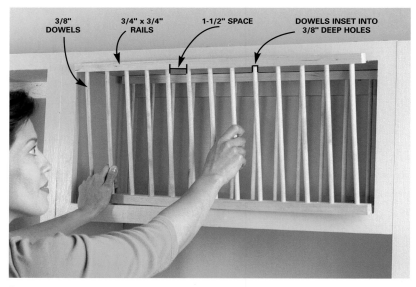

3/8" DOWELS   3/4" x 3/4" RAILS   1-1/2" SPACE   DOWELS INSET INTO 3/8" DEEP HOLES

Cut, assemble and install the two plate rack "ladders." Use short screws to secure the ladders in the cabinet opening. We set the rear ladder 4 in. away from the back of the cabinet and the front ladder snug against the back of the face frame.

together until the glue dries.

A drill press comes in handy, but you can get excellent results using the same tools we did: a cordless drill, a steady hand and a 3/8-in. drill bit with masking tape wrapped around it as a depth guide for the holes in the rails.

Install crown molding

Crown molding comes in many profiles and sizes; we installed rope molding (see Buyer's Guide, p. 134). If your face frames aren't wide enough on top to nail the molding to, nail strips of wood to the top edge to provide a nailing surface.

Raising the corner cabinet created a challenge where the moldings on each side butted into it. We held the upper part of the crown molding back a few inches, but extended the thin rope molding portion so it butted into the corner cabinet.

Position and mark each piece of crown molding as you work your way around the kitchen. Make small notches in the top corners of the face frames so the moldings lie flat against the sides of the cabinets when installed.

Cut crown molding by placing it upside down and securing it at the correct angle with a clamp and wood scrap.

Install open basket units

The "Base 18" baskets we installed (see Buyer's Guide, p. 134) came with two side tracks that could be cut narrower to accommodate cabinets ranging in width from 15-7/8 in. to 17-7/8 in. "Base 15" baskets fit cabinets with an inside width of 12-7/8 in. to 15-7/8 in. Measure carefully, cut the basket tracks to width, then install them as shown.

Remove cabinet hardware, then the rails where you want to create an open cabinet. A fine-tooth pull saw works well for removing dividers, since it lies flat against the cabinet frame as it cuts. Sand the area to create a smooth surface.

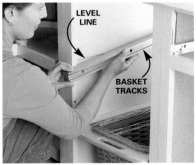

Cut the tracks to the proper width, then level them in both directions and screw them to the sides of the cabinet.

Buyer's Guide for Cabinet Facelift

All the products used in this project are readily available through catalogs, the Internet and specialty woodworking stores. Here are a few sources:

Cabinet doors and drawer fronts

A local cabinetmaker made our 13 maple doors and six drawer fronts for $1,500. Expect to pay about $20 per square foot for custom doors, slightly less for the drawer fronts. You could also have a company specializing in cabinet refacing measure and order the doors for you.

There are a variety of mail order sources you can explore:

● **Custom Kitchen Cabinet and Refacing Co.:** (888) 407-3322, www.reface.com

● **Jackson Custom Woodworks:** (866) 261-7643. www.jacksoncustom.com

● **Kitchen Door Depot:** (877) 399-5677, www.kitchendoordepot.com

● **Rockler Custom Door and Drawer Front Program:** (800) 279-4441, www.rockler.com

Crown molding, bun feet, baskets, wine glass molding

We ordered our maple rope crown molding (No. 53639, $77.99 per 8-ft. length), wicker baskets (No. 47527, $67.99 each), wine glass molding (No. 22210, $10.99 per 36-in. piece) and bun feet (No. 70410, $10.59 each) from Rockler (800-279-4441, www.rockler.com).

Outwater: (800-835-4400, www.outwater.com) and Woodworker's Supply: (800-645-9292, www.woodworker.com) sell similar items.

Miscellaneous

The porcelain pulls, dowels for the plate rack, primer and paint were bought at a home center.

We ordered the wall tile (Newport, Sage Green by Walker Zanger Ceramics, 877-504-0235, www.walkerzanger.com) from a local tile shop.

Thyme saver

Does your stew boil over every time you're distracted for five minutes looking for the right spice? Often spices are jammed into a drawer with only the tops visible. If you have this problem, take an hour to make this nifty rack that slips neatly into the drawer. Make it with leftover scraps of 1/4-in. and 1/2-in. plywood from my shop. Now spend less time cleaning the burners and more time stirring the pot!

EASY FOR EVERYONE

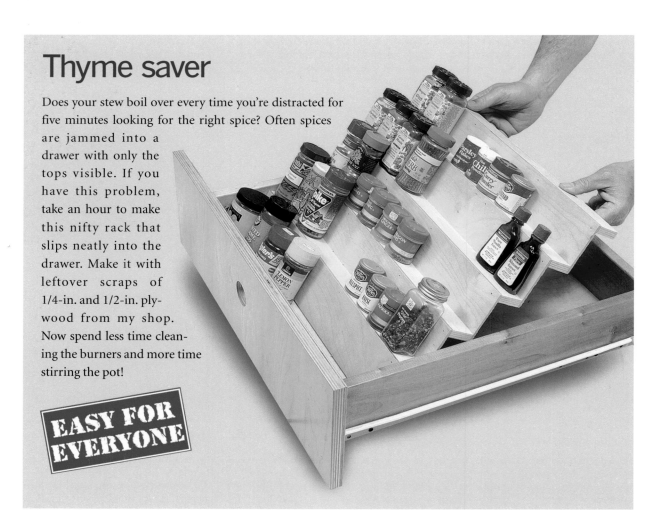

Swing-out wastebasket

Our hang-on-the-door swing-out wastebasket mounts on the inside of a vanity door with two plastic mirror clips. You can use any small wastebasket with a lipped edge, but the one we used is made by Rubbermaid. It's 10 in. wide, and will work on any vanity door more than 11 in. wide. This setup will work under your kitchen sink as well, using a larger wastebasket that will hold a grocery bag as a liner.

EASY FOR EVERYONE

project at a glance

skill level
beginner

special tools
drill

approximate cost
Less than $5

MIRROR CLIPS

1 Mount two plastic mirror clips to the back of your vanity door. Make sure they're level with each other, and low enough so the wastebasket's top edge will just clear the door opening. Also, space the clips far enough apart to prevent the wastebasket from sliding from side to side. You'll probably need to use shorter screws than those in the clip package so they won't come through the other side of the door.

2 Clear out space inside the cabinet to allow room for the basket when doors are closed, then hang the wastebasket on the clips.

Paths, Walls

& Fences

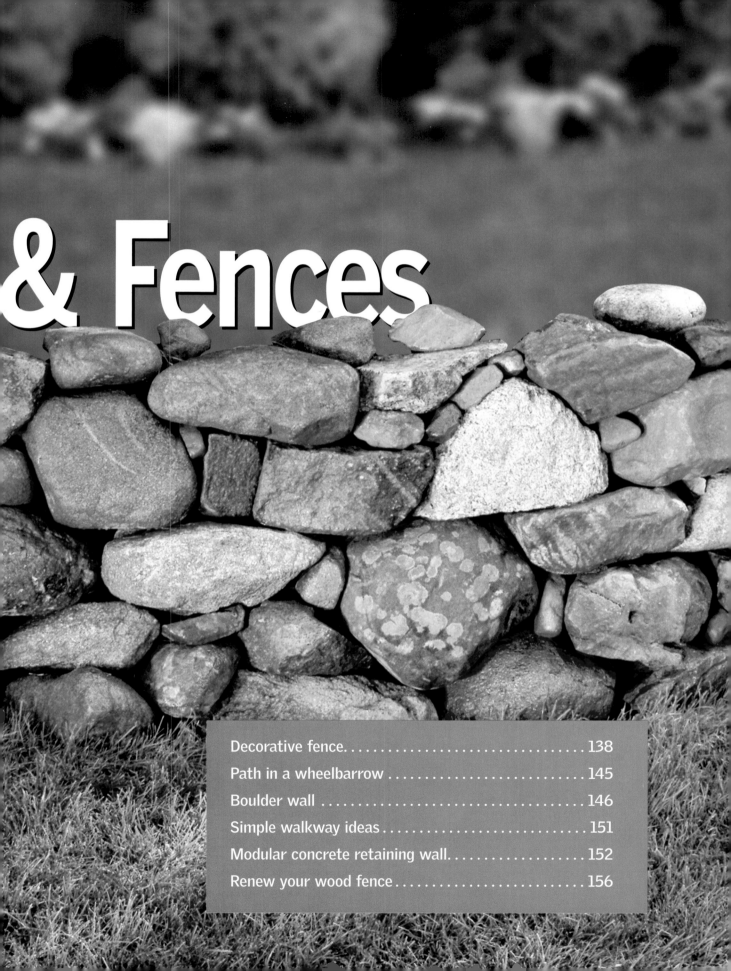

Decorative fence
Build a great-looking fence in two weekends.

Looking for more privacy, a corral for the kids and pets or an attractive border on the edge of your yard? Consider building your own fence—it's the ideal project for weekend carpenters of every ability level. You can build a simple fence with as few tools as a posthole digger, hammer, power saw and tape measure and little if any woodworking experience. On the other hand, you could pick a design that's so challenging only a skilled builder should attempt it.

The design we show here falls somewhere in the novice-to-intermediate difficulty range. It's primarily a privacy fence intended to enclose a backyard and garden in the middle of a busy neighborhood. However, we added lattice and a gate to make it more friendly and inviting. While these features complicate the project a bit, don't let them put you off. The basic design and assembly procedures that we'll demonstrate work well for both simple and complex fences. Once you master these basics, you'll be able to design

and build a fence that fits your home, the surrounding landscape and your ability level.

Wood fences aren't cheap
Even the simplest hand-crafted wood fence costs more than your garden-variety chain-link fencing. A wood fence will be even more expensive in the long run if you include the cost of periodic staining or painting. So for both economy and convenience, chain-link fencing is usually your best bet. But for beauty and versatility, wood wins hands down.

Neighborhood concerns
Most communities have ordinances that regulate fences, because they visually affect your neighbors' property as well as your own. So before you get too far into the planning process, call your local building

POSTHOLE
DIGGER

PRY BAR

STRONG
CORD

LEVEL

4x4
CORNER
POST

TAMPING
STICK

1 Stretch lines to mark the fence location, then dig
holes 8 in. in diameter for the corner posts using a
posthole digger. Use a steel pry bar to knock rocks loose
and break through tree roots. Remember to call your utility
company to check for buried lines before digging.

2 Plumb the corner posts with a level and tamp 6 in. of
soil around their bottoms to anchor them. Trim the
tops to the exact height later (Photo 7).

inspector and ask about local codes. Many locales limit fence height to 4 or 5 ft. (Our design is 6 ft. high, which isn't acceptable in some areas.) Many have "setback" requirements; that is, the fence has to be a certain distance from the property line. And the fence has to look at least as attractive from the outside as it does on the inside. (You can't face the least attractive side toward your neighbors.) Check whether a building inspector has to approve your plan and issue a building permit before you can start work.

Let your neighbors know what you're up to before you begin. Otherwise the sudden change may shock them, and you'll have to smooth ruffled feathers!

Allow two weekends to complete an average fence: one weekend to lay out and set the posts, and the second to assemble the fencing.

Fence-planning basics

Our fence design, like most, consists of repeating sections supported on both ends by 4x4 posts, spaced from 6 to 8 ft. apart. Two 2x4s span the distance

Plan Smart

Look through the design books of local fence-building companies to find creative ideas. Many companies will also sell you materials and offer free advice. And keep a sharp eye out for attractive designs in your own neighborhood.

between the posts, which, when fastened "on edge" (1-1/2 in. side facing down), are strong enough to support the fence boards without sagging (Figure A). The third (top) 2x4 primarily supports the lattice. When you use 2x4s to span more than 8 ft., they usually sag within a few years. The same thing will happen if you fasten the 2x4s "flat" (with the 3-1/2 in. side down).

Since the 4x4 posts and 2x4 framework provide the strength, you can add just about any pattern of fence boards and trim to finish the fence.

It's best to use a rot-resistant wood, either cedar, redwood, or pressure-treated lumber. Expect both redwood and cedar fences to last 15 to 20 years, or longer where weathering from sun and rain is less severe. Pressure-treated wood will last even longer. However, most treated species, when left unfinished, tend to warp, crack and split more readily than cedar and redwood. You'll have to apply paint, stain or another water repellent to keep a treated wood fence looking good. By the same token, both redwood and cedar will last longer and look better if you apply a water-repelling finish to them, too.

Rough-surfaced boards absorb stain better than smooth, while smooth wood accepts paint better. Two other factors can complicate your plans:

One. A design that requires exact post spacing. The 6-in. square lattice in our design meant that we had to accurately space our posts an exact multiple of 6 in. apart (6 ft. 6 in., 7 ft., etc.). Sure, we could fudge an inch or so either way, but not much more if we were to keep the lattice looking symmetrical.

Unless you're lucky, you'll end up with an odd-sized fence section or two. Put that section at the most obscure corner of your yard!

Two. A sloped landscape. Lattice also limits your options when it comes to following the sloped contours of the yard. The lattice looks best if it's level, so you'll have to "step" it up and down slopes (Figure B). The bottom of the fence doesn't matter as much; you can either follow the contour of the ground or step it as well (Figure B).

Without lattice or other details that require a level approach, a fence can simply follow the contours of the lot. To help choose the best option for your fence, sketch your fence design and try out the slope options on paper first.

Finally, keep in mind that your fence should look attractive on both sides. The sides of our fence are virtually identical.

The layout and corner posts

To look good, a fence has to be straight. So the first task is to find the fence corners and stretch tight string lines between them. If you're working near the property line, you'll have to find the official boundary markers or hire surveyors to reestablish them.

With the fence lines clearly marked, dig holes for the corner posts (Photo 1). Call your local utility before you dig so they can come out and mark buried gas, electrical, water and telephone lines.

Buy Smart

When buying fence boards, look for wood specifically labeled as such. They're usually rough-surfaced and slightly thinner than regular 1x4s and 1x6s, and they cost less. Quality varies widely, so check the stacks at several lumberyards or local fence companies.

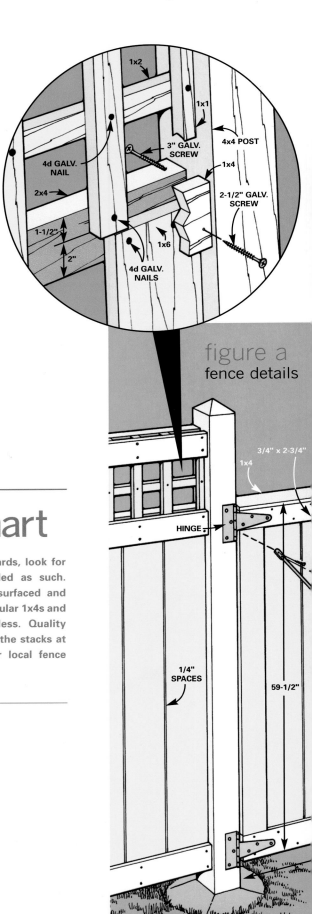

figure a
fence details

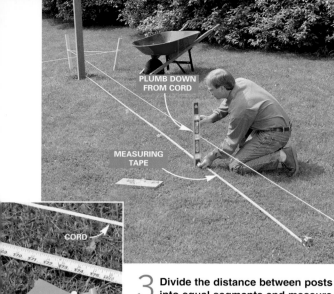

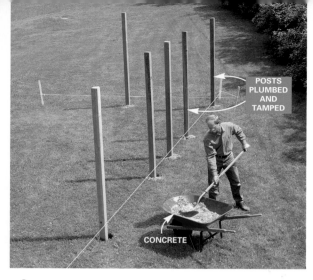

3 Divide the distance between posts into equal segments and measure and mark the exact location of each post along the string line. A nail with a ribbon makes highly visible markers.

4 Dig the holes, plumb and anchor the posts, then fill the holes with concrete to about 1 in. above ground level.

CORD

NAIL MARKER

PLUMB DOWN FROM CORD

MEASURING TAPE

POSTS PLUMBED AND TAMPED

CONCRETE

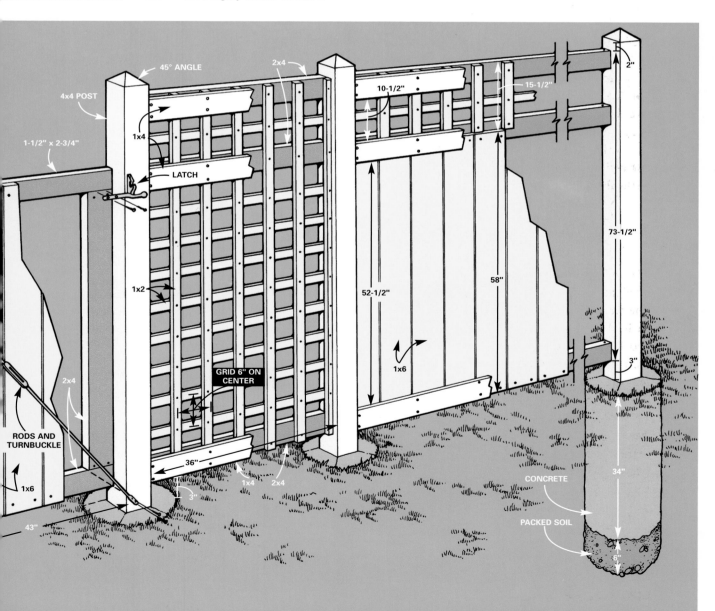

45° ANGLE

4x4 POST

1-1/2" x 2-3/4"

1x4

LATCH

1x2

GRID 6" ON CENTER

2x4

RODS AND TURNBUCKLE

1x6

36"

1x4   2x4

3"

43"

2x4

10-1/2"

15-1/2"

2"

52-1/2"

1x6

58"

73-1/2"

3"

34"

6"

CONCRETE

PACKED SOIL

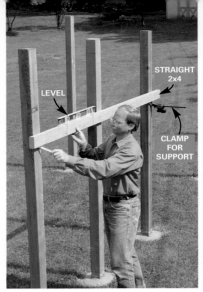

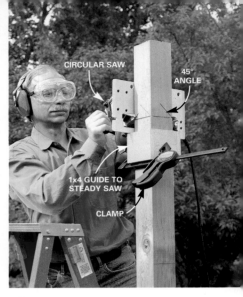

5 Smooth the concrete with a wood or metal float, angling the top away from the post for better drainage.

6 Mark the locations of the 2x4 framework on each post with a straight 2x4 and level. Then mark the finished height of each post.

7 Cut the post tops to height with a circular saw. Clamp a jig to the post to guide the saw.

figure b
options for slopes

Stepped top, angled bottom

Stepped top, stepped or contoured bottom

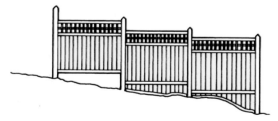

Angled top and bottom

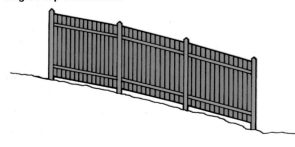

You'll work up a sweat hand-digging with a post hole digger, but it's our favorite tool for fence work. Renting a gas-driven post hole auger might save you a little time, but it'll still give you a workout.

You have to bury posts deep enough so that the steady force of the wind doesn't gradually tip them over. Bury 1 ft. of post for every 2 ft. it extends above ground. Our posts extended about 80 in. above ground and 40 in. below. Finally, drop in the corner posts and tamp 6 in. of soil around them to keep them plumb (Photo 2).

Now measure the distance between corner posts (a 50-ft. tape comes in handy here) and divide the distance into equal segments (Photo 3). Remember to allow 3-1/2 in. for each 4x4 post. Also allow space for special sections in your plan, like the gate and lattice adjacent to it.

Dig all the post holes and plumb the posts with your level, again tamping 6 in. of soil around each to hold them in place (Photo 4). After you fill the holes with concrete, check each of them again for plumb. It's

Handy Hints

As the concrete hardens, it'll shrink, opening a narrow gap between the post and concrete. Fill this crack with a bead of acrylic caulk to keep out water.

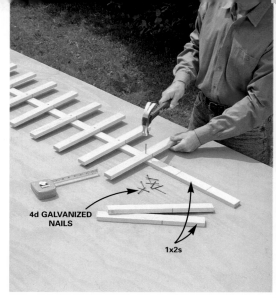

8 Clamp a jig to the post to cradle the 2x4 framework, and screw the 2x4s to the posts with 3-in. galvanized decking screws.

9 Cut the fencing boards to length and fasten them to the 2x4s with 6d galvanized nails. Space the boards 1/4 in. apart to allow for normal expansion.

10 Lay out the 1x2 lattice on 6-in. centers. Then fasten it with 4d galvanized nails.

TOP 2x4 LOCATION

MIDDLE 2x4

JIG FOR POSITIONING

6d GALVANIZED NAILS

1/4" SHIM SPACER

1x6 FENCE BOARD

4d GALVANIZED NAILS

1x2s

11 Nail the lattice in place with 6d galvanized nails. Use a framing square to align the vertical pieces and keep them straight.

12 Screw 1x4s over the board and lattice ends using 2-1/2 in. galvanized decking screws.

FRAMING SQUARE

1x4s

tough to move them once the concrete sets! Give the concrete two days to harden.

Assembling the framework

Layout work was painstaking, but now you move into the fun part where your fence comes together quickly. The framework for our fence consists of three 2x4s in each section (Figure A). Start from the highest point in your yard and mark the height of the middle 2x4 on each post, keeping the 2x4 level from post to post (Photo 6). Step it up or down 6 in. (to be consistent with the lattice) on slopes. Then measure up from the line to locate the top 2x4 and down to locate the lower. (The height of the lower 2x4 will vary if you angle it to follow the contours of the ground.)

13 Assemble the gate on a flat surface. We used screws to strengthen it and keep it perfectly square.

2" GALVANIZED SCREWS
1x6s
2x4s

14 Shim the gate to center it in the opening, and screw heavy-duty hinges to both the gate and post. Then add a turnbuckle to reinforce the gate, and a latch.

HINGE
SHIMS

Cut the post tops. Use a circular saw set at a 45-degree angle (Photo 7). Warning: Sawing from a ladder is difficult and can be dangerous. The guide (ours is painted yellow in Photo 7), made from four 4-1/4 in. long 1x4s nailed together and clamped to the post, made the cutting easier and safer.

Measure the 2x4s for each section, and cut them to length so they fit snugly between the posts (Figure A, inset). Although the sections are supposed to be equal, expect small variations. Predrill the 2x4s with a 5/32-in. bit before fastening them, so the 3-in. galvanized deck screws draw the 2x4s tight to the posts.

Fasten the fencing boards. Two 6d nails driven at the top and bottom are strong enough to hold each fencing board (Photo 9), particularly since a 1x4 covers them. Use hot-dipped galvanized nails for the best corrosion resistance.

We prestained the fence boards and lattice to save time. Stain won't last as long as paint, but it's easier to renew. We expect our stain to last about five years before it fades and cries out for another coat.

We made our lattice from 1x2s that we ripped from wider boards on a table saw. However, you can usually buy both the square and angled types of lattice preassembled at lumberyards, although in a much smaller grid. Preassemble it on a flat surface (Photo 10) before nailing it in place (Photo 11).

Finish the fence by covering the joints with 1x4s to match the 2x4s on the other side. Cut them accurately so they won't leave gaps at the ends (Figure A, inset).

Building the gate

Our gate is virtually identical to the fence, except we continued the 2x4s and 1x4s completely around the perimeter (Figure A). And we capped the top with a 1x3. For additional strength, we fastened the boards to the 2x4s with 2-in. galvanized decking screws and the 1x4s with 2-1/2 in. galvanized decking screws (Photo 13). But gates have a tendency to sag anyway, especially if the kids swing on them! So we screwed two threaded rods connected by a turnbuckle diagonally across the gate to reinforce it (Figure A).

Now put away the tools and let the dog loose.

Path in a wheel-barrow

EASY FOR EVERYONE

There's no heavy lifting, no fancy tools and it's really, really cheap!

This garden path is as easy to build as it is to look at and walk on. A bundle or two of cedar shakes, a roll of landscape fabric, a few bags of mulch and a couple of hours are all it takes to build it. You'll spend less than $5 per foot of 30-in.-wide path.

To create the path edging, we cut 18-in.-long cedar shakes in half, then pounded the 9-inch sections about halfway into the ground. Shakes are naturally rot-resistant and should last 5 to 10 years or more. And since they're tapered, they're easy to install. Bear in

Work Smart

Place a scrap 2x6 on top of each shake and pound on that if you find you're breaking shakes as you drive them in. The 2x6 will help distribute the blow more evenly across the top of the shake.

mind, shakes will split and break if you try to pound them into soil with lots of rocks, roots or heavy clay; this path works best in loose garden soil.

The landscape fabric helps prevent weeds from growing up into the path and creates a barrier so the dirt below remains separate from the path materials above.

The path material itself can be wood chips, shredded bark, decorative stone—just about anything.

Here's how to do it in three steps:

WEAR YOUR SAFETY GLASSES

CEDAR SHAKES

1 **Pound the cedar shakes into the soil using a small mallet. Stagger every other shake, overlapping the previous shake by about 1/2 in.**

2 **Trim or fold the fabric so it follows the contour of the cedar shake edging. On sloped ground, use U-shaped sod staples to hold the fabric.**

MULCH

3 **Install a 2- to 3-in. layer of wood chips, shredded bark or stone over the landscape fabric.**

Boulder wall

You don't have to be a stonemason to build a great-looking wall.

Building a dry stone retaining wall is hard work, but it's also fun. Maybe it's the low-tech appeal of doing what humans have done for thousands of years. Maybe it's the satisfaction of turning a pile of rocks into something beautiful and useful that will last for centuries. Maybe it's the challenge of fitting together a giant, three-dimensional puzzle. Whatever the reasons, many people find working with stone enjoyable and satisfying.

You can, of course, turn any pleasant project into drudgery by overdoing it. Two hours of wall-building is enjoyable exercise; six hours is an ordeal. To keep it fun, think of your wall as a summer hobby, to be plugged away at on Sunday afternoons, not a project to be completed in a weekend.

Why dry?

"Dry" simply means that mortar isn't used to cement the structure together. Rather, the stones are carefully fit into place and held there by gravity.

Mixing up and slopping on mortar are, of course, a nuisance. But that's not why we leave it out of our wall recipe. A dry stone wall, put together well, will actually outlast a mortared wall for two reasons: It can flex slightly, moving with the ground beneath it instead of cracking like a stiff mortared wall would; and since it doesn't rely on mortar, it won't fall apart as mortar wears away, as all mortar eventually does.

Do it right

Some dry stone retaining walls have stood for hundreds of years, even though they were thrown up carelessly. But building this way is a gamble. A poorly built wall may stand for decades. Then again, it may topple over next spring. Worse, it could come apart as kids play on it, resulting in broken bones. The method we show isn't the only way to build a dry stone wall, and it certainly isn't the easiest. But the extra effort pays off with safety and longevity.

Finding rocks

Gravel pits, quarries, farms and construction sites are good sources of low-cost or no-cost rock. But always ask before you take.

Getting rocks home is the hard part. Building a wall takes a lot of rock. (We used 10 tons to build our 35-ft. long, 3-ft. high wall.) So even if you have a full-size pickup truck, you'll need to make lots of trips.

1 Cut back the slope and dig a 1-ft. deep, 2-ft. wide trench at its base. Keep the topsoil and subsoil separate and pile both nearby; you'll need them for backfill. Fill the trench with a 6-in. bed of 3/4-in. stone.

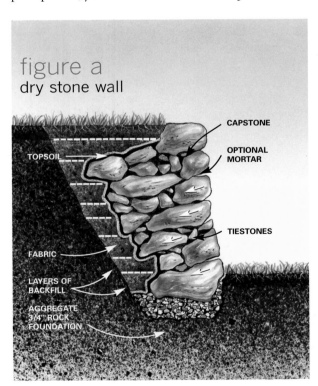

figure a
dry stone wall

CAPSTONE

OPTIONAL MORTAR

TOPSOIL

TIESTONES

FABRIC

LAYERS OF BACKFILL

AGGREGATE 3/4" ROCK FOUNDATION

A dry stone retaining wall is basically an organized pile of rocks that leans against an embankment and is held together by its own weight.

For the backyard builder, rocks fall into two categories: angular (like shale, sandstone, marble or slate) and rounded (usually granite). Angular rocks have a definite grain, sort of like wood. So the forces of geology break them into irregular blocks with flat sides and sharp, squarish edges. These flat surfaces make the rocks easier to fit together. They're also easier to split because they usually break along predictable lines.

Rounded rocks (like the ones we used) are much harder and have a less definite grain. They come in all shapes, but they tend to have humped surfaces. Fitting them together takes a lot more trial and error; you set one in place, find it's too wobbly and try another.

In most regions, Mother Nature has made choosing a rock-type simple; you just take what you can get. Still, there are a few things to keep in mind while filling your truck or trailer:

- You'll need a mix of sizes; everything from baseball-size on up. But don't play Hercules. If it's too big, leave it alone.
- The flatter a rock's surfaces are, the better. Block-shaped rocks are valuable; completely round rocks are almost worthless.
- Long rocks, which are used as "tiestones" (Photo 4), are treasures. The more you have, the stronger your wall.
- Wedge-shaped rocks are handy for "chinking" or filling in small gaps (Photo 5).

2 Lay your first course along the outer edge of the trench. Now's the time to roll into place any rocks that are too big to lift onto upper courses.

4x4

BACKFILL

LANDSCAPE FABRIC

3 Tuck landscape fabric in behind the first course, fold it over the rocks, shovel in backfill and tamp the soil down by pounding it with a post. You'll need to repeat this entire process after each course.

Rock shopping

If rocks are scarce in your area, or if you have no way to transport them, you can buy a load and have it dumped in your yard. Begin by looking in the Yellow Pages under "Stone" or by calling a landscaping supplier. But don't just phone in an order. One advantage of buying stone is that it usually gives you a choice of types and colors. So go and browse before you buy.

Prices vary widely, depending on what you get and whom you get it from. A farmer may deliver a load of fieldstone for little more than the cost of transportation. A few tons of richly colored granite from a landscaping supplier may cost you $1,000.

Planning your wall

Establish the course of your wall by laying out a garden hose and adjusting it until you establish the path you want the wall to follow. Then cut back the slope and dig the foundation trench.

Here are a few things to keep in mind as you plan your layout:

● If you have dirt hauled in (check the Yellow Pages under "Landscape") to create or enlarge a slope, it should be thoroughly soaked a couple of times—by a garden hose or rain—so it settles before you build against it.

● Big tree roots can slowly tear a wall apart; you may need to cut back any that threaten to reach your wall.

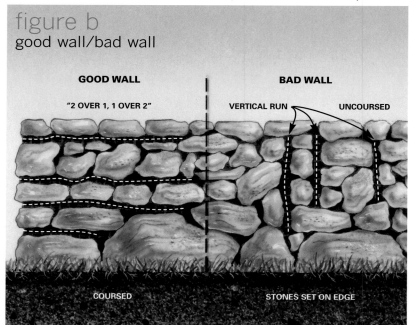

figure b
good wall/bad wall

GOOD WALL

"2 OVER 1, 1 OVER 2"

BAD WALL

VERTICAL RUN   UNCOURSED

COURSED   STONES SET ON EDGE

The left side of this wall will stand forever; the right may collapse with the next heavy rain.

THIRD COURSE

TIESTONES

LANDSCAPE FABRIC

SECOND COURSE

FIRST COURSE

LOOSE ROCK

2-LB. BLACKSMITH'S HAMMER

CHINKING STONE

4 Lay the fabric back against the slope and set the next course. Each course should be wider than the previous. Note: For clarity, we show three courses exposed here. You're better off completing an entire course before moving on to the next.

5 Drive chinking stones into the wall's face to fill gaps or secure loose rocks. Wear safety glasses to protect your eyes from shards of stone.

Foundation first

Soil moves as it gets soaked and dries, freezes and thaws. A dry stone wall is flexible and will survive centuries of minor shifting. But big shifts can make it crumble in just a few years.

That's why a simple, solid foundation and landscape fabric are good ideas. A trench lined with 3/4-in. stone provides drainage and absorbs some movement of the soil below (Photo 1). Landscape fabric (available from landscape suppliers), placed against the back side of the wall (Photo 3), keeps soil from working its way into the wall and gradually forcing stones apart.

Smart stone-setting

You build a dry stone wall by repeating three steps over and over again: Lay a "course" (a horizontal row of rocks); backfill with subsoil you removed when you cut back the slope; and "tamp" or pack down the backfill. Then on to the next course. Pretty simple, but not necessarily easy.

Work Smart

Carefully choose rocks for the face of the wall. If you have different colors, mix them into a patchwork. For a neat, geometric look, lay stones with their flat sides facing out; for a rustic look, leave rounded, irregular sides exposed.

Here are some time- and labor-saving tips:

- Building with stone is like putting together a jigsaw puzzle. So begin by spreading out the rocks just as you would the pieces of a puzzle.
- Put your best, wide, flat stones aside to be used as capstones (Photo 6).
- Use your biggest stones for the first course. That way you won't have to heave them up into place later.
- If, after the first course, you have a few biggies to raise onto the wall, use a wood plank to roll them up into place.
- Fitting stones together is mostly trial and error. Cut down on both by mentally measuring the shape and size of the stone you need first. Then go hunt for the perfect fit. You may even want to use a tape measure.
- Stone cutting is no fun. And doing it well is difficult. So we recommend you don't. But if you must, you can knock off troublesome crags or knobs with a hammer and cold chisel. *If you do, wear eye protection and keep others out of the flying-stone zone!*

6 Lay capstones, checking them with a level as you go. Capstones should bring the wall to a height roughly level with the embankment. Then tuck the fabric in behind the capstones, backfill and add topsoil.

Ten commandments of stonebuilding

1. Make "one over two, two over one" your wall-building motto. Lay the stones of one course over the vertical gaps between stones of the previous course; just like a bricklayer lays bricks. If you don't do this, you get "vertical run" and a weaker wall (Figure B).

2. Use tiestones, long rocks laid perpendicular to the face of the wall (Photo 4). You'll need one tiestone at least every 4 ft. on each course. But you can't have too many; the more tiestones, the stronger the wall.

3. All rocks on the face of the wall must slant down toward the inside of the wall. Those that don't will eventually fall out (Figure A).

4. Keep it roughly coursed. If you're working with very irregular stone, you're likely to build jagged, uneven courses. This makes the next course harder to fit together. Soon you have no courses at all and lots of vertical run. Try instead for roughly even courses, by avoiding peaks and filling in valleys with smaller stones (Figure B).

5. Lay rocks flat, not on edge (Figure B).

6. Use chinking, small stone wedges driven between larger rocks, to tighten up loose-fitting rocks and fill gaps in the wall's face (Figure A).

A freestanding wall

A freestanding dry stone wall is similar to a retaining wall, but with a few variations. You have to be more fussy about the fit of the stones. A retaining wall leans against a solid mound of earth. A freestanding wall leans in on itself, so the two faces must slant into each other and lock together. The key to a strong freestanding wall is "V-slant." Each course must be highest at the faces, with a gradual depression in the middle. With each stone tilting down toward the middle, gravity holds each in place and the entire wall together.

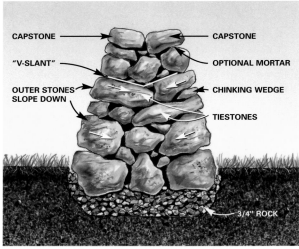

A freestanding dry stone wall should be as wide at its base as it is tall. Both faces should lean inward at least 2 in. for each foot of height. Amateurs shouldn't build freestanding walls more than 3 ft. tall.

7. Make it as thick as it is high. If your wall—especially a freestanding one—will rise 3 ft. above the ground at its base, the bottom course should be 3 ft. thick.

8. Don't build retaining walls more than 4 ft. high. The higher the wall, the more skill required to build it right.

9. Don't make the face of the wall perfectly vertical. To hold back all that earth, it must lean into the slope. A minimum of 2 in. of backward tilt for each foot of height is a good rule of thumb.

10. Mortar if you must. You should have large, tight-fitting capstones that will stay solidly in place by themselves. If not, cement them with a mortar mix like Quikrete or Sakrete (Figure A).

Simple walkway ideas

Steppingstone form

Don't discard that partial bag of concrete mix! Build your own steppingstone form from a 5-gallon bucket. Cut around a 5-gallon bucket just above the handle. Set the cutout ring on a sheet of plywood and fill it with concrete. When the concrete has set, remove the form—you now have your first homemade steppingstone.

project at a glance

skill level
beginner

special tools
**5-gallon bucket
trowel**

approximate cost
**$1 per
steppingstone**

Edge a concrete walk

Dress up a plain concrete walk with a border of bricks placed in a line or a basketweave pattern. Bluestone or flagstone pieces, cut at the quarry in pieces 6 in. to 1 ft. wide and at least 1 ft. long, also look handsome along the edges of a walk or a cement patio. Large Belgian pavers like those shown in the photo work well too: Their extra width keeps weeds away from the walk; their weight holds them firmly in place; and their warm, golden color and rough texture make a nice contrast with plain concrete.

No matter which type you choose, set the pavers in about 2 in. of pea gravel. It'll keep the pavers from settling or heaving and lets you easily adjust their height during installation.

project at a glance

skill level
beginner

special tools
shovel

approximate cost
$1 per paver

PAVERS

PEA GRAVEL

Modular concrete retaining wall

Get an attractive, hardworking wall with this DIY-friendly project.

Until concrete retaining wall systems muscled their way onto the scene 20 years ago, there were few do-it-yourself-friendly materials to choose from. Rock and stone were labor intensive to gather (or expensive to buy) and tricky to install. Treated timbers, despite claims to the contrary, often rotted within 15 years. Railroad ties looked like, well, railroad ties, and other options, like poured concrete

or mortared brick, were best left to the pros. But concrete retaining wall systems—easy to install, widely available, reasonably priced, long-lasting and available in a wide selection of colors and patterns—changed all that.

A retaining wall can solve

EASY FOR EVERYONE

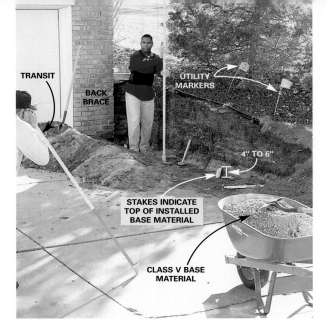

TRANSIT

BACK BRACE

UTILITY MARKERS

4" TO 6"

STAKES INDICATE TOP OF INSTALLED BASE MATERIAL

CLASS V BASE MATERIAL

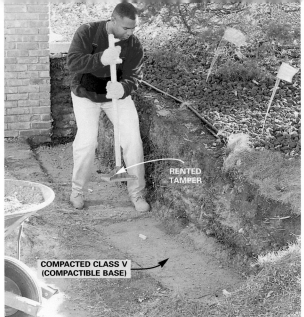

RENTED TAMPER

COMPACTED CLASS V (COMPACTIBLE BASE)

1 Excavate and level the area where you'll be installing the wall. Use a transit or a 4-ft. level taped to a straight 2x4 to establish a common stake height, indicating the top of your sand leveling bed (see Figure A). Create a flat area at least 4 to 6 in. deep and 24 to 28 in. wide for installing compactable base material. Provide a clear area of at least 12 in. behind the wall for installing the crushed rock as shown in Photo 7.

2 Install 4 to 6 in. of base material level to the tops of the stakes, then compact it until it's about 1 in. below the tops. Rent a hand tamper (about $5 a day) for small projects, or a gas-powered tamper (about $50 for a half day) for walls more than 30 ft. long.

many problems. It can convert steep, hard-to-mow hills into terraced, usable planting beds. It can prevent erosion, help level a patio, create tree borders or add visual interest to a rolling yard.

The retaining wall system we installed uses nylon pins to align and secure horizontal rows of 80-lb. blocks. Other block systems use lips, gravity and filled cores to connect rows and increase strength. Your system may differ, but most of the preparation and installation steps remain the same. Here's how to install your wall.

Don't skimp on time, tools or materials

The wall we built was a weekend-long project, and an exhausting one at that. It took a day to rip out the old, collapsing retaining wall, to dig farther into the hill to provide room for the backfill gravel and to help unload materials. It took another day to install the base, blocks and backfill.

Before launching into this project, contact your local building code official. Depending on the height and location of your wall, there may be structural, drainage and setback (the distance from wall to property line) considerations. A permit may be required.

Unless you own a heavy-duty truck (and back!), have your blocks, compactable base, sand and backfill gravel delivered. Blocks may cost slightly more at specialty landscaping stores than at home centers, but landscaping stores are often better equipped to deliver the small batches of base, sand and gravel that you'll need for this wall.

We used a transit level (Photo 1) to establish a flat base. But unless you own or rent one and know how to use it properly, just use a 4-ft. level taped to a long, straight 2x4, especially for short walls. The tamper, brick tongs and block chisel are available at rental yards.

Plan Smart

For safety's sake, call your utility companies and have them mark the location of underground wires and pipes; the service is usually free. For more information, call the North American One-Call Referral System at 888-258-0808.

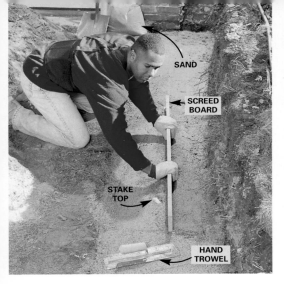

SAND

SCREED BOARD

STAKE TOP

HAND TROWEL

NATIVE SOIL

4' LEVEL

GRADE LEVEL

TORPEDO LEVEL

STRING LINE

BRICK TONG

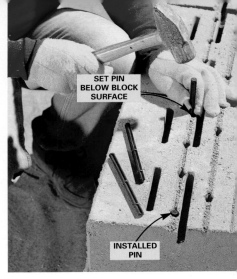

SET PIN BELOW BLOCK SURFACE

INSTALLED PIN

3 Provide a flat-as-a-pancake sand base for installing the first course of blocks. With the tops of the stakes as guides, use a long, straight screed board to level the sand. A hand trowel is good for fine-tuning small dips and humps.

4 Install the first course of blocks, using a taut string line to establish a straight row. Use a 4-ft. level to level blocks lengthwise and a torpedo level to level them front to back. Once the first row is installed, pack native soil to grade level on both sides to anchor the wall in place. The brick tong makes handling and positioning the 80-lb. blocks easier and safer.

5 Drive in the pins to lock courses to one another and help establish the 3/4-in. backset for each row. Use an extra pin to set the installed pins below the surface of the blocks so they don't interfere with blocks on the next row. To maintain wall strength, offset the vertical joints of the row you're installing at least 4 in. from those of the row below.

figure a
anatomy of a retaining wall

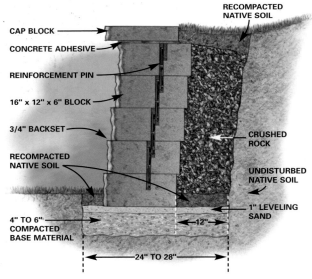

RECOMPACTED NATIVE SOIL

CAP BLOCK

CONCRETE ADHESIVE

REINFORCEMENT PIN

16" x 12" x 6" BLOCK

3/4" BACKSET

RECOMPACTED NATIVE SOIL

CRUSHED ROCK

UNDISTURBED NATIVE SOIL

1" LEVELING SAND

4" TO 6" COMPACTED BASE MATERIAL

12"

24" TO 28"

A retaining wall is only as straight and solid as its base. For a 4-ft. tall wall, excavate a trench deep enough to accommodate 4 to 6 in. of compacted base, 1 in. of leveling sand and half the height of the first course of blocks. Step succeeding courses back 3/4 in., overlap vertical joints at least 4 in. and secure one row to the next with pins. Backfill with crushed rock, except for the top, where you should install a 6-in. "cap" of native soil to help keep surface water from entering the rock-filled trench. Use concrete adhesive to secure the cap blocks.

Build straight and solid from start to finish

Starting with a solid, level and well-compacted base is an absolute necessity. Failure to do this will result in a weak, wavy wall. Bear in mind:

● If your wall is higher than 4 ft., most concrete block manufacturers require extra engineering and installation steps not shown here. These steps range from using special reinforcement fabric to installing a series of terraces rather than one tall wall. Most manufacturers provide good printed installation guidelines. If you purchase your blocks from a specialty landscape center, there may be an on-site designer or engineer to help you.

● Contact local utility companies to mark the location of underground wires and pipes. Telephone and cable TV wires are often buried just beneath the surface.

Plan Smart

If your wall borders a sidewalk or deck, you may need a code-compliant rail. Contact your local building code department.

HAND-PROTECTING BLOCK CHISEL

V-GROOVE

6 Cut blocks to size by first scoring the top and bottom with a block chisel, then turning the block on its side and finishing the task with a series of solid blows.

CRUSHED ROCK

7 Backfill behind the retaining wall with crushed gravel. Crushed, rather than smooth, gravel locks together and helps direct backfill pressure downward (rather than outward). The backfill also provides a fast path for water drainage and acts as a tree root barrier.

● In the Midwest, the compactible base material shown in Photo 2 is often referred to as "Class V" (as in the Roman numeral for five). In other regions, the rock may vary and the material may go by a different name. The important quality of the material is its different-sized rock and sand particles that interlock and compact to create a solid base. It's the same material used be-neath roadbeds and paver patios. Make sure you use the right stuff. It's NOT the same as the crushed gravel you use for backfill.

● The 16-in. wide x 12-in. deep x 6-in. high blocks we installed weigh 80 lbs. each. A brick tong (Photo 4) doesn't make them lighter, but it does make them less clumsy to handle, easier to position and less likely to crush fingers.

Work Smart

Install that first row of blocks dead level. Otherwise those dips and humps will haunt you with each succeeding course.

CONCRETE ADHESIVE

CAP BLOCKS

8 Install the cap blocks using two 1/4-in. beads of concrete adhesive to secure them in place. Cap blocks can be positioned with a slight overhang or back-set, or set flush with the wall face.

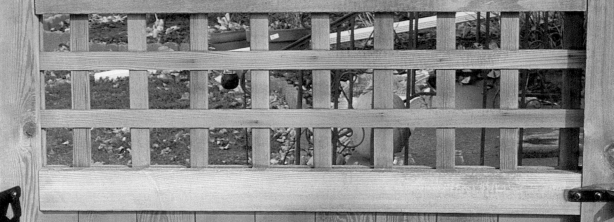

Renew your wood fence

Shabby to handsome in three easy steps.

When did your cedar fence lose its rich, warm glow? Who invited that discolored, shabby-looking impostor into the neighborhood? Don't worry—underneath that thin gray skin, the glow still remains. All you have to do is remove the surface layer of aged wood cells to expose a fresh layer of wood. With a power washer, it's as easy as washing your car. Then apply an exterior wood oil stain to preserve this new layer of wood. It'll prolong the life of your fence to boot.

project at a glance

skill level
beginner

special tools
power washer
staining supplies

approximate cost
varies

Wash

Repair

Stain

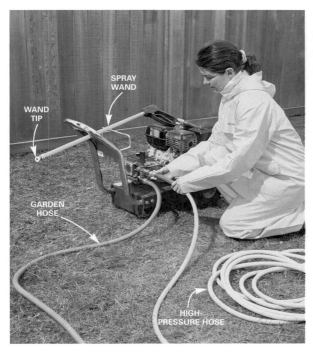

WAND TIP

SPRAY WAND

GARDEN HOSE

HIGH-PRESSURE HOSE

1 Connect a garden hose and the power washer hose to the machine. Snap a 25-degree tip onto the end of the wand. Turn on the water to the garden hose and pull the trigger on the spray wand until water squirts out. Now start up the power washer's engine.

2 Hold the tip of the wand about 18 in. from the fence and move it the length of the boards. Pull the trigger and keep the sprayer tip moving to avoid gouging the wood. Use a variety of attack angles to strip inside corners.

Power washing makes the huge cleaning task easy

Power washers are aggressive. They'll strip the wood as well as clean off the dirt and grime, but you can also erode the wood too deeply and ruin it. The key is to use the right sprayer tip and technique. In any case, the power washer's spray will slightly raise and roughen the grain on smooth wood. That's actually good—it allows more sealer to soak in and improves the finish.

SPRAYER TIP

Power washers cost about $40 to rent for four hours. Rent one that operates at 1,500 or 2,000 psi and avoid more powerful 3,000 or 3,500 psi units. Be sure to get both 15- and 25-degree spray tips. Have the rental people demonstrate the washer's use. It's an easy machine to run.

To avoid damaging the pump, don't run the power washer without first filling the pump and hoses with water. To do this, attach both hoses (Photo 1), snap in a 25-degree tip, turn on the garden hose spigot and hold down the trigger on the wand until water squirts out. Release the wand trigger and start the engine. If it's hard to pull the start cord, pull the wand trigger to release the water pressure.

Start spraying with the wand tip 18 in. from the wood surface. Move in closer as you swing the tip slowly along the length of the board (Photo 2). Keep the width of the fan spray aligned across the boards. The wood's color will brighten as the surface is stripped away. Watch closely and stop stripping when no more color change occurs. You don't have to remove too much surface to expose fresh wood, and continuing to spray won't improve the color.

It takes a little practice to arrive at the proper tip distance and speed of movement, but you'll catch on fast. It's better to make two or three passes than to risk gouging the surface trying to accomplish this job in one pass. As you gain experience, you can switch to a 15-degree tip. This tip cuts more aggressively and works faster than the 25-degree tip.

tip Clear the area along the fence by tying back plants that are growing alongside it. Wear water-repellent clothing—you will get wet from the spray.

3 Glue split and broken pieces when the wood has dried for at least 24 hours. Apply waterproof glue and clamp or tape the pieces firmly together.

4 Drive weather-resistant or stainless steel screws to tighten loose boards. Recess the head 1/4 in. and fill with a light-colored caulk.

5 Realign sagging gates with a turnbuckle. We spray-painted the shiny turnbuckle black to make it less conspicuous.

6 Brush a wood preservative into the posts around the base to help prevent rot at this vulnerable area.

Simple repairs add years to the life of your fence

With the fence clean, it's time to fix or replace damaged boards, refasten loose boards and countersink any protruding nails. Use waterproof glue (Photo 3) to repair any split and broken boards. Drive corrosion-resistant screws (Photo 4) instead of nails to pull loose pieces tightly together. If a gate is sagging, straighten it with a turnbuckle support (Photo 5). Also coat the posts (Photo 6) where they emerge from the ground or concrete with a wood preservative. This is the area that rots first.

7 Roll into the dry wood a soaking coat of semitransparent stain. Coat about 3 ft. of fence, then proceed to
the step shown in Photo 8.

8 Brush the stain (backbrush) into the wood grain and
all corners and gaps. Brush out any runs or drips.

Stain makes the fence look brand new

To preserve the natural color of the wood, use an exterior semitransparent oil stain. It seals the wood while allowing the grain and color variations to show through. And its pigments add an overall color tone. Make sure the stain contains ultraviolet inhibitors, which will slow down bleaching by sunlight, and a mildewcide to slow fungal growth. Look for samples applied to cedar at the paint store, or bring in your own piece of wood to test. A test sample is the best way to ensure a satisfactory result.

Before applying the stain, be sure the fence is dry. Allow at least 24 hours. If it's cool and humid, allow another 24 hours.

Use a paint roller with a "medium nap" cover (Photo 7) to apply a soaking coat to the wood. Let the wood absorb as much sealer as it can. Roll about a 3-ft. section

9 Work the stain into small and tight areas with a trim roller and a 2-in. brush. One generous coat should be enough.

of fence and then brush (Photo 8) the sealer into the wood. If the wood still appears dry, roll on additional sealer. Work the sealer into all recesses and corners. The roller applies the stain, but you need the brush to work it well into the wood's surface. Coat detailed areas with a trim roller and smaller brush (Photo 9). Keep wet edges to prevent lap marks.

Most semitransparent oil stains are guaranteed to last two to five years. (Solid-color stains last longer but are more difficult to renew.) Fences usually face severe weathering, so expect the finish to last no more than three years. Plan on recoating the fence within this time frame to keep your fence looking fresh. Before recoating, wash the fence with a garden hose sprayer and use a bristle brush on stubborn dirt deposits and stains. Let the fence dry and stain it using the same method.

Yard

& Garden

5 tips for a perfect lawn

Have the greenest grass on the block.

The average homeowner spends nearly four hours per week on yard work and mows their lawn 30 times a year. That's a good chunk of time, but believe it or not, your lawn pays you back for all this work. It serves as a gigantic air conditioner to help cool your home. It releases a tremendous amount of oxygen and captures tons of dirt and dust to keep you and your family healthier. It even gives you a nice place to play croquet. And the healthier your lawn is, the better it can keep up its end of the bargain.

To a great extent, it's not the amount of work you put into your lawn—it's when and how you do it. Here are five simple tips.

TIP #1

Use a sharp blade and adjust the cutting height based on the time of year

For cool-climate grasses, use a 1-1/2 in. cutting height for the first mowing of the year to remove dead grass and allow more sunlight to reach the crowns of the grass plants. Raise the blade during the heat of summer to 2 or more inches. Then lower the blade back to 1-1/2 in. for the last cutting of the year. For warm-climate grasses, these heights will be about 1/2 in. lower.

When adjusting your blade height, measure from a hard surface to the bottom of the mower deck, then add 1/4 in. (most blades sit 1/4 in. above the bottom of the deck). Cut your grass using a sharp blade; a dull one tears grass rather than cutting it cleanly. Damaged grass turns yellow, requires more water and nutrients to recover, and is more susceptible to disease. Sharpening and balancing a blade three times a year is usually enough to maintain a good cutting edge.

CLEAN CUT   RAGGED CUT

TIP #2

Give your lawn a few good soakings rather than lots of light sprinklings (but not at night)

Deep watering helps develop deep roots that tap into subsurface water supplies. Light sprinklings wet only the grass and surface of the soil; this encourages shallow root growth and increases the need for more frequent watering. As a general rule, lawns require 1 to 2 in. of water per week (from you or Mother Nature), applied at three- or four-day intervals. But this varies greatly depending on the temperature, type of grass and soil conditions. Lawns in sandy soils may need twice as much water, since they drain quickly. Lawns in slow-draining clay soils may need only half as much.

When your lawn loses its resiliency, or when it wilts, exposing the dull green bottoms of the blades, it needs water. Water until the soil is moist 4 to 5 in. down, then wait to water again until the top 1 or 2 in. of soil dries out. The best time of day to water is early morning. Water pressure is high, less water is lost to evaporation and your lawn has time to dry out before nightfall. Lawns that remain wet overnight are more susceptible to disease caused by moisture-loving mold and other fungi.

TIP #3

Mow only the top one-third of the grass blade (and don't rake up the clippings)

The top one-third of a blade of grass is thin and "leafy," decomposes quickly when cut and can contribute up to one-third of the nitrogen your lawn needs. While decomposing, this light layer of clippings also helps slow water evaporation and keeps weeds from germinating in the soil below. The bottom two-thirds of a blade of grass is tough, "stemmy" and slow to decompose. It contributes to thatch, which—when thick enough—prevents sunlight, air, water and nutrients from reaching the soil. Cutting more than the top third also shocks grass roots and exposes stems, which tend to burn in direct sunlight.

This means if 2 in. is your target grass length, cut it when it reaches 3 in. Since grass grows at different rates at different times of the year, "every Saturday" isn't necessarily the best time to mow. The ideal length for cool-climate grasses is 3 to 4 in.; for warm-climate, 1 to 2 in. Mow when the grass is dry and avoid mowing in the heat of the day when you're more likely to stress the grass—and yourself.

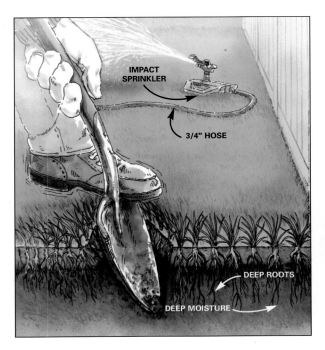

IMPACT SPRINKLER

3/4" HOSE

DEEP ROOTS

DEEP MOISTURE

ONE-THIRD OF GRASS HEIGHT

TIP #4

Apply fertilizers and weed killers at the right time of year

When applying weed killers and fertilizers, take into account variables such as geographic location, grass type, weed type and soil conditions. Here are a few general guidelines:

● The best defense against weeds is a thick, healthy lawn that doesn't provide weed seeds adequate sunlight or open space to germinate.

● Attack weeds in the early spring and summer before they have a chance to develop deep root systems, go to seed or reproduce.

● Eradicate grassy weeds like crabgrass with preemergent weed killers, which destroy germinating plants just as they sprout. Broadleaf weeds need to be attacked while they're young and actively growing; spraying the leaves of individual plants or patches of plants is most effective.

● Fertilize in early spring to jump-start root development. Fall feedings help repair summer damage and spur the root growth that goes on for several weeks even after the top growth stops; this helps grass survive the winter. Light feedings in between help maintain healthy growth. Make sure to read the package; some chemicals work only in the presence of moisture; others are rendered useless by water.

TIP #5

Aerate your lawn to help it "breathe"

Grass roots need oxygen as well as water and nutrients. Aerating—the process of removing small plugs of soil—produces multiple benefits. It improves air-to-soil interaction, allows water and fertilizer to penetrate the soil deeper, reduces soil compaction, and opens space for roots to grow. It removes some thatch and stimulates the breakdown of the remaining thatch. The best tool for this task is a gas-powered aerator, available at most rental centers.

Timing is critical. You can aerate in the spring. But fall—after the kids are through trampling the grass and there are fewer weed seeds to set up home in the open spaces—is the best time to aerate. It's usually best to aerate first, then apply any weed killers so the open holes are protected against weeds.

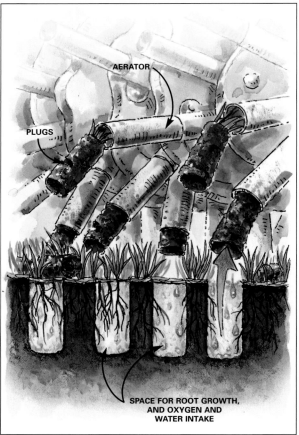

AERATOR

PLUGS

SPACE FOR ROOT GROWTH, AND OXYGEN AND WATER INTAKE

LAYER OF PREEMERGENT HERBICIDE

Micro irrigation

Reduce the time you spend watering to practically zero.

Whether you're growing roses to win prizes or just trying to keep a few flowerbeds looking good, you know what a chore watering is, lugging hoses around the yard and moving them every half hour or so. Micro irrigation—a network of plastic tubing and low-volume drippers and sprinklers that reach every part of the garden you want to water—takes the hassle out of watering.

The materials are inexpensive (you can get started for less than $100) and easy to install using nothing more than a pruning shears and a special hole punch tool. Once you lay out the tubing and connect the drippers, sprinklers or sprayers, you'll be able to water your plants by simply turning on the water and letting it run for an hour or two. Add a battery-operated controller for about $40 more and you won't even have to remember to turn on the water. It'll turn the water on and off automatically at the times you select.

Micro irrigation saves more than time and energy; it saves water by distributing it more efficiently. Because you use dozens of watering devices to replace one regular sprinkler, you have much greater control over where the water goes and how much is supplied to each plant. Instead of flooding the ground all at once, micro irrigation lets you apply a small amount over longer periods, allowing it to soak into the plants' root zone for maximum benefit. And since runoff and evaporation are kept to a minimum, micro irrigation uses less water.

In this article, we'll introduce you to the basics of micro irrigation, including planning tips and step-by-step installation instructions. For more details, especially in the planning phase, we recommend that you also read through one of the manufacturers' free planning guides or browse the Internet sites we've listed (see Buyer's Guide on p. 168).

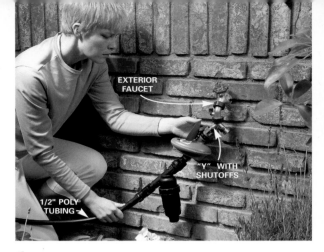

EXTERIOR FAUCET

"Y" WITH SHUTOFFS

1/2" POLY TUBING

1/2" POLY TUBING

1 Mount a "Y" with shutoff valves to your faucet. Then attach the optional timer, backflow preventer, filter, pressure regulator and adapter.

2 Connect the 1/2-in. poly tubing to the faucet end. Then lay the tubing through the garden according to your plan. Stake it down about every 5 or 6 ft.

Make a sketch and plan the system

The basic planning strategy is to pick the best watering device to serve each type of plant. Then determine a flow rate that supplies adequate water to every plant in the watering zone. Set up the system to run between one and two hours at a time, two or three times a week.

Start by measuring your garden and making a simple sketch. Choose the type and flow rate of the watering devices based on your soil and the plants' water needs. Mark these on the plan and draw in the tubing route to connect them. This will involve a little guesswork. See "Drippers, Bubblers, Sprinklers and Sprayers" on p. 168

for information that will help you choose the right watering device. Try to cover all the root zones of your plants. Don't worry about getting everything perfect at first. Add a few extra of each type of watering device and buy the watering devices, tubing and the basic parts shown in Figure B for the faucet hookup. Once you see how the system works, you'll find it's easy to relocate or add emitters to get a more balanced water flow or better coverage.

tip If this is your first venture into micro irrigation, start small and experiment to get a feel for how the system works. Choose one or two flowerbeds or a garden and install a simple one-zone system.

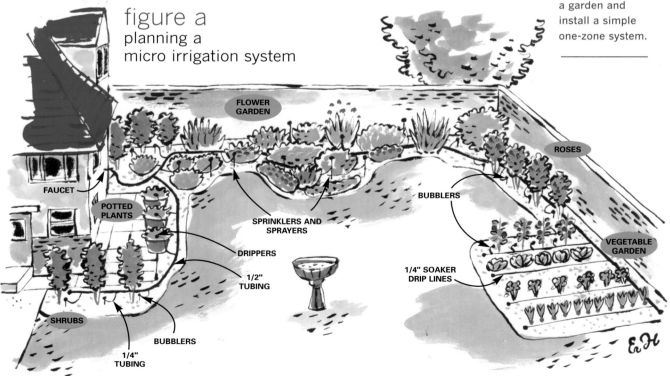

figure a
planning a
micro irrigation system

FLOWER GARDEN

ROSES

FAUCET

BUBBLERS

POTTED PLANTS

SPRINKLERS AND SPRAYERS

VEGETABLE GARDEN

DRIPPERS

1/2" TUBING

1/4" SOAKER DRIP LINES

SHRUBS

BUBBLERS

1/4" TUBING

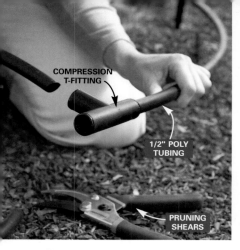

COMPRESSION T-FITTING

1/2" POLY TUBING

PRUNING SHEARS

HOLE PUNCH TOOL

1/2" POLY TUBING

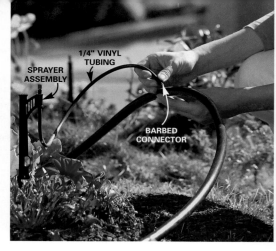

1/4" VINYL TUBING

SPRAYER ASSEMBLY

BARBED CONNECTOR

3 Cut the tubing with a pruning shears and install T- and 90-degree fittings where they're needed. Twist and press the tubing firmly into the fitting.

4 Punch holes in the tubing wherever you want to install a watering device. Push and twist until the tip of the punch creates a clean hole.

5 Press a barbed connector into the hole in the 1/2-in. tubing. If the 1/4-in. tubing isn't already attached, add a length of 1/4-in. tubing to reach your dripper, sprayer or sprinkler location.

Planning rules of thumb:

- Use 1/2-gph (gallons per hour) drippers in clay soil, 1-gph drippers in loam and 2-gph drippers in sandy soil.
- Add the gph rate of all drippers, bubblers, sprayers and sprinklers you plan to use. If you're using 1/2-in. tubing for the main line, limit the total to between 150 and 220 gallons per hour (check with the manufacturer).

- Limit the length of 1/2-in. tubing on one zone to a maximum of about 200 ft.
- Limit the total gph on a length of 1/4-in. tubing to 25 to 30.

As you add to the system, it's best to divide your yard into groups of plants that have similar watering requirements. With this strategy, you add a separate system (zone), starting at the water source, for each group of plants or area of the yard.

For help with planning a large, more complicated system (and for the best prices), work with a retailer that specializes in selling micro irrigation products (see Buyer's Guide on p. 168).

Begin at the outside faucet

Figure B and Photo 1 show the parts you'll need and the order in which to install them. The Y-splitter with shutoffs allows you to keep the drip system on all the time (and operated by a controller) and still use your regular garden hose (Photo 1). You don't have to use a controller, but you must use a backflow preventer. Some of these components are available with hose thread or pipe thread, so make sure to match the thread type when you buy parts. Joining hose thread to pipe thread will result in leaks.

Lay the 1/2-in. tubing

Next, run the 1/2-in. tubing to the garden bed (Photo 2) and position it according to your plan. The tubing will be more flexible and easier to work with if you let it sit in the sun for a while to warm up. Remember, you

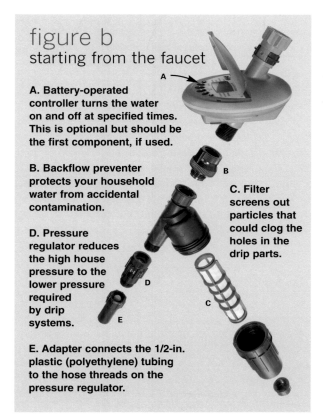

figure b
starting from the faucet

A. Battery-operated controller turns the water on and off at specified times. This is optional but should be the first component, if used.

B. Backflow preventer protects your household water from accidental contamination.

C. Filter screens out particles that could clog the holes in the drip parts.

D. Pressure regulator reduces the high house pressure to the lower pressure required by drip systems.

E. Adapter connects the 1/2-in. plastic (polyethylene) tubing to the hose threads on the pressure regulator.

Drippers, bubblers, sprinklers and sprayers

One of the first things you'll notice when you're browsing the brochures or Web sites is a wide variety of watering devices. Here are the basic types and a few things you need to know about each one. While the ones shown here are the most common, there are many other, more specialized emitters. See the micro irrigation catalogs for the other types and their uses.

Drippers (20¢ to 70¢ each)

Use these to water individual plants, or buy "inline" drippers and use them in a series with a 1/4-in. tube. Drippers work great for container plants too. They're color-coded for different flow rates between 1/2 gph (gallons per hour) and 4 gph. In general, use lower flow rates for less porous soil, like clay, to allow more time for the water to soak in. Buy pressure-compensating (PC) drippers to maintain a steady flow despite the water pressure.

Bubblers (45¢ to 70¢ each)

A cross between drippers and sprayers, many bubblers are adjustable for flows up to 35 gph and diameters to 18 in. Since they put out more water than drippers, they're good for larger plants like roses, tomatoes and shrubs.

Soaker drip line (20¢ to 35¢ per linear foot)

Also called emitter tubing, drip line consists of 1/2-in. or 1/4-in. tubing with built-in drippers. It's available with emitters spaced different distances apart for different flow rates. Drip line is great for vegetable gardens or rows of plants. You can use it to encircle shrubs and large plants, or lay it out in a grid pattern as a substitute for sprinklers in a densely planted flowerbed. Use 1/4-in. drip line for maximum flexibility.

Sprinklers (45¢ to $2 each)

These are miniature versions of sprinklers you might use in the yard. Most have flow rates between 14 and 40 gph and cover a radius of 3 to 30 ft. Since most sprinklers have a relatively high flow rate, you can't use more than about 15 or 20 in one zone of 1/2-in. tubing.

Sprayers (45¢ to $1.70 each)

These are like sprinklers without moving parts. You can choose a spray pattern from a quarter circle up to a full circle, or buy sprayers with adjustable spray patterns. They spray from 4 to 34 gph and up to a radius of about 12 ft. Use sprayers to water ground cover or densely planted flowerbeds.

Buyer's Guide

- DIG Irrigation Products: (800) 322-9146. www.digcorp.com. Free planning guide available where DIG products are sold. Products available at retail and online stores.

- DripWorks: (800) 522-3747. www.dripworks.com. Free design service. Catalog and mail order sales. Excellent Web site and online sales.

- The Drip Store: (866) 682-1580. www.dripirrigation.com. Step-by-step online tutorial, forum and shopping for all your micro irrigation needs.

- Raindrip: (877) 237-3747. www.raindrip.com. "Micro-Watering Handbook" is free where RAINDRIP products are sold. Free phone advice. Call and ask for Dr. Drip to answer your micro irrigation questions.

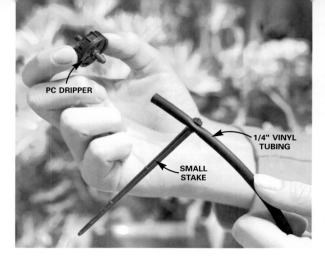

PC DRIPPER

1/4" VINYL TUBING

SMALL STAKE

6 Press pressure-compensating (PC) drippers, sprinklers or sprayers onto the end of the 1/4-in. tubing. Use a stake to support the dripper and anchor it in the root zone of the plant.

HOSE END CAP

STAKE

7 Flush the system by running water through it. Then use end cap fittings to close the open ends of the 1/2-in. tubing.

can cover the tubing with decorative mulch later to hide it. Cut the tubing with a pruning shears. Use T-fittings to create branches and elbows to make 90-degree bends (Photo 3). Be aware that there are a few different sizes of what's called "1/2-in." tubing, depending on which brand you use. Buy fittings to match the brand of tubing you're using. If you need to join two different brands of tubing or you're not sure which you have, you can buy universal fittings that will work on all diameters of tubing. Use special plastic tubing clamps to nail the tubing to the house or deck.

You can bury 1/2-in. poly tubing in a shallow trench to conceal it as it crosses a path or small section of lawn, but for longer lengths, especially in high-traffic areas, we recommend substituting 1/2-in. PVC pipe instead. Buy adapters to connect the 1/2-in. poly tubing to the ends of the PVC pipe. Check with your local plumbing inspector before burying any pipe to see whether special backflow prevention is required.

Connect the emitters

Now add the various types of emitters for the particular plants—drippers, sprayers, sprinklers or drip line. The technique is simple. Use a hole punch tool to poke a hole in the tubing wherever you want to add a watering device (Photo 4). You can insert a dripper directly into the hole in the 1/2-in. tubing or use a barbed connector and connect a length of 1/4-in. vinyl tubing. Then connect a watering device to the end of the 1/4-in. tube (Photo 6).

You can buy sprinklers and sprayers as assemblies that include a barbed connector, a short

BARBED CONNECTOR

length of 1/4-in. tubing and a plastic stake (Photo 6), or buy the parts separately and assemble them yourself. Remember to buy a selection of 1/4-in. barbed fittings, including T-fittings, elbows, connectors and hole plugs. You can press any of these fittings into a punched hole in the 1/2-in. line and connect 1/4-in. tubes to feed the emitters. T-fittings allow you to run 1/4-in. tubing in opposite directions from the main line or to branch off a 1/4-in. tube. Use connectors to extend a 1/4-in. tube that's too short. If you punch a hole in the wrong spot or want to remove a fitting, push a hole plug into the hole to seal it.

When your installation is complete, run water through the tubing to flush out any dirt. Then cap the ends (Photo 7). Now you're ready to turn on the water and see how your new micro irrigation system works. Let the water run for an hour. Then check around your plants to make sure the root zone has been thoroughly wetted. Fine-tune the system by adjusting the length of time you water or by adding or relocating watering devices.

Maintain your system

- Clean the filter once a month (more often if you have well water with a lot of sediment).
- Inspect the drippers occasionally to make sure they're working.
- In cold climates, prepare for winter by removing the shutoff Y-splitter, backflow preventer, controller, filter and pressure regulator and bringing them inside. Remove end plugs and drain or blow the water out of the system. Replace the caps and plug the faucet end of the tubing as well.

Simple deck

Just follow these step-by-step photos.

We can't promise you a beachfront view, but we know you'll enjoy relaxing on this simple deck wherever you choose to build it. Since it's at ground level and is freestanding, you don't have to fuss with challenging railings or footings. All you need are basic carpentry tools and a relatively flat area in your yard or garden. The foundation is nothing more than 4x6 treated timbers buried in the soil, with decorative treated joists and construction-grade cedar decking and a bench. Follow the instructions along with the photos for detailed measurements and building techniques.

materials list

QTY.	SIZE	DESCRIPTION
2	4x6 x 12'	treated timbers
9	2x6 x 10'	cedar joists
2	2x6 x 10'	cedar for blocking
1	2x12 x 10'	cedar bench supports
2	2x6 x 10'	cedar bench tops
22	2x6 x 12	cedar decking
32		metal corner brackets
3 lbs.		galv. joist hanger nails
2 lbs.		No. 8 galv. box nails
10 lbs.		16d galv. casing nails
1 lb.		3-in. galv. deck screws

project at a glance

skill level
beginner

special tools
circular saw
jigsaw

approximate cost
$900

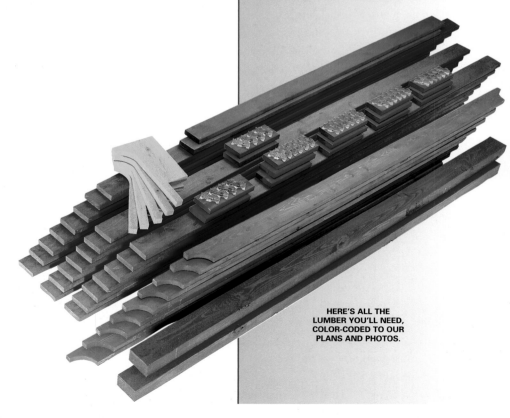

HERE'S ALL THE LUMBER YOU'LL NEED, COLOR-CODED TO OUR PLANS AND PHOTOS.

EASY FOR EVERYONE

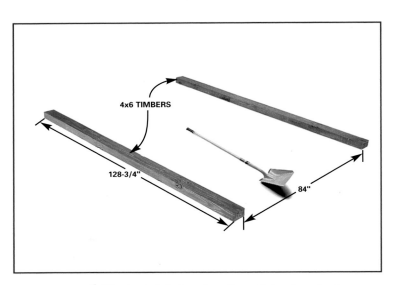

4x6 TIMBERS

128-3/4"

84"

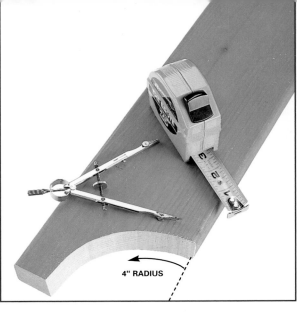

4" RADIUS

1 Dig the 4x6 timbers into the soil, leaving about 1-1/2 in. of the top exposed. The timbers must be parallel and the diagonal measurements must be equal.

2 Cut each treated 2x6 joist to 10 ft. Cut the decorative curve on each end, as shown, before installing them onto the 4x6 treated timbers.

FIRST BLOCK IS 13-1/4"

ALIGN FACE OF FIRST JOIST WITH END OF TIMBER

REMAINDER OF BLOCKS ARE 14-1/2"

Tool List

- Shovel
- Square
- Tape measure
- Level
- Compass
- Chalk line
- Jigsaw
- Hammer
- Circular saw
- Hearing and eye protection, gloves

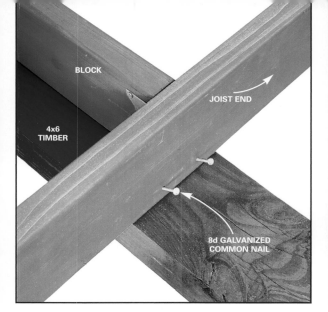

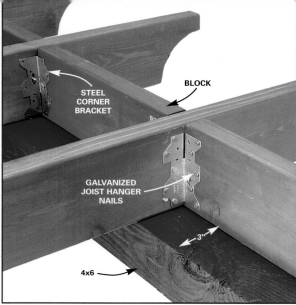

3 Lay out the joist spacing so the joists are on 16-in. centers. Cut the blocks to fit between the joists. The first set of blocks (one on each side) will be 13-1/4 in., while the remainder will be 14-1/2 in. long. Toenail each joist to the timber as shown. Be sure the ends of all the joists align with each other as you toenail them in place.

4 Nail your steel corner brackets to the joists and each block between with 1-1/4 in. galvanized joist hanger nails. The blocks add stability and give the deck a finished look.

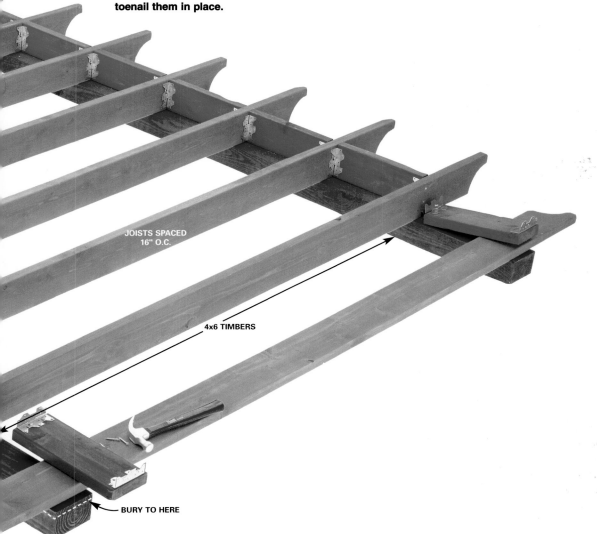

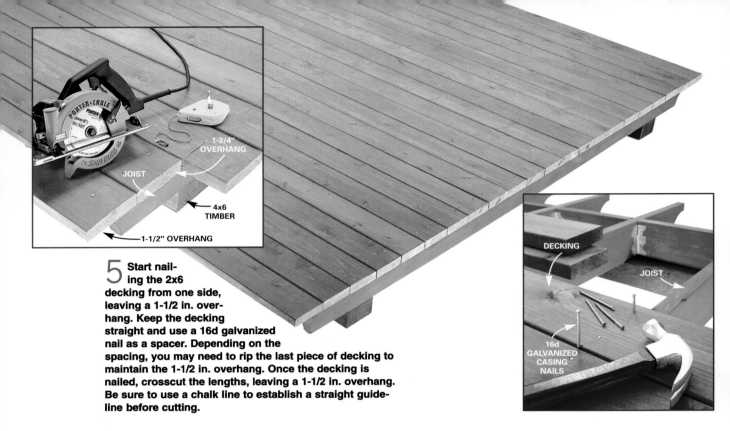

5 Start nailing the 2x6 decking from one side, leaving a 1-1/2 in. overhang. Keep the decking straight and use a 16d galvanized nail as a spacer. Depending on the spacing, you may need to rip the last piece of decking to maintain the 1-1/2 in. overhang. Once the decking is nailed, crosscut the lengths, leaving a 1-1/2 in. overhang. Be sure to use a chalk line to establish a straight guideline before cutting.

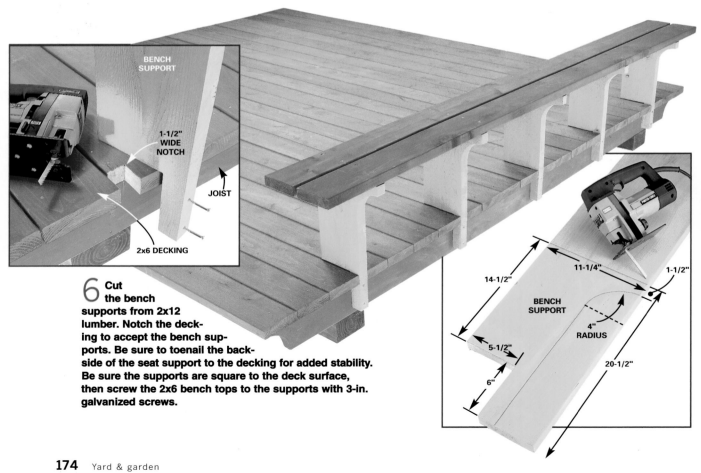

6 Cut the bench supports from 2x12 lumber. Notch the decking to accept the bench supports. Be sure to toenail the backside of the seat support to the decking for added stability. Be sure the supports are square to the deck surface, then screw the 2x6 bench tops to the supports with 3-in. galvanized screws.

10 secrets to colorful container gardens

Container gardens are the perfect way to liven up your front entrance, create a small herb garden or soften the look of your deck, porch or patio. They can provide instant color in drab areas, and you can create your own mini-garden in an hour or less. Best of all they're easy to care for and maintain.

Here are 10 tips for successful container gardens, plus some tried and true plant combinations to help you get started.

1. Pick the right pot.

The most important issue is size. Generally a pot should be one-third the height of the mature plants for things to look balanced. Classic round pots with tapered sides are more practical for planting and transplanting than containers with handles, odd shapes or narrow necks. If you plan to move the pots frequently, use lightweight foam or fiberglass pots. If you need a pot that won't topple in the wind use concrete or ceramic.

2. Buy or mix the right type of soil.

The soil should be a mixture of peat moss, compost and a little sand, with small amounts of puffy perlite or flaky vermiculite to lighten the mix and aid drainage. Packaged potting soil often includes fertilizer, which further simplifies the planting process. Tailor your soil to the specific needs of the plants you'll be growing.

3. Plant what you love.

You can plant annuals, perennials, vines, vegetables, herbs, ground covers, bulbs, shrubs and even trees. So think about what you want to achieve. If you want a quick splash of spring color, plant a pot of tulip bulbs in the fall. If you want an arrangement that will grace your outdoor living space for years, plant a juniper or Japanese maple. If you're looking for low maintenance, think in terms of ornamental grasses.

4. Start with healthy plants.

You want vigorous youngsters that will quickly mature into strong adults. Look for plants with fresh green leaves and sturdy stems. Select young plants with a large number of buds, which are more apt to adapt quickly to a new location and container.

A few tried-and-true combinations

- Geranium and petunia
- Globe amaranth and portulaca
- Caladium and impatiens
- Salvia and sweet alyssum
- Bronze fennel, dichondra and coleus
- Tulip and pansy
- Japanese maple and English ivy
- Ornamental grass, sweet potato vine and impatiens

5. Pick the best combination of flowers.

You can place as many plants together as you like, but consider combining just two or three varieties for your first few attempts. The plants should have similar watering and sunlight requirements. For twosomes, select a tall, upright plant along with a mounding or cascading plant. For threesomes, begin with a tall upright plant to structure the design, add a second plant that will fill the area with foliage and color, then select a third plant that will gently cascade over the edges. But most of all have fun experimenting.

8. Keep them well watered.

If the top inch or two of soil feels dry, the plant probably needs watering. When plants are small, a watering can with a sprinkler head is often adequate. As the root system expands, water may tend to run over the soil and flow over the top of the pot or seep into a gap between pot and soil. To counteract this, water with warm water, which soaks in faster than cold water. Or poke small holes into the soil with a pencil or screwdriver and water thoroughly.

6. Plant them right.

Spread a layer of pebbles or pot shards over the drain holes of the container to keep soil in while letting excess water drain out. Add soil until the pot is about three-quarters full, then gently shake or rock the pot to help the soil settle. Place the root ball of your plants on the soil, then add or subtract soil until the base of each stem is just below the rim of the pot. Continue filling soil around the plants until the soil is within 1 in. of the rim; within 2 in. if you're adding ornamental mulch.

7. Keep them well fed.

The roots of container-grown plants can't wander far and wide in search of nutrients; it's up to you to supply them. You can use either water-soluble plant food (about once every two weeks) or granular fertilizer (scratched into the soil surface every 6 to 8 weeks).

Plants vary in their nutritional needs, so no one fertilizer or schedule suits all plants. However, container plants are easy to monitor. Yellow leaves, slow growth and poor flowering are the most common signs of nutritional deficiencies. Brown leaf edges are a symptom of over-feeding and fertilizer burn.

9. Pinch and groom them.

With annual flowers, pinch or clip off old blossoms to prolong overall flowering. When an entire stem seems to have borne its last bud, clip that off too. When removing old blossoms or stems always use a scissors or pruning shears; tugging at plants with fingers can injure roots.

10. Monitor the roots.

When a plant stops growing or refuses to take up water, check for crowded roots. If the pot is full, transplant the arrangement into a larger container. Some arrangements can be split and transplanted into two or more pots.

Timber frame garden arbor

You can cut perfect, old-style joints with standard tools . . . and keep all the fasteners out of sight.

This timber garden arbor can be your place to get away for a quiet retreat or serve as a delightful lawn sculpture that you gaze at through your kitchen window.

Building it is enjoyable too. The main structure goes together like an old-fashioned timber frame with tenons and notches you cut into wooden 6x6s with your circular saw and handsaw. The main posts are anchored in the ground with concrete, and the roof and sides are made of dimensional treated lumber screwed to the treated 6x6s. Our project cost about $450 and took about three days to build with plenty of break time. After waiting about three weeks to give the wood ample time to dry out, we applied an exterior oil stain.

Shopping for treated lumber

When you're looking for lumber at the home center, make sure to pick out 6x6s that are fairly dry and free of twists and large cracks. The same goes for the other treated dimensional lumber you'll need for this project. However, don't be disturbed by the "green" color of the wood at this stage. A quality semi-transparent oil stain will give you a nice, warm wood tone.

You may want to rent a 10-in. circular saw

You can cut the notches into the 6x6s (Photo 1) with a standard 7-1/4 in. circular saw and a sharp handsaw, but a 10-in. circular saw will make quick work of it. Be aware, however, that these saws are heavy and a bit awkward to handle. If you decide to use the smaller circular saw and handsaw, use the handsaw to get the extra depth you can't get with the circular saw and to clean up the notches.

Stand the two end assemblies and fill in the concrete

To get this structure to behave and end up square, measure the holes carefully and dig each one about 16 in. deep and 12 in. wide with a posthole digger. Tip: What do you do with the extra dirt? I always lay a tarp right next to where I'm digging and dump the soil right onto it. Then I can drag it around to any location on

the lot that needs a bit of fill.

Join the front posts as a pair (Photo 2), then do the same with the rear. Stand the rear assembly (get a friend to help) and stick the bottoms of the posts into the rear holes. Now drive some stakes into the ground

1 Cut the 6x6s to length and then cut the notches in the tops with your circular saw. First cut lengthwise, then make the crosscut and finish the cut with your hand-saw. Clean the bottom of the notch with a sharp chisel.

2 Screw temporary 59-in. long 2x4 crossties to the posts near the top and 16 in. up from the bottom.

3 Tip and drop the rear assembly into the 16-in. deep x 12-in. diameter holes. Screw temporary supports to stakes and then to the assembly to plumb it. Once the rear assembly is level and plumb, drop the front assembly into the holes and screw it to the back assembly with temporary 2x2 horizontal supports top and bottom. Square the legs by measuring and making the diagonals equal between opposite legs.

materials list

DESCRIPTION	QTY.
6x6 x 10' treated posts and lintels	6
2x2 x 8' supports	2
2x4 x 8' treated beam flanges, ridge beam and ridge supports	2
2x4 x 10' braces, supports	6
2x6 x 8' treated seat slats	2
2x6 x 12' treated rafters	2
2x8 x 12' treated beam and brackets	1
2x10 x 8' treated seat braces	1
5/4x6 x 8' roof and side lattice	11
Simpson A-23 steel angles	4
Simpson TP39 tie plates	2
80-lb. bags of concrete mix	3
1/4" x 3-1/2" lag screws, washers	16
10d nails	2 lbs.
1-5/8" screws	2 lbs.
3" deck screws	2 lbs.

cutting list

KEY	PCS.	SIZE & DESCRIPTION
A	4	5-1/2" x 5-1/2" x 105-1/2" treated posts
B	2	5-1/2" x 5-1/2" x 42-1/2" treated side lintels
C	2	5-1/2" x 5-1/2" x 76" treated front and back lintels
D	8	1-1/2" x 7-1/4" x 12" post brackets
E	2	1-1/2" x 3-1/2" x 45" center beam flanges
F	1	1-1/2" x 7-1/4" x 45" center beam
G	2	1-1/2" x 3-1/2" x 22-1/2" ridge beam supports
H	1	1-1/2" x 3-1/2" x 45" ridge
J	4	1-1/2" x 5-1/2" x 62" rafter
K	14	1" x 5-1/2" x 45" roof lattice
L	4	1-1/2" x 9-1/4" x 12" seat braces
M1	2	1-1/2" x 5-1/2" x 37" outer seat slats
M2	2	1-1/2" x 5-1/2" x 45" inner seat slats
N1	4	1" x 2-11/16" x 80" vertical side lattice
N2	4	1" x 2-11/16" x 37" horizontal side lattice

figure a
arbor assembly

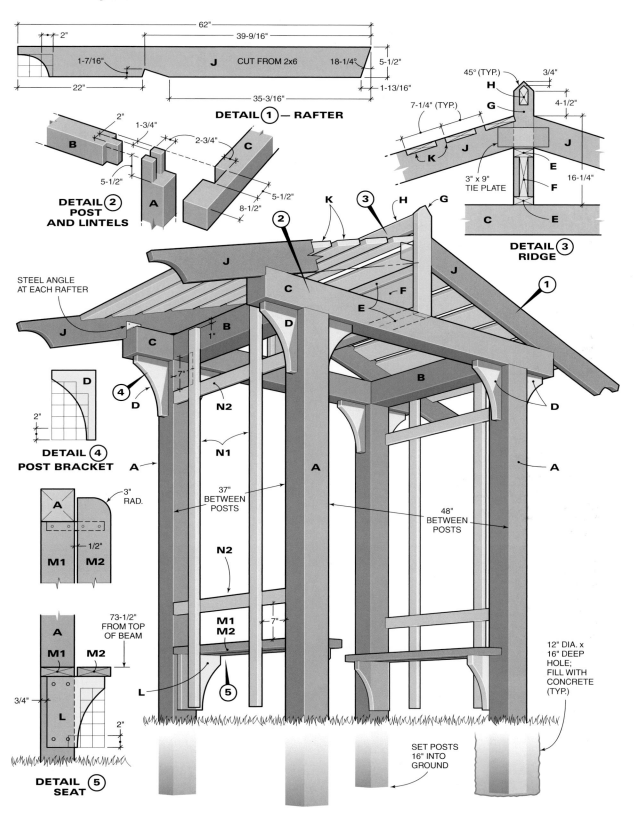

DETAIL 1 — RAFTER

62"
39-9/16"
2"
1-7/16"
J CUT FROM 2x6
18-1/4°
5-1/2"
22"
1-13/16"
35-3/16"

DETAIL 2 POST AND LINTELS

2"
B
1-3/4"
2-3/4"
C
5-1/2"
A
5-1/2"
8-1/2"

DETAIL 3 RIDGE

45° (TYP.)
3/4"
H
G
7-1/4" (TYP.)
4-1/2"
K
J
J
E
F
3" x 9" TIE PLATE
16-1/4"
C
E

STEEL ANGLE AT EACH RAFTER

DETAIL 4 POST BRACKET

D
2"

DETAIL 5 SEAT

A
M1 M2
3" RAD.
1/2"

A
M1 M2
73-1/2" FROM TOP OF BEAM
3/4"
L
2"

K
3
2
J
C
H
G
B
1"
D
E
F
J
1
B
D
A
N2
7"
4
D
N1
37" BETWEEN POSTS
48" BETWEEN POSTS
A
A
N2
M1 M2
7"
L
5

12" DIA. x 16" DEEP HOLE; FILL WITH CONCRETE (TYP.)

SET POSTS 16" INTO GROUND

while one person holds the assembly. Plumb the posts with temporary braces fastened to the stakes and posts, then level the horizontal ties at the bottom with shims. Once this assembly is secured, insert the front post assembly into the front post holes and fasten it to the rear assembly with the 2x2 horizontal side supports as shown in Photo 3. With the front secured to the rear assembly, make sure the front posts are at right angles to the rear posts and the diagonal measurements between the posts are equal. Add additional braces if necessary.

Mix the concrete for your posts in a tub or wheelbarrow. Mix no more than two bags at once and then mix more as needed. We used about three 80-lb. bags, but the amount depends on the hole diameter and depth. Dump the concrete into each hole and then pack it around the posts with a scrap 2x2. Bring the concrete up to grade level (Photo 4) and then berm it slightly to keep water from collecting at the bottom of the post every time it rains.

4 Mix concrete and pour it into each hole around the post. Let the concrete set for two days before continuing.

5 Remove the braces, cut the side lintel tenons with your circular saw and handsaw, and lower each into the front and back post notches. Screw the joints together with 3-in. deck screws.

6 It's easier to cut the notches in the front and back lintels with a 10-in. circular saw. You can rent one for about $40 a day to make quick work of the post cutting.

7 Break out the chips and clean the bottom of the notch with a sharp chisel. Finish smoothing it with a coarse file.

Lock the lintels together with 3-in. screws

The tenons and mortises are traditionally held together with dowel pins, but because this structure is exposed to the weather, it's best to lock them into place with 3-in. galvanized screws driven at angles from above. As you place each lintel, you may find that you'll need to either squeeze or separate the top ends of the posts a bit to get them to fall into place. This is because one or more of the posts may be slightly out of plumb. Screw in the brackets (D) as shown in Photo 10.

8 Lift the front and back lintels onto the tops of the posts and push them back until they're flush with the posts. You may need to persuade it a bit with a hammer and a block of wood. Screw the lintels into place with 3-in. screws angled in from the top.

Make the center beam from 2x4s and a 2x8

Screw the 2x4 parts (E) to the center 2x8 (F) to create an I-beam that'll run from front to back and support the roof members. Get the beam positioned 1-1/2 in. from the outer edge of both front and rear lintels (Photo 11). Screw it into place

9 Cut the post brackets with a jigsaw and then smooth the curves with your belt sander (80-grit works best).

10 Screw brackets to posts with 3-in. deck screws. Drill a pilot hole to avoid splitting the brackets.

11 Cut and assemble the parts for the center beam and then center and screw it to the front and back lintels.

with 3-in. screws. Next cut the ridge supports and the ridge and fasten them as shown in Photo 12. The top ridge has a 45-degree bevel on each top edge. Make a mark 7/8 in. down from the top edge of the 2x4 ridge board on each side. Temporarily nail the ridge to the sawhorse tops, set your circular saw at a 45-degree bevel and cut along the line on one side. Then pull the nails and reposition it to cut the other side. Screw the ridge to the ridge supports, making sure it rests 3/4 in. down from the top of the ridge supports.

Cut the remaining roof parts and assemble them as shown in Photos 13 – 15.

12 Screw the ridge support (G) to the center beam and then fasten the ridge to the support with 3-in. deck screws.

13 Cut the rafters (J) as shown in Figure A using your jigsaw and circular saw. Complete one, then use it as a pattern for the rest.

14 Measure down 4 in. from the top of the ridge support, make a horizontal mark with your square and align the top edges of the rafters with your mark. Screw the rafters to the support and then use Simpson A-23 angles on the backside of the bird's-mouth notch to connect the rafter to the beam.

Sand the arbor to get rid of rough edges

"Sand it?" you say? Well, this isn't a fine piece of furniture, but you will have a few rough edges and corners that could give you splinters. Just go around and examine the corners and edges and sand them smooth with 100-grit sandpaper. You may have to wait a week or more to sand if your treated wood is still moist because it will just gum up your paper. Once the project is dry to the touch, find an oil stain that suits your taste and brush it on. Have a rag or two handy to catch the drips and runs, and use dropcloths if you're staining over a walkway. One coat should be sufficient, and you'll need to recoat your arbor in about three years.

15 Clamp a temporary support 1 in. down from the top of the rafter to guide the roof lattice board. Tap in nails every 7-1/4 in. to space the boards. Nail into the edge of the rafters with 10d casing nails.

16 Predrill and screw the seat braces to the inside faces of the four posts using 1/4-in. x 3-1/2 in. lag screws.

17 Fasten the 2x6 seat slats to the braces with 3-in. deck screws. Leave a 1/2-in. space between the boards and round over the outside edge of the inner slat with a 3-in. radius cut.

18 Rip 5/4x6 decking in half and round over the edge with a block plane and sandpaper. Screw the vertical lattice to the side lintels and the back of the seat. Finish the lattice by screwing the horizontal lattice pieces to the inside face of the vertical pieces with 1-5/8 in. deck screws.

3-hour cedar bench

Build it in one afternoon!

The beauty of this cedar bench isn't just that it's easy to assemble and inexpensive—it's that it's so doggone comfortable. You can comfortably sit on your custom-fit bench for hours, even without cushions. In this story, we'll show you how to build the bench and how to adjust it for maximum comfort.

Sloping the back and the seat is the secret to pain-free perching on unpadded flat boards. But not all bodies are the same, and it's a rare piece of furniture that everyone agrees is seatworthy. This bench has a bolted pivot point where the back and seat meet that lets you alter the backrest and seat slopes to fit your build during one of the final assembly steps (Photo 10). The materials will cost about $85, and cutting and assembly will only take about three hours. Follow the step-by-step photo series for details on the simple construction.

project at a glance

skill level
beginner

special tools
circular saw
screw gun
drill

approximate cost
$85

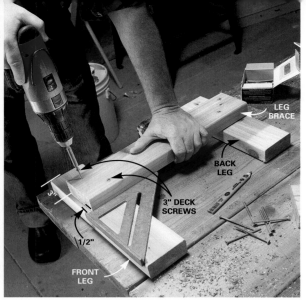

1 Cut out the bench parts following the measurements in Figure A. Use a square to guide the circular saw for accurate, square cuts. Cut 45-degree angles on the ends of the seat and back supports 1 in. down from the ends as shown (also see Photos 4 and 5).

2 Fasten the leg brace to the legs 3 in. above the bottom ends. Angle the 3-in. screws slightly to prevent the screw tips from protruding through the other side. Hold the brace 1/2 in. back from the front edge of the front leg. Use a square to make sure the brace and legs are at exact right angles.

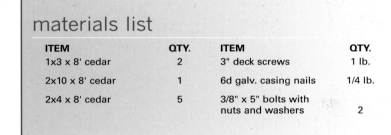

figure a
bench parts

materials list

ITEM	QTY.	ITEM	QTY.
1x3 x 8' cedar	2	3" deck screws	1 lb.
2x10 x 8' cedar	1	6d galv. casing nails	1/4 lb.
2x4 x 8' cedar	5	3/8" x 5" bolts with nuts and washers	2

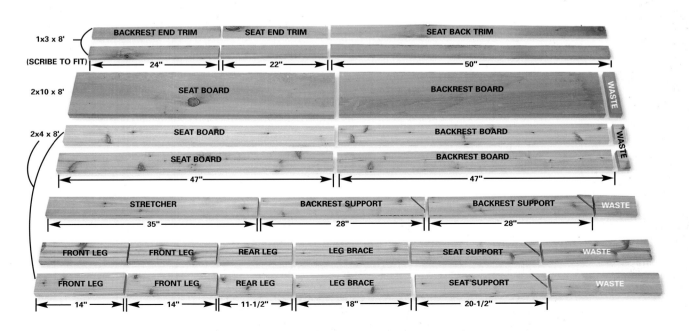

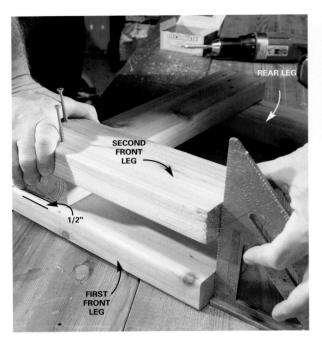

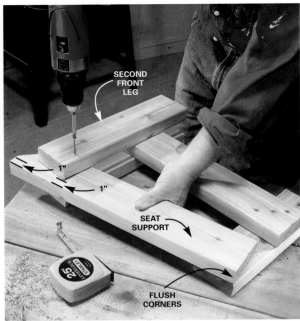

3 **Align the second part of the front leg with the first one using a square and screw it to the leg brace as shown.**

4 **Slip the seat support between the two front legs, positioning it as shown. Drive a single 3-in. screw through the front leg into the seat support.**

Build it from eight 8-ft. long boards

A circular saw and a screw gun are the only power tools you really need for construction, although a power miter saw will speed things up and give you cleaner cuts. Begin by cutting the boards to length. Figure A shows you how to cut up the eight boards efficiently, leaving little waste.

After cutting the pieces to length, screw together the leg assemblies (Photos 2 – 6). Be sure to use a square to keep the leg braces square to the legs (Photo 2). That way both leg assemblies will be identical and the bench won't wobble if it's put on a hard, flat surface. We spaced the leg brace 1/2 in. back

from the front of the legs to create a more attractive shadow line. Then it's just a matter of connecting the leg assemblies with the stretcher (Photo 7), screwing down the seat and backrest boards and adjusting the slopes to fit your body.

The easiest way to adjust the slope is to hold the four locking points in place with clamps and then back out the temporary screws (Photo 10). To customize the slopes, you just loosen the clamps, make the adjustments, retighten and test the fit. When you're satisfied, run a couple of permanent screws into each joint. If you don't have clamps, don't worry—you'll just have to back out the screws, adjust the slopes, reset the screws and test the bench. Clamps just speed up the process.

Round over the edges

We show an option of rounding over the sharp edge of the 1x3 trim, which is best done with a router and a 1/2-in. round-over bit (Photo 12). Rounding over the edges can protect shins and the backs of thighs and leave teetering toddlers with goose eggs on their melons instead of gashes. So the step is highly recommended. If you don't have a router, round over the

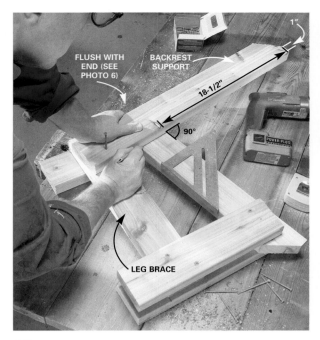

5 Position the backrest support on the leg assembly as shown, making sure it's at a right angle with the seat support, and mark the position on the seat support. Then drive a 3-in. screw through the middle of the backrest support into the leg brace.

6 Clamp the backrest support, seat support and rear leg as shown using the line as a guide. Drill a 3/8-in. hole through the center of the assembly. Drive a 3/8-in. x 5-in. bolt fitted with a washer through the hole and slightly tighten the nut against a washer on the other side.

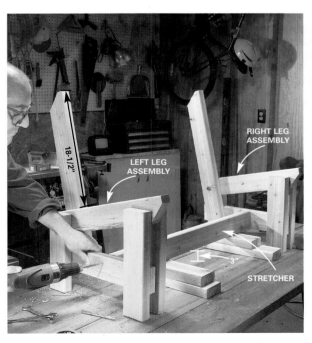

7 Assemble the other leg assembly to mirror the first as shown. (The back support and rear leg switch sides.) Prop the stretcher 3 in. above the workbench, center it between the front and rear bench legs and screw the leg braces into the ends with two 3-in. deck screws.

8 Center the first 2x4 seat board over the leg assemblies and flush with the front ends of the seat supports. Screw it to the seat supports with two 3-in. deck screws spaced about 1 in. away from the edges. Line up the 2x10 with the first 2x4, space it about 5/16 in. away (the thickness of a carpenter's pencil) and screw it to the seat supports with two 3-in. deck screws. Repeat with the rear 2x4.

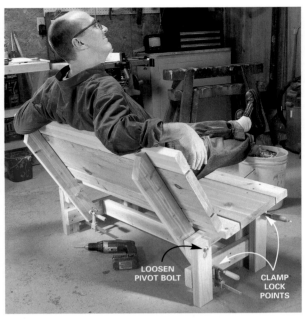

9 Rest the bottom backrest 2x4 on carpenter's pencils, holding the end flush with the seat boards and screw it to the seat back braces. Then space and screw on the center 2x10 and the top 2x4 backrest boards.

10 Sit on the bench and decide if you'd like to tilt the seat or the backrest or both to make the bench more comfortable. To make seat or back adjustments, loosen the bolts and clamp the bottoms of the seat back supports and the fronts of the seat supports. Then back out the four screws at those points. Loosen the clamps, make adjustments, then retighten and retest for comfort. When you're satisfied with the fit, drive in the four original screws plus another at each point. Retighten the pivot bolts.

edge either by hand-sanding or with an orbital or belt sander. In any event, keep the casing nails 1 in. away from the edge to prevent hitting the nailheads with the router bit or sandpaper (Photo 12).

Building a longer bench

We demonstrate how to build a 4-ft. long bench, plenty of space for two. But you can use the same design and techniques for building 6- or 8-ft. long benches too. You'll just have to buy longer boards for the seat, back, stretcher and the trim boards. While you're at it, you can use the same design for matching end or coffee tables. Just match the double front leg design for the rear legs, and build flat-topped leg assemblies with an overall depth of 16-3/4 in.

Seal the legs to make it last

If you want to stain your bench, use a latex exterior stain on the parts after cutting them to length. After assembly, you won't be able to get good penetration at the cracks and crevices. Avoid clear exterior sealers, which will irritate bare skin. But the bench will last outside for more than 20 years without any stain or special care even if you decide to let it weather to a natural gray. However, the legs won't last that long, because the end grain at the bottom will wick up moisture from the ground, making the legs rot long before the bench does. To make sure the legs last as long as the bench, seal the ends with epoxy, urethane or exterior woodworker's glue when you're through with the assembly.

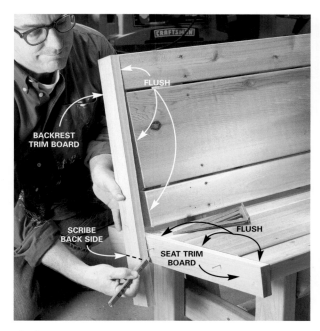

FLUSH

BACKREST
TRIM BOARD

SCRIBE
BACK SIDE

FLUSH

SEAT TRIM
BOARD

TURN ROUTER
SIDEWAYS
HERE

1"

1/2"
ROUND-OVER
BIT

11 Tack the seat trim boards to the seat with the ends flush with the front and top. Scribe and cut the trim boards to fit. Nail the boards to the seat and backrest boards with 6d galvanized casing nails, keeping the nails 1 in. back from the seat edges.

12 Ease the edges of the trim boards with a router and a 1/2-in. round-over bit. Hold the router sideways to get at the seat/back corner.

A bench with a past

About 15 years ago, I decided to throw together some simple outdoor benches so my growing family could relax outside and enjoy the yard. But they had to be better looking and more comfortable than the flat benches they were replacing. I wanted them to feel more like a chair, be light enough to move around easily and stand up to the elements. After much experimentation, I came up with a version of this design and used it to make three benches. At times they'll be arranged around the fire ring, or for larger social gatherings, placed on the patio or deck. Most often, however, all three encircle the herb garden, our favorite outdoor hangout.

After all those years without any shelter or finish, the benches are showing their age. The crisp, new look has long passed, now replaced with puppy teeth marks, a few cracks, a deep gray hue and even some rot at the bottom of the feet. But they're still as sturdy and comfortable as the day they were made. This new version has a few improved features. I wanted to make it easier to build (no fancy angles and fewer parts), even more comfortable (adjustable to fit), and even more durable (the feet bottoms are sealed).

— Travis Larson, Editor

Folding grill table

A fold-up companion for your barbecue.

After this collapsible cedar table was built, our family wondered how we ever grilled without it. The legs nest under the top for quick storage or easy carrying. All you need to build it is a drill, a saw, basic hand tools, a short stack of cedar boards and half an afternoon.

The table is made entirely from 1x4 cedar boards. You can make the table from eight 6-foot boards, but buy 10 to allow for possible miscuts and to give you more choice for the top slats.

Cut the parts

You can use a handsaw to cut the parts, but an electric jigsaw speeds up the job significantly. Use a square to help make straight cuts (Photo 1). To ensure matching legs and frame parts, clamp two boards together and mark and cut them at the same time (Photo 2). Cut slats one or two at a time. You'll cut the stretchers after bolting on the legs.

To assemble the frame, drill two holes in the ends of the longer frame boards and add a countersink hole for the screwheads to nestle into. Cut the slats and place them top-side up on a flat surface (Photo 3).

EASY FOR EVERYONE

1 Cut the boards for the top and the frame that supports it using a jigsaw or handsaw and a square. (See the exploded view diagram below.)

2 Clamp the leg boards together (rough side in) and cut both of them at once to create identical leg pairs. Drill the 3/8-in. bolt hole in the upper end before unclamping.

materials list

QTY.	DESCRIPTION
2	2-1/2" x 3/8" carriage bolts
2	3-1/2" x 3/8" carriage bolts
4	3/8" wing nuts and flat washers
1	Box 1-5/8" deck screws
10	1x4 x 6' cedar boards
1	Pint Penofin wood finish
1	Drill with countersink

cutting list

KEY	NAME	QTY.	DIMENSIONS IN INCHES
A	Top slat	12	1x4 x 19
B	Long side piece	2	1x4 x 41-1/2
C	Short side piece	2	1x4 x 15-3/4
D	Leg	4	1x4 x 28-3/4 (15° angled end cut)
E	Leg stretchers	2	1x4 x 15-3/4 (Cut to fit)
F	Leg spacers	2	1x4 x 6-3/4
G	Leg stop blocks	4	1x4 x 4-3/8 (15° angled end cut)

(Note: All parts cut from "1x4 S3S" cedar, so each board is a "fat" 3/4 thick and 3-1/2 wide, with two smooth edges, one smooth side and one rough side.)

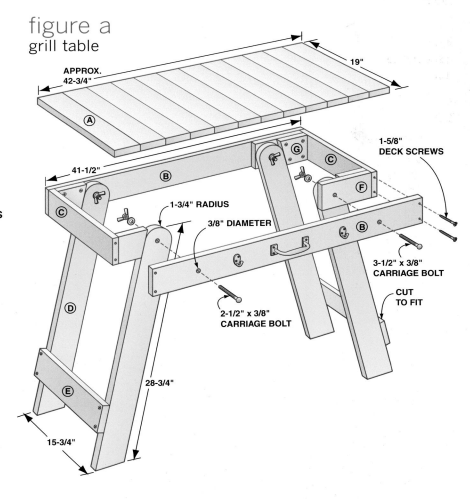

figure a
grill table

APPROX. 42-3/4"

19"

Ⓐ

41-1/2"

Ⓑ

Ⓒ

1-3/4" RADIUS

3/8" DIAMETER

Ⓖ

Ⓒ

1-5/8" DECK SCREWS

Ⓕ

Ⓑ

3-1/2" x 3/8" CARRIAGE BOLT

CUT TO FIT

Ⓓ

2-1/2" x 3/8" CARRIAGE BOLT

Ⓔ

28-3/4"

15-3/4"

3 Lay the frame on the top boards and lightly trace the frame shape so it's easy to see where to drill holes. Space the top boards with about 1/16-in. gaps between them.

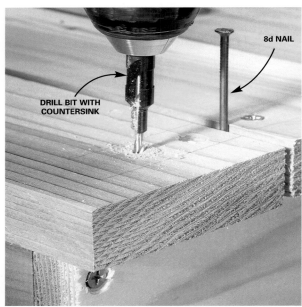

DRILL BIT WITH COUNTERSINK

8d NAIL

4 Drill two holes on each top board end with a countersink bit and screw them to the frame. A nail is handy for creating even spacing.

Center the frame on the slats to create a 3/4-in. overhang on all four sides. Then lightly trace the frame shape on the slats with a pencil.

Lift off the frame, and drill and countersink screw holes in the slats using the traced lines as a guide. Then screw the slats to the frame (Photo 4). Lightly tap a couple nails between the slats while screwing them to the frame to create the approximate 1/16-in. spacing between the slats. The end slats will overhang the frame approximately 3/4 in. to match the slat overhang along the frame sides.

Attach the legs

Flip the tabletop upside down and screw the pair of angled blocks to the corners of one end (Photo 5). Butt the rounded leg ends against the spacer blocks, then drill and bolt on the outer leg pair with the shorter 2-1/2-in. carriage bolts, washers and wing nuts. Now attach the inner leg pair to the other frame, first screwing in the spacer blocks to allow the legs to nest inside the other pair (Photo 6). Add the angled blocks, then drill and bolt on the second leg pair with the longer 3-1/2-in. carriage bolts.

With the legs flat on the underside of the table, measure for the stretchers, cut, drill and fasten them to the legs (Photo 7). To pull out the legs, lift the more widely spaced pair first so the second pair can be raised without catching on the first pair's stretcher (Photo 8).

Sand, finish, then grill

Sand the table with 100-grit paper and, with a sanding block or rasp, slightly round the top edges of the slats. Put on your favorite finish; we used two coats of Penofin penetrating oil finish (cedar color). Pull out the legs, tighten the wing nuts and grill away.

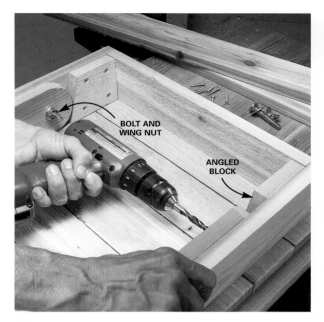

BOLT AND
WING NUT

ANGLED
BLOCK

SPACER
BLOCK

3-1/2"

4-3/8"

ANGLE
BLOCK

5 Screw a pair of angled blocks in one end of the
frame, then butt the rounded ends of the legs
against the blocks. Drill through the frame and bolt on
the legs.

6 Screw the spacer blocks in the other frame end.
These allow the other pair of legs to nest inside the
first pair. Then drill and bolt on the second pair of legs.

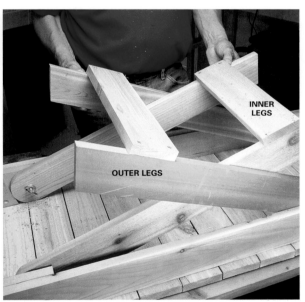

INNER
LEGS

OUTER LEGS

7 Screw stretchers across each pair of legs. For best fit
and overall results, mark and cut the stretchers
based on the actual spacing between the legs.

8 Test the fit of the legs in the frame by pulling the
legs up from the frame. If they bind and scrape,
sand the sides for a smoother fit.

Patio planters

Give your potted plants a simple, stylish home—outdoors or in.

This planter is designed to make your patio or deck gardening much easier. Instead of filling it with dirt and planting each flower or plant individually, you simply set prepotted plants right into the planter. You can conveniently switch plants as the season changes or unload the planter and move it to a new location.

We designed this project to fit any pot with an 11-in. diameter or less and a maximum height of 10-1/2 in. To create the illusion of a fully planted box, you just fill in around the pots with wood chips, bark or other mulch covering. The base or bottom of the planter has 7/8-in. holes drilled every 6 in. to drain

away any excess water. The side boards have a 1/4-in. space between them to ventilate the mulch and keep it from getting soggy.

Buying the right lumber

You'll notice the legs are treated pine and not cedar like the sides and top apron. Treated pine is less likely to split along the grain (a nasty problem with cedar). Pick treated 2x12 material for the legs with as few large knots as possible. You'll be able to cut around knots on a single board, so bring a tape measure when you select the lumber. Choose straight cedar for the sides and remember that some knots here can add to the overall beauty.

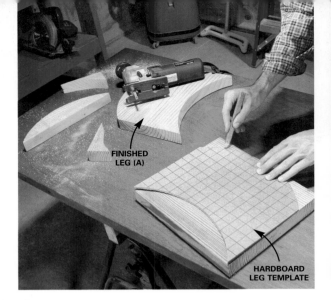

FINISHED LEG (A)

HARDBOARD LEG TEMPLATE

12" SPEED SQUARE

SUPPORT BLOCK

C

D

1 Using a full-size template made from Figure A, trace the outline of the planter legs onto pressure-treated 2x12 pine boards. Sand the edges with a finish or belt sander followed by 100-grit hand-sanding to gently ease the edges.

2 Make straight cuts using a 12-in. Speed square held firmly against the back of the 2x6.

E

A

C

F

D

figure a: leg template

(enlarge 400% or until overall leg height equals 13 in.)

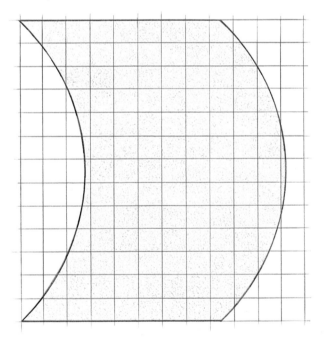

cutting list

KEY	QTY.	SIZE & DESCRIPTION
Large planter		
A	4	1-1/2" x 11-1/4" x 13" treated pine legs
B	1	1-1/2" x 11-1/4" x 48" treated pine base
C	4	1-1/2" x 5-1/2" x 48" cedar side panels
D	4	1-1/2" x 5-1/2" x 14-1/4" cedar end panels*
E	2	1-1/16" x 4-1/2" x 57" cedar side aprons
F	2	1-1/16" x 4-1/2" x 20-1/4" cedar side aprons*
Small planter		
A	4	1-1/2" x 11-1/4" x 13" treated pine legs
B	1	1-1/2" x 11-1/4" x 36" treated pine base
C	4	1-1/2" x 5-1/2" x 36" cedar side panels
D	4	1-1/2" x 5-1/2" x 14-1/4" cedar end panels*
E	2	1-1/16" x 4-1/2" x 45" cedar side aprons
F	2	1-1/16" x 4-1/2" x 20-1/4" cedar side aprons*

*Cut to fit

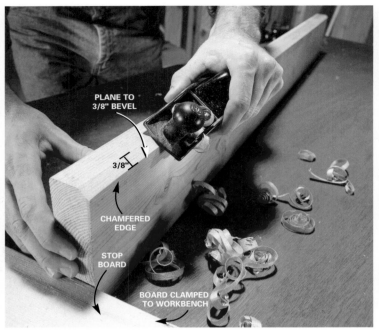

PLANE TO 3/8" BEVEL

3/8"

CHAMFERED EDGE

STOP BOARD

BOARD CLAMPED TO WORKBENCH

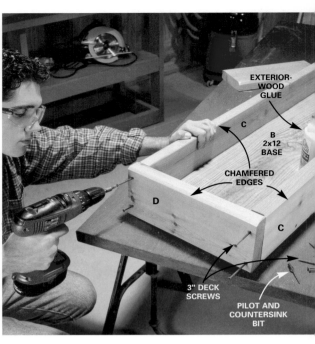

EXTERIOR-WOOD GLUE

C

B 2x12 BASE

CHAMFERED EDGES

D

C

3" DECK SCREWS

PILOT AND COUNTERSINK BIT

3 Plane only the edges where the side boards C and D meet. This chamfered edge should be about 3/8 in. wide when completed. Clamp a board to the edge of your workbench to stop the workpiece from drifting while you stroke the edge of the board with the plane.

4 Cut your 2x12 base to length, then screw the lower sides (C) to the base. Align the base and sides so they're flush on the bottom sides. Predrill for each screw using a pilot/countersink combination bit. Then screw the ends to the sides.

Plan Smart

We've shown you two planters of different lengths, but you can adapt them to fit your unique space. You can even change the width by nailing a treated 2x2 to the side of the 2x12 base piece and lengthening other parts accordingly to accommodate a slightly wider pot. To build either the small or large planter shown, follow our clear step-by-step photos and refer to the Cutting List for lumber lengths.

Feel free to use other species of wood such as redwood, cypress or even a plantation-grown tropical wood like ipe (available at some lumberyards).

Use paint, stain or a combination of both

We chose an exterior enamel paint for the legs and apron pieces to accent the deck oil stain/sealer on the base and sides. Stain is a better choice than paint for the base and sides because they'll be exposed to more moisture than the legs and top. The photo at left shows the excellent results you can get by staining the entire project with an exterior oil deck stain.

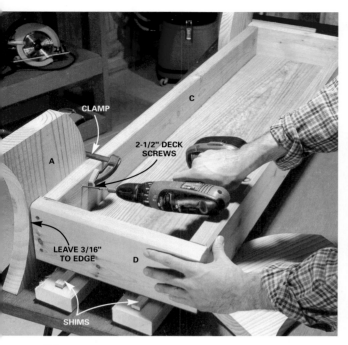

CLAMP

2-1/2" DECK
SCREWS

A

C

LEAVE 3/16"
TO EDGE

D

SHIMS

C

C

B

A

D

DRILL 7/8"
DRAIN HOLES
EVERY 6"

5 Shim the base up 1-3/4 in. on each side using scrap pieces of wood, then clamp the legs one at a time to the sides (C). Screw the sides to the legs with 2-1/2 in. deck screws. Use three screws per leg.

6 Clamp the upper sides flush to the tops of the legs. Be sure to align the upper and lower side ends before drilling and screwing this piece in place. Again, use three 2-1/2 in. deck screws per leg. Next, screw the upper end panels (D) to the upper sides. Make sure the chamfers face each other on each side.

5/4 x 6"
CEDAR DECK
BOARD

6d GALVANIZED
CASING NAILS

F

E

E

C

D

F

7 Rip the 5/4 x 6 in. deck boards to 4-1/2 in. to make the top apron frame. Use a rip guide on your circular saw or a table saw if you have one. Plane and sand the cut edge to match the factory-machined edge of the deck board.

8 Glue and nail the side apron pieces (E) flush with parts C below. Next, nail the apron end pieces to the end panels (D). You'll notice the inside edge of F will be about 1/4 in. out from the inside of the planter to adequately cover the tops of the legs.

EASY FOR EVERYONE

Stair-step plant display

Show off your favorite plants with this simple cedar stand.

We tend to buy plants first and worry about good spots for them later. So unfortunately, many of the prettiest plants get lost in the corners of a deck and sunroom and don't get the attention (or the light) they deserve.

To help solve this problem and to spotlight some favorite plants, we came up with this simple display stand. It's made from cedar 1x2s that are cut into just two lengths, stacked into squares and nailed together. We used western red cedar with the rough-sawed side exposed. You may have to check several suppliers to find a good selection of 1x2s. Assembly is simple and fast, because there's nothing to measure as you build—just keep everything square and use the wood pieces themselves for spacing and alignment.

project at a glance

skill level
beginner

special tools
power or hand
  miter saw
basic hand tools

approximate cost
$15–$20

Here's what you'll need

For supplies, you'll need seven 8-ft.-long cedar 1x2s, some exterior glue, like Titebond II, a few dozen 4d galvanized finish nails, and some 100- or 120-grit sandpaper. You'll also need a hammer, a tape measure and a framing square, plus a saw that can cut the 1x2s to a consistent length. A power miter saw is great for this (you can rent one) but you could also use a handsaw in a miter box. An exterior finish for the wood is attractive, but not really necessary.

Begin by trimming any rough or out-of-square ends from your 1x2s. Almost all the ends will show, so they need to look good. Cut the 1x2s into 16 20-in. pieces and 27 10-3/4-in. pieces. It's important that the two groups of pieces are consistent in length, so rather than measuring each one,

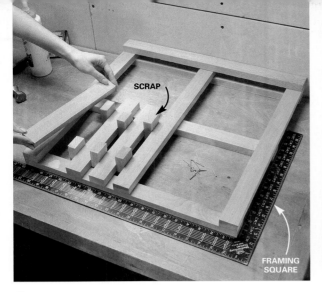

SCRAP

FRAMING SQUARE

SEVENTH LAYER

1 Assemble the first two layers without nails or glue to get the spacing right and to make sure everything is square. Use scrap pieces of 1x2 as spacers. Once everything is square, glue and nail all the intersections.

2 Build up the stand "log-cabin style" until you get to the seventh layer, which has two platforms. When that's nailed down, continue until the 12th layer, which has the final platform.

clamp a "stop block" to your bench the appropriate distance from the blade of your saw, and push the 1x2 up against it for each cut.

How to build it

Begin making your stand by arranging the lowest two layers without nails or glue (Photo 1). Lay out the bottom three 20-in. pieces against a framing square, then lay three more 20-in. pieces and three 10-3/4-in. pieces on top of them as shown in Photo 1.

Adjust the spacing, using scrap pieces to create the gaps, and make sure everything is square. The second layer should have a plant platform in one corner and nothing in the other three. When everything looks good, nail the pieces together, using one nail and a dab of glue at every intersection. Keep the nails 3/4 in. away from the ends of the boards to prevent splitting.

Add five more layers each consisting of two long and one short piece, with glue and a nail at every overlap. Check the sides with the square as you go to keep them straight. At the seventh layer, add two more platforms, with the 10-3/4-in. pieces running perpendicular to the pieces on the first platform. Add another five layers, with just two 10-3/4-in. pieces per layer, then fill in the top layer to create the final display platform (Photo 2). When you're done nailing, sand all the outside edges of your stand and apply an exterior stain or preservative. Wait a few days for the finish to dry completely, then start moving in the plants!

figure a
exploded view

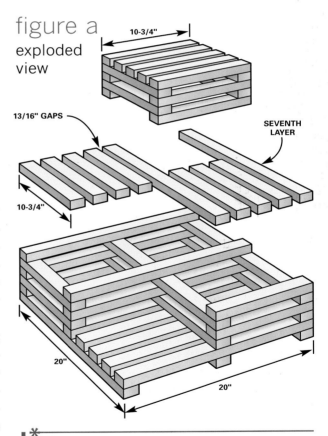

10-3/4"

13/16" GAPS

10-3/4"

SEVENTH LAYER

20"

20"

tip Always nail at least 3/4 in. in from the end, and if the wood still splits, predrill the nail holes using a bit the size of the nail or the nail itself with the head snipped off. Your boards may also differ in thickness from those shown, which were 13/16 in. thick. If so, simply adjust the spacing between the boards.

Copper trellis
A garden project with a twist.

The first reaction of my neighbor when she saw this trellis was, "Wow! I love it!" The second reaction was, "How in the world did you make it?"

Well, there's a trick to bending the wire, that's for sure, but once you understand it, this trellis goes together pretty easily. When you're done, you've got an elegant garden ornament that looks great even when the plants that climb on it have died back.

Give it a year or two outdoors and the wood will turn gray and the copper will turn a beautiful dark brown, and then eventually green. It wouldn't be hard to customize this trellis, forming the copper wire into initials or even more fanciful shapes.

Materials and tools

The copper scrollwork is made from No. 6 solid-copper wire, which is used for grounding electrical panels and is available at most home centers. This wire is stiff enough to hold its shape on the trellis, but soft enough to bend easily. The rest of the trellis is made from 2x2s and 1/2-in. copper pipe.

In the tool department, you'll need a drill and a 5/8-in. spade bit, a pair of medium to large wire-cutting pliers (test 'em out on the copper wire to see if they can cut it), a miter box or electric miter saw and an electric sander.

When you're shopping for the 2x2s, the best choice is clear D-grade cedar, typically stocked for deck railings. You can use pressure-treated lumber, which will be more economical, but

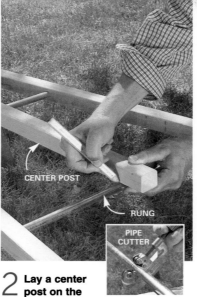

1 Drill holes in the legs using a wood scrap cut at 80 degrees to guide you. With all four legs clamped together, it's easy to get the holes to line up.

2 Lay a center post on the rungs, which are cut from copper pipe, and mark the rung holes directly on the post. Be sure the post is centered top-to-bottom and side-to-side.

3 Your bending jig for the wire scrolls is a piece of scrap wood with a copy of the scroll pattern (p. 184) tacked to it. Two finish nails in the middle hold the pieces of copper wire.

you may have to sort through a large number of 2x2s to find straight, relatively knot-free ones. If you have a table saw, you can often cut fairly knot-free 2x2s from the edges of a wider board.

Made from treated lumber, this trellis will cost around $70. Using clear cedar will bump it to $90.

Begin with the legs and rungs

Begin with the four legs, the wooden center posts and the copper pipe rungs that connect them.

Place your four 2x2 legs on sawhorses, get the top ends even and clamp them all together. Mark one end as the top, and measure from that end at 28 in., 41-1/2 in. and 59 in. to mark where you will drill the holes. Use a square to transfer the marks to all four legs and to the adjacent side of one leg. Make an angle guide by cutting a piece of scrap wood at an 80-degree angle (Photo 1). An inexpensive protractor works fine to set the angle. Drill angled holes at each mark, using your guide, so you're drilling three holes in each leg (Photo 1). Mark your drill bit to indicate the 1-in. depth for the holes, and be sure the

project at a glance

skill level
beginner

special tools
drill
wire cutter
miter saw
electric sander

approximate cost
$90

drill is always "leaning" toward the top of the legs. Flip each leg 90 degrees, clamp them together and repeat the whole process. The marks you made on the second side of one leg will allow you to transfer your hole locations. Be careful—the drill may be a bit jumpy as the second hole meets the first.

Cut six pieces of pipe (C, D and E), as shown in Photo 2. Note in the Cutting List (on p. 184) that there are two sets of pipe rungs; one set is slightly longer. Cut the longer set now. Temporarily assemble one side of the trellis—two legs and three pieces of pipe. Tap the legs to get the pipe seated. The tops of the legs should be within 1/4 in. of each other. Cut the center posts (B) to length, and use a miter box or miter saw to cut points on the ends. A line marked around all four sides will help guide you. Lay the center post on top of the assembled side. Be sure the post is centered and equidistant from the legs. Mark the post for the pipe holes, then transfer the marks to the other three center posts and drill the holes at 90 degrees. Drill from one side until the point of the spade bit pokes through, then drill the other side. This gives you cleaner holes.

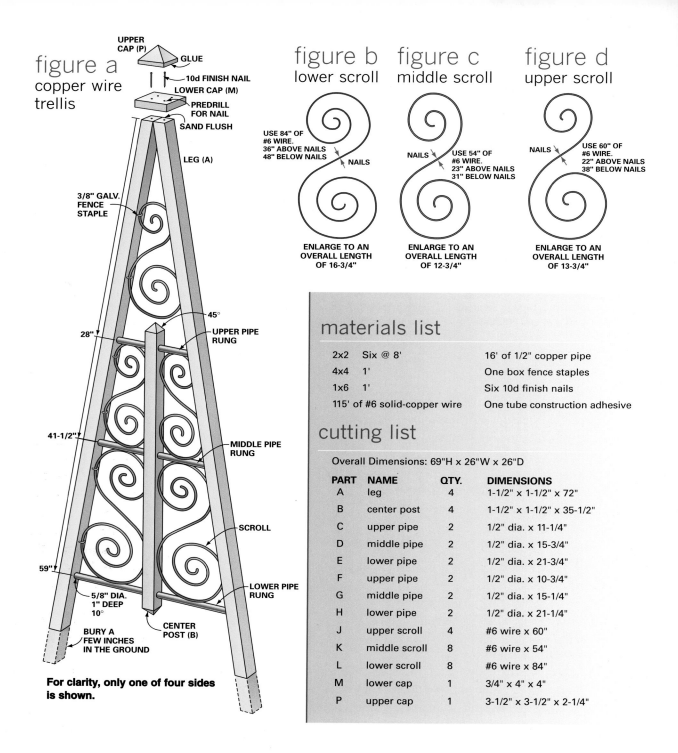

figure a
copper wire trellis

UPPER CAP (P)
GLUE
10d FINISH NAIL
LOWER CAP (M)
PREDRILL FOR NAIL
SAND FLUSH
LEG (A)

3/8" GALV. FENCE STAPLE

45°
28"
UPPER PIPE RUNG

41-1/2"
MIDDLE PIPE RUNG

SCROLL

59"
LOWER PIPE RUNG

5/8" DIA. 1" DEEP 10°
CENTER POST (B)

BURY A FEW INCHES IN THE GROUND

For clarity, only one of four sides is shown.

figure b
lower scroll

USE 84" OF #6 WIRE. 36" ABOVE NAILS 48" BELOW NAILS

NAILS

ENLARGE TO AN OVERALL LENGTH OF 16-3/4"

figure c
middle scroll

NAILS
USE 54" OF #6 WIRE. 23" ABOVE NAILS 31" BELOW NAILS

ENLARGE TO AN OVERALL LENGTH OF 12-3/4"

figure d
upper scroll

NAILS
USE 60" OF #6 WIRE. 22" ABOVE NAILS 38" BELOW NAILS

ENLARGE TO AN OVERALL LENGTH OF 13-3/4"

materials list

2x2	Six @ 8'	16' of 1/2" copper pipe
4x4	1'	One box fence staples
1x6	1'	Six 10d finish nails
115' of #6 solid-copper wire		One tube construction adhesive

cutting list

Overall Dimensions: 69"H x 26"W x 26"D

PART	NAME	QTY.	DIMENSIONS
A	leg	4	1-1/2" x 1-1/2" x 72"
B	center post	4	1-1/2" x 1-1/2" x 35-1/2"
C	upper pipe	2	1/2" dia. x 11-1/4"
D	middle pipe	2	1/2" dia. x 15-3/4"
E	lower pipe	2	1/2" dia. x 21-3/4"
F	upper pipe	2	1/2" dia. x 10-3/4"
G	middle pipe	2	1/2" dia. x 15-1/4"
H	lower pipe	2	1/2" dia. x 21-1/4"
J	upper scroll	4	#6 wire x 60"
K	middle scroll	8	#6 wire x 54"
L	lower scroll	8	#6 wire x 84"
M	lower cap	1	3/4" x 4" x 4"
P	upper cap	1	3-1/2" x 3-1/2" x 2-1/4"

Be careful inserting the pipe

Assemble two sides. The easiest approach is to put the pipes through the center posts, get them centered and then place the ends of the pipes in the legs. Be careful as you insert the pipe in the center post. It's possible to split out a chunk of the wood as the pipe exits the post. When you're done, the tops of the legs should be within 1/4 in. of each other.

Lay an assembled side upside down on sawhorses so the remaining holes in the legs are pointing up and supported. Using a bolt, an old screwdriver or similar tool, mash the end of the pipe where you can see it at the bottom of each hole. This will lock the pipe in place and make room at the bottom of the hole for the other pipes.

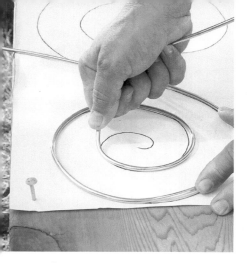
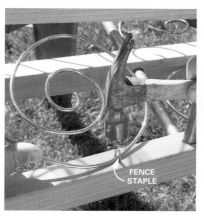

4 Bend the scrolls with your hands, following the pattern. The copper wire is soft enough to bend easily. When you've bent one side, weight it down and bend the other.

5 Attach the scrolls with small fence staples. You can bend the scroll out of the way temporarily to make room for the hammer.

FENCE STAPLE

6 Sand the top where all four legs come together, using coarse sandpaper, so they form a flat surface for nailing on the cap.

Cut the remaining pipe rungs (F, G and H) and then fit the rungs and remaining center posts between the two assembled sides to form the complete trellis structure. If any of the joints are loose, put a bit of epoxy in the hole.

Bend the scrolls

Now the fun part: making the wire scrollwork. Make your bending jig out of a 2x12 or a scrap piece of plywood at least 11 in. x 18 inches. Enlarge the patterns in Figures B, C and D until the dimensions are correct, and tack a pattern to the jig (Photo 3). Nail two 10d finish nails on either side of the scroll shape to hold the wire (see Figures B, C and D).

Cut one piece of wire to the appropriate length for the scroll you're working on. Measure from one end to find the point that goes between the two finishing nails (see pattern drawing), mark that spot and lay the wire on the jig so your mark is between the two nails. Using your hand only, bend the wire to the shape on the pattern (Photo 4). There should be a few inches of extra wire on each end to give you something to hold. When you've got the first half bent to shape, snip the end. Put a weight or a clamp on the part you've done, then bend the other side. You don't have to be fussy about matching the pattern; close is good enough.

If your first scroll was a success, cut the remaining pieces of wire and bend the rest of the scrolls. For each of the three different shapes, I suggest doing one for practice before cutting all the remaining wire. If you

have trouble, cut the wire a little long and you'll have more to work with.

Final assembly

Lay the trellis on its side and use fence staples to attach the scrolls to the 2x2s (Photo 5). Be sure to get the pairs of scrolls on each side of the trellis to be symmetrical (a right and a left), and to reverse the direction between the lower and middle scrolls (see Figure A).

When all the scrolls are attached, stand the trellis up, find yourself something to stand on, and sand the tops of the legs flat and even (Photo 6). If the pieces vibrate too much, tape them all together with duct tape or packing tape.

Cut the cap pieces (M and P). For the facets on the topmost cap piece (P), start with a 1-ft.-long piece of 4x4 so you have enough wood to hold on to while you cut the facets. Then trim off the finished cap piece. You can also buy deck caps at a home center to avoid the cutting completely. When both cap pieces are cut, drill pilot holes in M, nail it on, then glue on part P with construction adhesive or epoxy.

Install the trellis in your garden. Dig the bottoms of the legs into the earth and get the trellis plumb. You'll have to do it pretty much by eye. If your location is windy, anchor the bottoms of the legs into the ground. One way is to bend a couple of 3-ft. pieces of 1/8-in. rod into a U-shape, so they can be driven in around the legs. Then fasten them to the legs with fence staples and cover with dirt or mulch.

Plant markers

Unique, simple and really cheap.

That favorite plant of yours deserves more recognition than a Popsicle stick with black ink spelling out its name. Try making these unique plant markers, which hold a label or a seed packet with bent copper wire set in a decorative base. They're easy to assemble, so let your creativity flow. Decorate them with rocks, glass beads or even seashells. They're also great gifts for friends and relatives, and at $2 apiece, you can make dozens of them.

You've probably got all the tools you'll need around the house to make these markers. A 2-gallon bucket and a wooden spoon are all you need for mixing the mortar. We used a 4- x 8- x 2-in. disposable plastic container as a form, but you could also try a cut-off milk carton or a bread pan. You should

EASY FOR EVERYONE

1 Bend the copper wire. Hold a dowel 8 in. up from the end of a 5-ft. piece of wire folded in half. Wrap the wire around it as shown, forming a loop. Move the dowel over 3-1/2 in. (or the width needed to fit your seed packet) and wrap it again, making a second loop in the opposite direction. Cut the wire off even with the first leg, and bend a 1/2-in. 90-degree turn at the bottom of each leg to anchor it in the mortar.

2 Add the mortar. Mix up the mortar to the consistency of cookie dough, slowly adding water to the dry mix as needed. Mix the mortar thoroughly, let it sit for about 3 minutes, then remix, adding a dash more water if needed. Coat the plastic form with cooking spray. After filling the container, give it a few quick shakes to settle the mortar. Then form a mound using a spoon or small trowel so it resembles a loaf of baked banana bread.

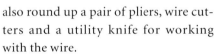

also round up a pair of pliers, wire cutters and a utility knife for working with the wire.

For supplies, you'll need a bag of premixed mortar (60 lbs. is plenty), a dust mask, a can of nonstick cooking spray, and 12-2 electrical cable with the plastic sheathing stripped off the wires.

For decoration, use rocks, glass beads or seashells—about 1/3 lb. of rocks per holder. Craft stores are loaded with materials. We added a latex bonding agent to the mortar. It's not absolutely necessary, but it'll make the mortar stick better to smooth rocks and glass. Buy it from a masonry supplier and follow the directions for mixing.

3 Push the copper marker into the mortar so the 90-degree bends are about 1/2 in. up from the bottom and centered. If the mortar is too wet to support the wire, have a cup of coffee and let it stiffen up a little.

Now arrange the rocks or beads to your liking. When arranging the rocks, it's best to start at the edges and work toward the center. Embed the decorations at least halfway into the mortar so they're held tight. If you don't like how a rock looks, remove it, rinse it off and reposition. Once you're done with the arrangement, let the marker set for at least 24 hours before removing it from the form.

Container water gardens

Great ponds in small packages.

Container gardens with aquatic plants create more mystery than plants potted in soil. They make you want to go outside and have a look. Plus, they're extremely low maintenance. Top them off with water before you go on vacation, and they're still bright and beautiful when you come home. And if you add a spouting ornament or water movement of any kind, the kids will love it even more than you do.

Container water gardens are inexpensive and easy to build, too. So here's how to get into the swim of things with a container water garden.

EASY FOR EVERYONE

project at a glance

skill level
beginner

special tools
drill

approximate cost
$50-$100

KITTY LITTER

PEA GRAVEL

WATER TUBE CONNECTOR

MOUNTING SPIKE

1 Drill a small hole in the rim of the container to mount the spouting ornament. If you need to bend the support spike to level or position the spouter, grip it with two pairs of pliers so you don't crack the ornament.

2 Spread the soil of the lily or other deep-water plants in one half of the container, then add kitty litter to create a level floor.

What you need

For a basic garden, you need at least an 18- to 20-in. plastic container that's 7 to 8 in. deep, a small submersible pump, a spouting ornament, plants, clear vinyl tubing, clean kitty litter, pea gravel or small pebbles and a nylon stocking. Most items are readily available at larger garden centers or on-line.

How to do it

The photos show you how. Here are a few handy additional tips:

● The floor is two tiered to allow for different types of plants; the lilies planted on the deep side have stems that float upward and extend horizontally, while the "marginal" plants—those that grow upright and favor shallower water—stand on the higher side. The partition that separates the two sides can be made from stone, bricks or other heavy material.

● Pea gravel both beautifies your water garden and acts as a lid over the unpotted soil so it can't circu

late and darken the water. Rinse the pea gravel before adding it to the container.

● For extra protection, place the pump in a nylon stocking before putting it in the cup, then stuff the extra nylon over the pump. This filtering is crucial; otherwise pebbles and kitty litter will be drawn into the pump and clog it. A well-filtered pump will run for months; a clogged pump must be dug up, which fouls the water.

● Small submersible pumps have adjustable pressure, so before burying the pump, place it in a bucket of water, plug it in and adjust the pressure of the jet of water coming out of the spouter.

● Fill a couple of buckets with tap water, then let them sit for a day or two to allow chlorine to evaporate and water temperature to moderate. Pour the water in gradually—it should be as clear as a mountain stream.

● Aquatic plants thrive on direct sunlight, so a bright sunny spot is ideal. If possible, position the container near an electrical outlet for the pump.

Plan Smart

Wind can wreak havoc with tall plants by pushing the containers off their pedestals. Finding a wind-free space helps solve this problem and ensures the fountain arc from the spouting ornament looks and sounds the way you want it to.

MARGINAL PLANTS

FLAGSTONE PARTITION

PLASTIC COVER

LOWER SIDE

PEA GRAVEL

3 Add a partition to divide the container into halves. Plant the shallow-growing marginal plants and spread more kitty litter over the soil. On the low side, nestle a plastic cup for the pump in the kitty litter, keeping it covered with plastic to prevent gravel from falling in.

4 Spread pea gravel over the kitty litter. Keep the floor on the lily side lower to allow the lily stems room to extend upward when you add water.

Handy Hints®

You can overwinter hardy water lilies by wrapping them in a damp towel and storing them in a cool basement or garage corner. Other plants are relatively inexpensive and grow rapidly, so in cold climates, buy them anew each year and treat as annuals.

Maintenance, Care, and something fishy

Taking care of water gardens is a breeze. Top them off as water evaporates and scoop off the occasional dead leaf or bit of algae.

Plants maintain water clarity by absorbing decaying matter through their roots as food. But if the water starts looking gunky, remove the plants, rinse the container and refill.

For any plants needing a boost, press a fertilizer pellet into the potting soil. You can also add a Mosquito Dunk (about $1 each at garden centers) a couple times in the summer to kill mosquito larvae without posing harm to people or pets.

Smaller containers will only need a small piece.

For a small container, plant a dwarf lily so the pads don't completely cover the surface as they grow. For larger water gardens, you can add a floating plant like water hyacinth, duckweed or water lettuce.

A dish-style garden is too small for koi or goldfish, but larger containers, like whiskey barrels or larger terra-cotta pots, are ideal. (Note: Water in metal containers usually gets too warm for fish.) Fish help keep the garden clean by eating algae, decaying plant material and mosquito larvae. Make certain to read up on fish so you give them the proper care and learn how they will impact your garden.

MOSQUITO DUNK

FERTILIZER PELLETS

SECTION OF 1/2" TUBING

3/8" TUBING

SUCTION CUPS

NYLON FILTER

5 Connect the pump to the spouter with vinyl tubing. Use a transition piece of 1/2-in. tubing if necessary to connect the 3/8-in. tube to the pump. Press the pump into the cup so that the suction cups anchor it to the bottom.

6 Cover the pump with a nylon stocking filter to keep gravel from clogging the pump, and then cover the pump with pea gravel.

The Super-Simple Approach

If you want an instant water garden, simply slip a plastic barrel liner into a decorative wooden barrel, set some pavers of various heights in place to act as pedestals and then perch a few potted aquatic plants on top. Just make sure to position the plants at the depth indicated on the plant tag or information sheet. The only drawback to this approach is that the container won't look as natural close up—you can see the plastic pots below the surface. You can even add a spouter

LINER

PAVER PEDESTALS

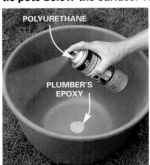

POLYURETHANE

PLUMBER'S EPOXY

to the barrel; the pump can simply sit on a pedestal without a cup.

If you can't find a plastic barrel liner, you can make a watertight terra-cotta container by plugging the drain hole with plumber's epoxy (left) and applying two coats of polyurethane.

Small soothing fountain

Inexpensive, simple to build and a great place for the neighborhood birds to freshen up—now that's a fountain!

This quaint fountain is proof that good things come in small packages. You can build it in an afternoon for under $80. It's a "disappearing fountain" so there's no exposed standing water. This means there's less maintenance since there's less chance debris and critters will wind up in the water. Yet it provides the soothing sight and sound of running water people love. Another bonus—since birds love moving water, there's a chance you'll attract some of these outdoor friends.

You can personalize your fountain in a number of ways:

● Surround it with any type of rock. We used a natural wall stone, but you can use modular concrete retaining-wall blocks, boulders or flagstone.

● Top it off with any type of small stone. We used a decorative rock called "Western Sunset." You can use pebbles, lava stone or special rocks you've collected in your travels.

● Use any bowl, dish or plate you want for the water to splash into. We used three pieces so the water cascades from one piece into the next.

Let's Get Started

You can use a whiskey barrel liner from a local home center for the catch basin, but any large plastic container will do (see Photo 1 on p. 60). Some garden centers sell special pond liners just for this purpose.

Regardless of your soil conditions, nestle your catch basin or liner into a bed of sand. This helps protect the bottom of the tub from sharp rocks and makes it easier to level the tub and the first course of rock.

We constructed our fountain so we could gain access to the pump by removing a handful of rocks along with the hardware cloth trap door (Photo 5). This allows us to easily remove the pump for maintenance and for storing it indoors over the winter.

multiple spray patterns **All four of these interchangeable fountainheads, which provide different looks, came in one package. Use just one or switch them around from time to time for a new look and feel.**

EASY FOR EVERYONE

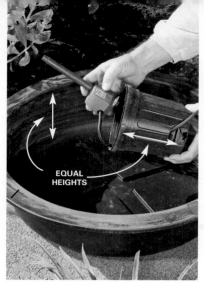

PLASTIC TUB

2" BED OF SAND

EQUAL HEIGHTS

PUMP ACCESS OPENING

1 Select a location where you'll enjoy your fountain, hollow out a 2-in.-deep area, then level in a bed of sand large enough to accommodate the plastic tub and the rock or block that will surround it.

2 Locate a sturdy plastic flower pot the same height as your plastic tub, cut a hole in the side near the bottom and feed the cord for the electric pump through it. Position this pot right side up in the center of your tub.

3 Cut a hole in the wire hardware cloth (available at home centers) large enough for the pump to fit through, then position the cloth over the tub and bend the edges over the tub lip.

Use a bag of sand as a workbench when drilling the holes in your bowls and dishes (Photo 6). It'll provide a cushion and help prevent breakage.

Many large garden centers and home centers sell water garden pumps and accessories. Or you can contact:

- Little Giant Pump Co., (888) 956-0000, www.littlegiant.com.
- MacArthur Water Gardens, (800) 695-4913, www.macarthurwatergardens.com.

figure a   how it all goes together

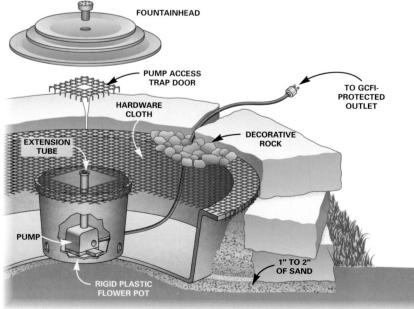

FOUNTAINHEAD

PUMP ACCESS TRAP DOOR

HARDWARE CLOTH

TO GCFI-PROTECTED OUTLET

EXTENSION TUBE

DECORATIVE ROCK

PUMP

1" TO 2" OF SAND

RIGID PLASTIC FLOWER POT

Operating Tips

Keep your fountain liner full of water and check the level every day or so, especially in hot weather. You can use any thin stick as a dipstick to check the water level.

Plug your pump into a GFCI-protected outlet—ideally one located next to the fountain. If you use an extension cord, leave it exposed so you know where it is, and be careful with sharp garden tools and mowers.

As a precaution, unplug the fountain when you're not around to watch it (or put it on a timer). If the pump runs dry, it'll burn out.

Most pumps will accept a variety of fountainheads. Bear in mind that with some spray patterns, all the water may not drain back into the tub. You'll have to refill your tub much more often with this type of fountain.

SMALL OPENING FOR PUMP STEM

REMOVABLE TRAP DOOR

4 Surround the tub with flagstone or concrete retaining-wall blocks to match the rest of your landscape. The upper course should be about 2 in. higher than the top of the tub.

5 Cut a small piece of hardware cloth a few inches larger than the access hole to create a removable trap door, then cut a small opening for the pump stem. Cover the top of the hardware cloth with decorative stone.

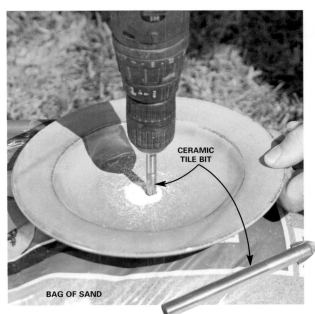

CERAMIC TILE BIT

BAG OF SAND

OTHER FOUNTAINHEADS

6 Drill a hole in your fountain dish by first scoring the glaze in the center of the bowl with a light tap of a nail (remember, light!), then boring a hole using a ceramic tile bit. If you need to enlarge the hole, use a larger bit or small file.

7 Install the fountainhead of your choice. Most pumps can accommodate a range of heads including mushroom-shaped, cup-shaped and fan-shaped patterns. Then fill the tub, plug in the pump and relax.

ti*p Have a little fun selecting your fountain dishes. It's the perfect opportunity to use those I-never-use-'em-but-I-can't-bear-to-throw-'em-out bowls, plates and even teapots.

Resources

Roll-out pantry
Page 12: Accuride pantry slides available through Rockler, (800) 279-4441, www.rockler.com

Corner swing-and roll-out trays
Page 15: Piano hinges and bottom slides available through Rockler, (800) 279-4441, www.rockler.com

Page 17: Front moldings manufactured by House of Fara, (800) 334-1732, www.houseoffara.com

Toe-kick drawers
Page 20: Drawer slides and Titbond Melamine glue available through Woodworker's Hardware, (800) 383-0130, www.wwhardware.com

Family message center
Page 22: Wrap-around and self-closing hinges available through Rockler, (800) 279-4441, www.rockler.com

Low-cost TV cabinet
Page 30-38: Toggle clamps, TransTint dye, drawer slides, edge banding and wood knobs available through Rockler, (800) 279-4441, www.rockler.com

Rotating garage shelves
Page 46: Lazy Susan hardware available through Rockler, (800) 279-4441, www.rockler.com

Open kitchen shelves
Page 56: Shelf pins, sleeves and rubber pads available through Rockler Woodworking and Hardware, (800) 279-4441, www.rockler.com

Entryway pocket screw coat locker
Page 73: Kreg pocket screw jig dealer information Kreg Tool Co., (800) 447-8638, www.kregtool.com

Traditional maple bookcase
Page 82: Clamp & Tool Guide available through www.amazon.com (under "Tools and Hardware" heading).

Modular concrete retaining wall
Page 153: The blocks used in this project are manufactured by Versa-Lok, www.versalok.com

Container water gardens
Page 209: Pond Care 95 Fountain Water Pump Kit (part #705G) available at www.renapump.com. Spouting wren ornament available through www.marylandaquatic.com

Metric conversions

Use the tables on this page to convert the "English" or "standard" measurements in this book into metric form.

In the "English system to metric system" and "Metric system to English system" charts below, multiply the number in the first column by the number in the third column to arrive at the conversion number in the middle column.

English system to metric system

To change:	Into:	Multiply by:
Inches	Millimeters	25.4
Inches	Centimeters	2.54
Feet	Meters	0.305
Yards	Meters	0.914
Miles	Kilometers	1.609
Square inches	Square centimeters	6.45
Square feet	Square meters	0.093
Square yards	Square meters	0.836
Cubic inches	Cubic centimeters	16.4
Cubic feet	Cubic meters	0.0283
Cubic yards	Cubic meters	0.765
Pints	Liters	0.473
Quarts	Liters	0.946
Gallons	Liters	3.78
Ounces	Grams	28.4
Pounds	Kilograms	0.454
Tons	Metric tons	0.907

Metric system to English system

To change:	Into:	Multiply by:
Millimeters	Inches	0.039
Centimeters	Inches	0.394
Meters	Feet	3.28
Meters	Yards	1.09
Kilometers	Miles	0.621
Square centimeters	Square inches	0.155
Square meters	Square feet	10.8
Square meters	Square yards	1.2
Cubic centimeters	Cubic inches	0.061
Cubic meters	Cubic feet	35.3
Cubic meters	Cubic yards	1.31
Liters	Pints	2.11
Liters	Quarts	1.06
Liters	Gallons	0.264
Grams	Ounces	0.035
Kilograms	Pounds	2.2
Metric tons	Tons	1.1

Also Available from Reader's Digest

Complete Do-It-Yourself Manual

Completely revised and redesigned with over 3,000 color photos and illustrations, facts on the latest tools and techniques, and updated user-friendly instructions for a wide range of projects. This definitive do-it-yourself guide to home repair, maintenance, and improvements is designed to save you time and money.

ISBN(13) 978-0-7621-0579-3 • $35.00

New Fix-It-Yourself Manual

The indispensable bible for keeping a home in tip-top shape, it is the time-and money saver every homeowner needs. It functions as a repair manual, an evaluation guide, a compendium of household hits, emergency reference, and homeowner's encyclopedia.

ISBN(13) 978-0-89577-871-0 • $35.00